Roadmap for DevOps in Cyber-Physical Systems

Sebastiano Panichella · Paolo Arcaini ·
Myra B. Cohen · Aitor Arrieta
Editors

Roadmap for DevOps in Cyber-Physical Systems

Challenges and Future Directions (Communications of Shonan Meetings)

Springer

Editors
Sebastiano Panichella
University of Bern
Bern, Switzerland

Italian Institute of Artificial Intelligence for Industry (AI4I)
Torino, Italy

Myra B. Cohen
Department of Computer Science
Lowa State University
Ames, IA, USA

Paolo Arcaini
National Institute of Informatics
Tokyo, Japan

Aitor Arrieta
Mondragon University
Mondragon, Spain

ISBN 978-981-95-1785-5 ISBN 978-981-95-1786-2 (eBook)
https://doi.org/10.1007/978-981-95-1786-2

This Springer imprint is published by the registered company Springer Nature Singapore Pte Ltd.
The registered company address is: 152 Beach Road, #21-01/04 Gateway East, Singapore 189721, Singapore

The spirit of innovation in science and engineering is fueled not just by knowledge, but by relentless curiosity and the freedom to question, explore, and imagine. The following quotes reflect the mindset we hope this book will inspire in its readers:

Study hard what interests you the most in the most undisciplined, irreverent and original manner possible.

I would rather have questions that can't be answered than answers that can't be questioned.

If you find science boring, you're learning it from the wrong teacher!

—Richard P. Feynman

You cannot teach a man anything; you can only help him find it within himself.

—Galileo Galilei

It does not make sense to try to be one of the most brilliant scientists. It makes much more sense, and it is also more fun to try to be one of the most curious and passionate among them.

There are no "basic" or "applied" researchers—only research in different states. Like atoms, researchers shift between a ground state of fundamental inquiry and an excited state of real-world application. It's the context—curiosity, need, or opportunity—that provides the energy for the transition. Through it all, the researcher remains the same.

—Sebastiano Panichella

Preface

Cyber-physical systems (CPS)—spanning domains from autonomous transportation to next-generation healthcare—are reshaping society by blending the digital and physical worlds. As these systems grow in complexity and autonomy, their development and operation require a new paradigm that goes beyond traditional engineering practices. The integration of DevOps into CPS development offers a promising avenue to manage this complexity, enabling continuous evolution, higher trustworthiness, and increased adaptability. However, applying DevOps in CPS is not straightforward. It introduces unique challenges rooted in hardware-software interaction, safety-critical demands, and dynamic environments.

This book, *Roadmap for DevOps in Cyber-Physical Systems: Challenges and Future Directions (Communications of Shonan Meetings)*, was written to address these challenges head-on. It is intended for researchers, practitioners, and students who are shaping or studying the next generation of dependable CPS. Our goal is to provide a comprehensive and forward-looking resource that highlights both the obstacles and opportunities of applying DevOps practices in this demanding context.

The motivation for this book emerged from years of research and engagement in European initiatives focused on dependable CPS engineering. We gratefully acknowledge the support of the COSMOS and Adeptness EU projects,[1] whose involved communities provided key insights and momentum for this volume.

Bern, Switzerland — Sebastiano Panichella
Tokyo, Japan — Paolo Arcaini
Ames, USA — Myra B. Cohen
Mondragon, Spain — Aitor Arrieta

[1] https://www.cosmos-devops.org and https://www.adeptness.eu.

Acknowledgements

We want to express our sincere gratitude to the organizations that supported and contributed to the success of the Shonan Meeting No. 204: DevOps for Cyber-Physical Systems (see Figs. 1 and 2, held at the Shonan Village Center from November 6 to 10, 2023.[2,3] This meeting brought together experts from around the world to discuss the challenges and opportunities at the intersection of DevOps and Cyber-Physical Systems. The vibrant discussions, collaborative spirit, and shared commitment to advancing the field were made possible through the generous support of our partners.

We extend our thanks to the following organizations:

- Shonan Village Center for hosting the event in an inspiring environment conducive to focused collaboration.
- COSMOS H2020 Project (https://www.cosmos-devops.org/) and Adeptness H2020 Project (https://adeptness.eu/) for providing a strong foundation of research, tools, and expert participation.
- University of Bern (Switzerland), National Institute of Informatics (Japan), Iowa State University (USA), and Mondragon University (Spain) for supporting the cooperation of the research meeting as well as the writing of this book.
- We are especially grateful to all the participants—researchers and practitioners from academia and industry—for their valuable insights and contributions, which helped to shape this book and other related initiatives.
- We thank the Horizon 2020 (EU Commission) and the SERI (State Secretariat for Education, Research, and Innovation) support for the project InnoGuard,[4] Marie Sktodowska-Curie Actions Doctoral Networks (HORIZON-MSCA-2023-DN), and the SNSF project entitled "SwarmOps: Human-sensing based MLOps for Collaborative Cyber-physical systems" (Project No. 200021_219732). We also thank the Hasler Foundation for the projects "Bridging the Reality Gap in Testing

[2] https://shonan.nii.ac.jp/docs/No.204.pdf.

[3] https://shonan.nii.ac.jp/seminars/204/.

[4] https://www.innoguard.eu/index.html.

Fig. 1 Overview of the participants to the Shonan meeting no. 204: DevOps for Cyber-Physical Systems

Fig. 2 Outcome of the Shonan meeting no. 204: DevOps for Cyber-Physical Systems

Unmanned Aerial Vehicles" (Project No. 23064)[5] and "Advancing Unmanned Aerial Vehicles Reliability and Societal Trust Through Integrated Testing and Formal Verification" (Project No. 2025-02-27-311). P. Arcaini is supported by the ASPIRE grant No. JPMJAP2301, JST; and also by Engineerable AI Techniques for Practical Applications of High-Quality Machine Learning-based Systems Project (Grant Number JPMJMI20B8), JST-Mirai.

[5] https://skhatiri.github.io/Aerialist-Project/.

Contents

Contributors

Aldeida Aleti Monash University, Melbourne, Australia

Shaukat Ali Simula Research Laboratory, Oslo, Norway

Paolo Arcaini National Institute of Informatics, Tokyo, Japan

Aitor Arrieta Mondragon University, Mondragon, Spain

Wesley K. G. Assunção North Carolina State University, Raleigh, USA

Domenico Bianculli University of Luxembourg, Luxembourg, Luxembourg

Christian Birchler University of Bern, Bern, Switzerland

Birthe Böhm Siemens AG, Erlangen, Germany

Antonio Cicchetti Malardalen University, Västerås, Sweden

Myra B. Cohen Iowa State University, Ames, IA, USA

Alexander Egyed Johannes Kepler University, Linz, Austria

Mattia Fazzini University of Minnesota, Minneapolis, MN, USA

Alessio Gambi Austrian Institute of Technology, Vienna, Austria

Robbert Jongeling Malardalen University, Vasteras, Sweden

Sajad Khatiri Università della Svizzera italiana–University of Bern, Bern, Switzerland

Stefan Klikovits Johannes Kepler University, Linz, Austria

Lei Ma University of Alberta, Edmonton, Canada;
The University of Tokyo, Tokyo, Japan

Annibale Panichella Delft University of Technology, Delft, The Netherlands

Sebastiano Panichella University of Bern, Bern, Switzerland

Violet Ka I Pun Western Norway University of Applied Sciences, Bergen, Norway

Cosmina Cristina Raţiu Johannes Kepler University, Linz, Austria

Vincenzo Riccio University of Udine, Udine, Italy

Volker Stolz Western Norway University of Applied Sciences, Bergen, Norway

Catia Trubiani Gran Sasso Science Institute, L'Aquila, Italy

Hironori Washizaki Waseda University, Shinjuku, Japan

Zhehua Zhou University of Alberta, Edmonton, Canada

Introduction

Sebastiano Panichella, Paolo Arcaini, Myra B. Cohen, and Aitor Arrieta

Abstract The book *Roadmap for DevOps in Cyber-physical Systems: Challenges and Future Directions* offers a holistic discussion of DevOps practices tailored specifically for cyber-physical systems (CPS). Each of the chapters focuses on going beyond conventional DevOps considerations, with the specific focus of meticulously examining the complexity, challenges, and needs of integrating software development (Dev) and operations (Ops) within CPS contexts. Through practical insights from real-world examples and case studies, the book takes readers through the challenges across the DevOps lifecycle in CPS, offering tangible solutions to bridge theory and practice. Key DevOps phases and topics include process automation, configuration management, automated testing, and operations deployment. Furthermore, the book provides a path forward, outlining and anticipating emerging trends such as runtime verification, uncertainty-aware DevOps, and responsible DevOps practices for CPS. By emphasizing standardization and providing a forward-looking perspective, this book provides readers with the background on the state-of-the-art of DevOps for the dynamic context of CPS.

1 DevOps in Cyber-physical Systems: Context and Motivation

Emerging Cyber-physical Systems (CPS)—from robotics to transportation to medical devices—are playing and will play a crucial role in the quality of life of people

S. Panichella (✉)
University of Bern, Bern, Switzerland
e-mail: spanichella@gmail.com

P. Arcaini
National Institute of Informatics, Tokyo, Japan

M. B. Cohen
Iowa State University, Ames, IA, USA

A. Arrieta
Mondragon University, Mondragon, Spain

S. Panichella et al. (eds.), *Roadmap for DevOps in Cyber-Physical Systems*,
https://doi.org/10.1007/978-981-95-1786-2_1

and the future of the global economy [15]. One specific example is the public transport system, in which the percentage of fully automated operations are expected to increase from today's 30–70% by 2030 [33, 40]: CPS is a key enabler for this transformation. Increasing automation to such an extent, however, gives rise to many challenges, at the crux of which lies hardware and software symbiosis. Several new challenges arise from the increasing complexity of CPS software, seamless connectivity, abundant compute power, and hardware heterogeneity [10, 13, 34].

Emerging CPS systems are characterized by an *evolving development cycle that never ends* [11, 28, 34], and practitioners in the field are facing a fundamental development challenge: *observability, testability* [24–26], *and the predictability* [23] *of the behavior of emerging CPS is highly limited and, unfortunately, their usage in the real world can lead to fatal crashes sometimes tragically also involving humans* [19, 21, 32].

DevOps practices and tools are potentially the right solutions to this problem, but they were not originally developed to be applied in CPS domains [22, 40]. For instance, in emerging safety-critical, dependable CPS—e.g., self-driving cars—requirement engineering for *DevOps has been largely unaddressed in the literature* [17].

This book focuses on these challenges[1] by discussing the existing and new DevOps methodologies, techniques, emerging Digital Twins technologies, and tools that can enable the effective, continuous development and evolution of CPS [8, 9, 14]: this will increase the level of **reliability**, **trustworthiness**, and **adaptability** in CPS [22].

From a reader's point of view, this book provides insights into this broad and still very open problem as follows:

- **Holistic Approach to DevOps in Cyber-Physical Systems**: The book provides a comprehensive and in-depth exploration of the challenges as well as contemporary and future directions of implementing DevOps practices specifically tailored for CPS. It goes beyond traditional DevOps considerations, addressing the unique aspects and complexities of integrating software development and operations in the context of CPS.
- **Practical Insights and Solutions**: Readers will benefit from practical insights into addressing challenges in different stages of the DevOps lifecycle for CPS. The book identifies problems and offers tangible solutions, drawing on real-world examples and case studies. It aims to bridge the gap between theory and practical implementation in the dynamic context of CPS.
- **Forward-Looking**: Focusing on future directions, the book anticipates emerging trends and advancements in DevOps for CPS. By examining topics such as runtime verification, uncertainty-aware DevOps, and responsible DevOps, the book provides readers with the knowledge to adapt and innovate in the ever-evolving domain of CPS.

[1] Stemming from the COSMOS and Adeptness EU projects—https://www.cosmos-devops.org and https://www.adeptness.eu.

The next section (Sect. 2) summarizes the main envisioned DevOps Pipeline we believe can address the limitations of current solutions for CPS. Then, an overview of the chapters and their summaries clarifies how each book chapter discusses in detail most of the relevant challenges, automation, topics, and needs we identified as relevant for realizing DevOps for CPS. Lastly, Sects. 3 and 4 focus on other key aspects: the former details the terminology employed throughout the book, while the latter encapsulates the primary impacts and implications of both recent research and anticipated future developments in the field outlined in the following technical chapters.

2 Envisioned DevOps Pipeline for CPS

DevOps is a software development methodology that emphasizes collaboration, communication, and integration between software developers and IT operations [1, 37, 38, 40, 41]. The goal of DevOps is to improve the speed and quality of software delivery by automating and streamlining the processes involved in the software development lifecycle [1, 16, 37, 40]. The typical DevOps pipeline consists of several phases, each of which plays a crucial role in ensuring the successful delivery and deployment of software. These phases include planning, development, building, testing, deployment, operation, and monitoring [1–7, 9, 22, 29–31, 35, 36]. As follows, we detail the main phases of a typical DevOps Pipeline [1, 22, 37, 38, 40, 41], then we detail how the book discusses (in the various chapters) the ways to extend it for CPS contexts.

Planning Phase (1): The objective of this phase is to define the software project's scope, requirements, and objectives. The *Main Activities of the Planning phase* are as follows.

1. Gather requirements from stakeholders.
2. Create user stories and acceptance criteria.
3. Plan sprints[2] and iterations.
4. Design architecture and (DevOps) infrastructure.

Development Phase (2): The objective of this phase is to write and manage code for the software application. The *Main Activities of the Development phase* are as follows.

1. Write code based on requirements and user stories.
2. Perform code reviews and pair programming.
3. Commit code to version control systems such as Git.[3]
4. Ensure adherence to coding standards and guidelines.

[2] A sprint is a fixed-time period in which a team works on a set of tasks from the product backlog to deliver the next shippable product increment

[3] https://git-scm.com/.

Building Phase (3): This phase aims to compile and package the code into deployable artifacts. The *Main Activities of the Building phase* are as follows.

1. Use build automation tools such as Maven,[4] Gradle,[5] or Jenkins.[6]
2. Compile code and resolve dependencies.
3. Create versioned artifacts (e.g., JAR,[7] WAR[8] files).
4. Ensure reproducibility of builds.

Testing Phase (4): This phase aims at validating the functionality, performance, and security of the software. The *Main Activities of the Testing phase* are as follows.

1. Write and execute unit tests, integration tests, and end-to-end tests.
2. Perform automated testing using tools.
3. Conduct performance testing and load testing.

Deployment Phase (5): The objective of this phase is to deploy the software to production and other environments. The *Main Activities of the Deployment phase* are as follows.

1. Use deployment automation tools (e.g., Ansible, Kubernetes, etc.).
2. Deploy to staging and production environments.
3. Implement continuous deployment or continuous delivery strategies.
4. Rollback in case of deployment failures.

Operation Phase (6): This phase aims to ensure the software runs smoothly in production environments. The *Main Activities of the Operation phase* are as follows.

1. Monitor application performance and availability.
2. Manage infrastructure and resources tools (e.g., tools such as Terraform, AWS CloudFormation, etc.).
3. Perform routine maintenance and updates.
4. Handle incidents and troubleshoot issues.

Monitoring Phase (7): Continuously monitor the software and infrastructure to ensure reliability and performance. The *Main Activities of the Monitoring phase* are as follows.

1. Use monitoring tools such as Prometheus, Grafana, Nagios, or other dedicated frameworks [23].
2. Collect and analyze logs and metrics [24].
3. Set up alerts and notifications for anomalies [23].
4. Perform root cause analysis and implement improvements.

[4] https://maven.apache.org/.

[5] https://gradle.org/.

[6] https://www.jenkins.io/.

[7] https://docs.oracle.com/javase/8/docs/technotes/guides/jar/jarGuide.html.

[8] https://docs.oracle.com/cd/E19199-01/816-6774-10/a_war.html.

Feedback loop Phase (8): Each phase of the DevOps pipeline is interconnected, and continuous feedback loops are essential to ensure iterative improvement and quick resolution of issues. Part of such feedback involves the actual users using/observing the systems in operational environments [12]. By following these feedback loops, organizations can achieve more efficient and reliable software delivery.

DevOps for CPS. The DevOps movement, along with its principles, practices, and toolchains, has been shown to deliver dramatic improvements in the time-to-market of traditional systems [22]. However, most of the ***world's giant enterprises are interested in finding ways to scale/apply DevOps practices*** [18, 39] ***across large, complex CPS composed of hardware, firmware, and software*** [20, 22]. This book discusses the contemporary challenges as well as ongoing and future technological innovations [18, 27, 27, 39] that are necessary to overcome the strain on developing and evolving high-quality, trustworthy CPS by employing ***two key technologies (see Fig.*** 1***): DevOps and Artificial Intelligence (AI)***. These technologies offer the potential to address CPS development,[9] verification, and evolution [18, 27, 27, 39, 40].

Each chapter of the book focuses on areas beyond conventional DevOps (see Fig. 1), focusing specifically on the complexity, challenges, and needs of integrating software development (Dev) and operations (Ops) within CPS contexts. With practical insights drawn from real-world examples and case studies, the book guides readers through the various challenges of the DevOps lifecycle in CPS, offering concrete solutions to bridge theory and practice. Key topics include process automation, configuration management, DevOps testing, and operations deployment. In the following section, we provide an overview of the main chapter topics and a general summary of each of them.

2.1 Chapters Overview and Summary

The chapters of this book focus on areas beyond conventional DevOps, specifically on the complexity, challenges, and needs of integrating software development (Dev) and operations (Ops) within CPS contexts. With practical insights drawn from real-world examples and case studies, the book guides readers through the various challenges of the DevOps lifecycle in CPS, offering concrete solutions to bridge theory and practice. Key topics include process automation, configuration management, DevOps testing, and operations deployment. Additionally, the book looks ahead to emerging trends such as runtime verification, uncertainty-aware DevOps, and responsible DevOps practices for CPS.

As follows, we summarize the main chapters' topics in the context of relevant DevOps phases for CPS, shown in Fig. 1:

[9] https://www.ibm.com/blogs/research/2018/01/designing-cyber-physical-systems/.

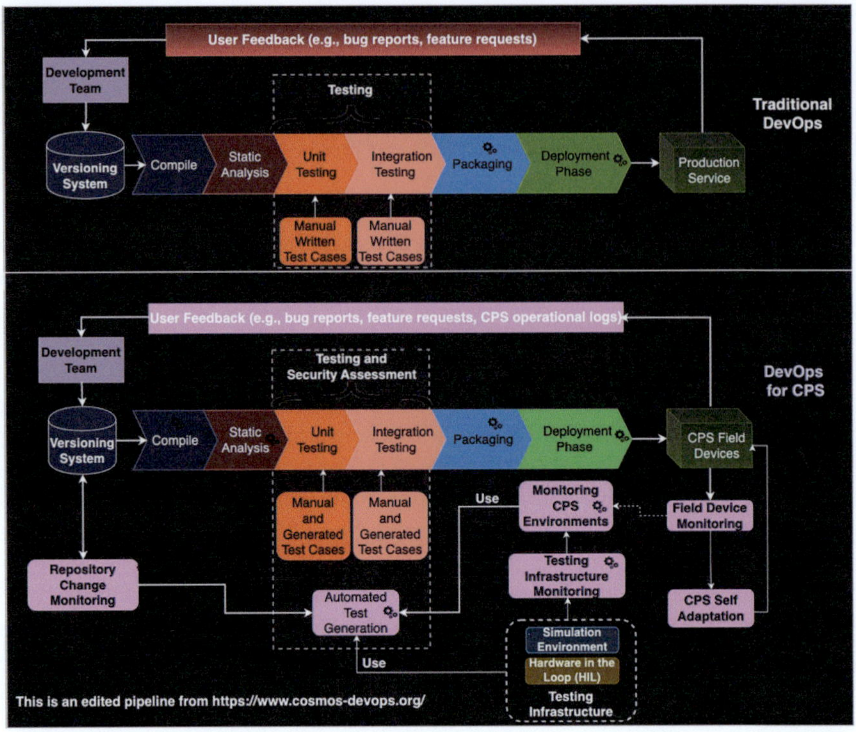

Fig. 1 DevOps pipeline for Cyber Physical Systems. The upper part of the figure shows the typical DevOps pipelines used today; the lower part of the figure shows how DevOps workflows need to be adapted for CPS contexts. Adapted from the insights and development activities of the COSMOS EU project (www.cosmos-devops.org)

- **Chapter** ***Introduction***: This chapter provides an overview of the context, motivation, and chapters of the book, terminology/macros, list of abbreviations, and general implications.
- **Chapter** ***Challenges and Needs of DevOps for Cyber-physical systems***: This chapter discusses challenges and needs, stemming from the COSMOS[10] and Adeptness EU projects so that all other chapters can be understood in terms of the research context and general gaps from the field. The challenges are discussed as part of the envisioned pipeline visualized in Fig. 1.
- **Chapter** ***Cross-domain Traceability and Consistency Management in DevOps for Cyber-physical Systems***: This chapter discusses DevOps challenges for CPS in terms of code management systems, configuration management systems, and misconfiguration modeling types of pipeline and process multi-tools, multi-disciplines, multi-artifacts traceability, and related topics.

[10] https://www.cosmos-devops.org/.

- **Chapter** ***DevOps Testing for Cyber-physical Systems***: This chapter discusses DevOps challenges for CPS in terms of test generation, real-world data augmentation, regression testing, mutation analysis, flakiness and reality gap problems, oracle coverage, test adequacy, and related topics.
- **Chapter** ***Uncertainty-Aware DevOps for Cyber-physical Systems and Runtime Verification***: This chapter discusses DevOps challenges for CPS in terms of design time operation, sources of uncertainty, and related topics.
- **Chapter** ***Deployment for Cyber-physical Systems: The Relations between the Testing and Monitoring DevOps Phases***: This chapter focuses on field testing, operational, and deployment challenges (or issues) of CPS and autonomous cyber-physical systems (ACPS). The chapter comprehensively addresses such topics, starting by discussing relevant testing, operational, and deployment challenges (e.g., the usage of digital twins, the reality gap problem, and issues when conducting runtime monitoring, etc.) as well as solutions to address them.
- **Chapter** ***Responsible DevOps for Cyber-physical Systems***: This chapter discusses DevOps challenges for CPS in terms of human interaction (Developer, End-user, Data scientist, etc.), sustainability, bias, ethics, fairness, inclusiveness, privacy, explainability, and related topics.
- **Chapter** ***Standardization for DevOps and Cyber-physical Systems***: This chapter discusses DevOps challenges for CPS in terms of standardization status and solutions for DevOps for CPS, and related topics.
- **Chapter** ***Future Directions of DevOps for Cyber-physical Systems***: This chapter discusses future directions of DevOps for CPS, primarily concerning the main findings and lessons learned from the various chapters more thoroughly.
- **Chapter** ***Conclusion***: This chapter concludes the book with final remarks.

3 Main Terminology and Abbreviations

In this section, we provide a list of the main terminology and acronyms that ware used throughout the book:

- *Cyber-Physical System* (CPS): it is a system in which a digital component interacts with the physical environment. In a typical CPS, the digital component perceives the environment through *sensors*, performs some computation, and modifies the environment through *actuators*.
- *DevOps*: it is a software development methodology that tightly integrates software development with its operation.
- *Development phase*: it is a phase of the DevOps pipeline that consists in the writing and management of the software.
- *Operation phase*: it is a phase of the DevOps pipeline that handles the execution of the software in the production environment.
- *Planning phase*: it is a phase of the DevOps pipeline that defines the requirements, scope, and objectives of the software project.

- *Building phase*: it is a phase of the DevOps pipeline that compiles and packages the code.
- *Testing phase*: it is a phase of the DevOps pipeline that assesses the software in terms of functional correctness, performance, and security.
- *Monitoring phase*: it is a phase of the DevOps pipeline that monitors the software during operation to check its reliability and performance.
- *Test input*: it is a particular input of the software used to assess its correctness.
- *Oracle*: it specifies the expected value of a test execution and determines whether a test should be considered *passing* or *failing*.
- *Digital Twin* (DT): a digital replica of the structure and of the functionalities of a physical entity.
- *Non-functional property (non-functional requirement)*: it is a property not related to the expected functionality of the software but to some expected quality like performance, security, etc.
- *Code management system*: it is a system that manages different versions of the software under development, and provides functionalities to keep track of changes, merge them, etc.
- *Uncertainty*: Lack of precise knowledge about the system's state, behavior, environment, or outcomes due to various sources. CPS are integrations of computation, networking, and physical processes–meaning they interact with both predictable digital systems and inherently variable physical environments. As such, uncertainty in CPS can arise from multiple domains.
- *Autonomous cyber-physical systems (ACPS)*: advanced systems that integrate computational algorithms with physical processes, enabling them to perform tasks with minimal human intervention. These systems combine sensors, actuators, computational intelligence, and communication networks to interact with and control their physical environments in real-time. The key aspect of ACPS is autonomy, meaning that they are capable of making decisions and adapting to changes in their environment without direct human control. Examples of ACPS are Unmanned Aerial Vehicles (UAVs or Drones), Self-Driving Cars (SDCs), and in general, Autonomous vehicles (AVs).
- *Deep Neural Network*: DNN.
- *Internet of Things*: IoT.
- *Software Development Lifecycle*: SDL.
- *Mean Time to Recovery*: MTTR.
- *Continuous Integration and Continuous Delivery (or Deployment)*: CI/CD.

4 Summary of Main Impact and Implications

This introductory chapter provides a roadmap for what readers can expect throughout the book, outlining the key themes, challenges, and innovations explored in the context of DevOps for CPS. The book discusses how traditional DevOps practices are expected to be extended and adapted to meet the specific demands of CPS.

Readers will have the opportunity to read chapters that explore a wide range of topics, such as the integration of AI and DevOps in CPS, automation of verification and validation, and the use of machine learning to enhance dependability. Several chapters present cutting-edge approaches such as reactive artifact linking to improve traceability across tools and domains, and frameworks for handling uncertainty in both design and runtime phases. The book also introduces the concept of "Uncertainty-aware DevOps", offering a vision for CPS that continuously adapts through monitoring and feedback mechanisms.

In addition, readers will explore how ethical and social dimensions-such as fairness, privacy, and sustainability–can be embedded into DevOps pipelines through "Responsible DevOps" practices. The final chapters examine the relevance and application of international standards (e.g., ISO, IEEE) to both DevOps and CPS, proposing pathways for harmonizing these frameworks to ensure interoperability, consistency, and accelerated development.

Overall, this chapter sets the stage for a forward-looking exploration of how DevOps can evolve to support the lifecycle of CPS in a way that is automated, resilient, secure, and ethically grounded. Readers can expect practical insights, research directions, and real-world case studies that bridge the gap between theory and application in this[11,12] emerging domain.

Competing Interests The authors have no conflicts of interest to declare that are relevant to the content of this chapter.

Acknowledgements We thank the Horizon 2020 (EU Commission) and the SERI (State Secretariat for Education, Research, and Innovation) support for the project InnoGuard, Marie Sktodowska-Curie Actions Doctoral Networks (HORIZON-MSCA-2023-DN), and the SNSF project entitled "SwarmOps: Human-sensing based MLOps for Collaborative Cyber-physical systems" (Project No. 200021_219732). We also thank the Hasler Foundation for the projects "Bridging the Reality Gap in Testing Unmanned Aerial Vehicles" (Project No.23064) and "Advancing Unmanned Aerial Vehicles Reliability and Societal Trust Through Integrated Testing and Formal Verification" (Project No. 2025-02-27-311). P. Arcaini is supported by the ASPIRE grant No. JPMJAP2301, JST; and also by Engineerable AI Techniques for Practical Applications of High-Quality Machine Learning-based Systems Project (Grant Number JPMJMI20B8), JST-Mirai.

References

1. Puppet and devops research and assessments (dora). 2016 state of devops report (2016)
2. A. Arrieta, J. Ayerdi, M. Illarramendi, A. Agirre, G. Sagardui, M. Arratibel, Using machine learning to build test oracles: an industrial case study on elevators dispatching algorithms, in *2021 IEEE/ACM International Conference on Automation of Software Test (AST)*. (IEEE, 2021), pp. 30–39

---

[11] https://www.innoguard.eu/index.html.

[12] https://skhatiri.github.io/Aerialist-Project.

3. A. Arrieta, M. Otaegi, L. Han, G. Sagardui, S. Ali, M. Arratibel, Automating test oracle generation in devops for industrial elevators, in *2022 IEEE International Conference on Software Analysis, Evolution and Reengineering (SANER)* (IEEE, 2022), pp. 284–288
4. A. Arrieta, G. Sagardui, L. Etxeberria, J. Zander, Automatic generation of test system instances for configurable cyber-physical systems. Softw. Qual. J. **25**(3), 1041–1083 (2017). (Sept.)
5. A. Arrieta, S. Wang, U. Markiegi, G. Sagardui, L. Etxeberria, Search-based test case generation for cyber-physical systems, in *2017 IEEE Congress on Evolutionary Computation (CEC)* (2017), pp. 688–697
6. J. Ayerdi, A. Iriarte, P. Valle, I. Roman, M. Illarramendi, A. Arrieta, Marmot: metamorphic runtime monitoring of autonomous driving systems. ACM Trans. Softw. Eng. Methodol. **34**(1), 1–35 (2024)
7. J. Ayerdi, S. Segura, A. Arrieta, G. Sagardui, M. Arratibel, Qos-aware metamorphic testing: An elevation case study, in *2020 IEEE 31st International Symposium on Software Reliability Engineering (ISSRE)* (IEEE, 2020), pp. 104–114
8. C. Birchler, S. Khatiri, B. Bosshard, A. Gambi, S. Panichella, Machine learning-based test selection for simulation-based testing of self-driving cars software. Empir. Softw. Eng. **28**(3), 71 (2023)
9. C. Birchler, S. Khatiri, P. Derakhshanfar, S. Panichella, A. Panichella, Single and multi-objective test cases prioritization for self-driving cars in virtual environments. ACM Trans. Softw. Eng. Methodol. **32**(2), 28:1–28:30 (2023)
10. C. Birchler, S. Khatiri, P. Rani, T. Kehrer, S. Panichella, A roadmap for simulation-based testing of autonomous cyber-physical systems: challenges and future direction (2025)
11. C. Birchler, S. Klikovits, M. Fazzini, S. Panichella, ICST tool competition 2025 - self-driving car testing track, in *IEEE/ACM International Conference on Software Testing, Verification and Validation* (ICST, 2025)
12. C. Birchler, T.K. Mohammed, P. Rani, T. Nechita, T. Kehrer, S. Panichella, How does simulation-based testing for self-driving cars match human perception? in *ACM International Conference on the Foundations of Software Engineering* (2024)
13. C. Birchler, C. Rohrbach, T. Kehrer, S. Panichella, SensoDat: simulation-based sensor dataset of self-driving cars, in *21st IEEE/ACM International Conference on Mining Software Repositories, MSR 2024, Lisbon, Portugal, April 15-16, 2024*. ed. by D. Spinellis, A. Bacchelli, E. Constantinou (ACM, 2024), pp. 510–514
14. C. Birchler, C. Rohrbach, H. Kim, A. Gambi, T. Liu, J. Horneber, T. Kehrer, S. Panichella, TEASER: simulation-based CAN bus regression testing for self-driving cars software, in *38th IEEE/ACM International Conference on Automated Software Engineering, ASE 2023, Luxembourg, September 11-15, 2023* (IEEE, 2023), pp. 2058–2061
15. H. Chen, Applications of cyber-physical system: a literature review. J. Ind. Integr. Manag. **02**(03), 1750012 (2017)
16. CollabNet, Anti-patterns in the continuous delivery (cd) practice (2014)
17. K. Czarnecki, Requirements engineering in the age of societal-scale cyber-physical systems: the case of automated driving, in *2018 IEEE 26th International Requirements Engineering Conference (RE)* (2018), pp. 3–4
18. A. Di Sorbo, F. Zampetti, A. Visaggio, M. Di Penta, S. Panichella, Automated identification and qualitative characterization of safety concerns reported in uav software platforms. ACM Trans. Softw. Eng. Methodol. **32**(3) (2023)
19. T. Guardian, Self-driving uber kills arizona woman in first fatal crash involving pedestrian (2018)
20. P. Helle, W. Schamai, C. Strobel, Testing of autonomous systems—challenges and current state-of-the-art, in *INCOSE International Symposium* (2016), pp. 571–584
21. F. Ingrand, Recent trends in formal validation and verification of autonomous robots software, in *3rd IEEE International Conference on Robotic Computing, IRC 2019, Naples, Italy, February 25-27, 2019* (2019), pp. 321–328
22. D.S. Johnson, H. Koehneman, D. LaFortune, D. Leffingwell, S. Magill, S. Mayner, A. Ofer, R. Stroud, A. Wallgren, R. Yeman, *INDUSTRIAL DEVOPS—Applying DevOps and Continuous Delivery to Significant Cyber-Physical Systems* (National Academies Press, 2017)

23. S. Khatiri, F.M. Amin, S. Panichella, P. Tonella, When uncertainty leads to unsafety. empirical insights into the role of uncertainty in unmanned aerial vehicle safety. Empirical Softw. Eng. (2025)
24. S. Khatiri, S. Panichella, P. Tonella, Simulation-based test case generation for unmanned aerial vehicles in the neighborhood of real flights, in *International Conference on Software Testing, Verification and Validation* (2023), pp. 281–292
25. S. Khatiri, S. Panichella, P. Tonella, Simulation-based testing of unmanned aerial vehicles with aerialist. in *International Conference on Software Engineering (ICSE)* (2024)
26. S. Khatiri, P. Saurabh, T. Zimmermann, C. Munasinghe, C. Birchler, S. Panichella, SBFT tool competition 2024—cps-uav test case generation track, in *IEEE/ACM International Workshop on Search-Based and Fuzz Testing, SBFT@ICSE 2024* (2024)
27. S. Khatiri, A.D. Sorbo, F. Zampetti, C.A. Visaggio, M.D. Penta, S. Panichella, Identifying safety-critical concerns in unmanned aerial vehicle software platforms with SALIENT. SoftwareX **27**, 101748 (2024)
28. S. Khatiri, T. Zohdinasab, P. Saurabh, D. Humeniuk, S. Panichella, ICST tool competition 2025—CPS-UAV test case generation track, in *IEEE/ACM International Conference on Software Testing, Verification and Validation*. (ICST, 2025)
29. V. Riccio, G. Jahangirova, A. Stocco, N. Humbatova, M. Weiss, P. Tonella, Testing machine learning based systems: a systematic mapping. Empir. Softw. Eng. **25**, 5193–5254 (2020)
30. V. Riccio, P. Tonella, Model-based exploration of the frontier of behaviours for deep learning system testing, in *ESEC/FSE '20: 28th ACM Joint European Software Engineering Conference and Symposium on the Foundations of Software Engineering, Virtual Event, USA, November 8-13, 2020*. ed. by P. Devanbu, M.B. Cohen, T. Zimmermann (ACM, 2020), pp. 876–888
31. V. Riccio, P. Tonella, When and why test generators for deep learning produce invalid inputs: an empirical study., in *45th IEEE/ACM International Conference on Software Engineering, ICSE 2023, Melbourne, Australia, May 14-20, 2023* (IEEE, 2023), pp 1161–1173
32. The-Washington-Post. Uber's radar detected elaine herzberg nearly 6 seconds before she was fatally struck, but "the system design did not include a consideration for jaywalking pedestrians" so it didn't react as if she were a person (2019)
33. H. Thompson, M. Reimann, Platforms4cps key outcomes and recommendations (2018)
34. M. Törngren, U. Sellgren, *Complexity Challenges in Development of Cyber-Physical Systems* (Springer International Publishing, Cham, 2018), pp. 478–503
35. P. Valle, A. Arrieta, L. Han, S. Ali, T. Yue, Defining and generating multi-level and uncertainty-wise test oracles for cyber-physical systems. Softw. Syst. Model. 1–26 (2025)
36. P. Valle, V. Riccio, A. Arrieta, P. Tonella, M. Arratibel, An industrial experience report on applying search-based boundary input generation to cyber-physical systems. Empir. Softw. Eng. **30**(4), 1–34 (2025)
37. C. Vassallo, G. Schermann, F. Zampetti, D. Romano, P. Leitner, A. Zaidman, M. Di Penta, S. Panichella, A tale of CI build failures: an open source and a financial organization perspective, in *Proceedings of International Conference on Software Maintenance and Evolution (ICSME)* (2017), pp. 183–193
38. C. Vassallo, F. Zampetti, D. Romano, M. Beller, A. Panichella, M. Di Penta, A. Zaidman, Continuous delivery practices in a large financial organization, in *Proceedings of International Conference on Software Maintenance and Evolution (ICSME)* (IEEE, 2016), pp. 519–528
39. F. Zampetti, R. Kapur, M. Di Penta, S. Panichella, An empirical characterization of software bugs in open-source cyber–physical systems. J. Syst. Softw. **192**, 111425 (2022)
40. F. Zampetti, D.A. Tamburri, S. Panichella, A. Panichella, G. Canfora, M.D. Penta, Continuous integration and delivery practices for cyber-physical systems: an interview-based study. ACM Trans. Softw. Eng. Methodol. **32**(3), 73:1–73:44 (2023)
41. F. Zampetti, C. Vassallo, S. Panichella, G. Canfora, H. Gall, M. Di Penta, An empirical characterization of bad practices in continuous integration. Empir. Softw. Eng. (2019)

Challenges and Needs of DevOps for Cyber-Physical Systems

Sebastiano Panichella, Paolo Arcaini, Myra B. Cohen, and Aitor Arrieta

Abstract This chapter examines the challenges of applying DevOps and artificial intelligence (AI) to Cyber-physical systems (CPS). While DevOps has improved time-to-market for traditional systems, scaling these practices to complex CPS with hardware-in-the-loop, software controllers, and firmware presents significant obstacles. This chapter provides a broad overview of these challenges, with subsequent chapters offering detailed solutions: (1) developing CPS-specific DevOps automation, integrating software and Hardware-in-the-Loop (HiL) testing, and using machine learning for dependability; (2) automating verification, validation, and security analysis and testing in DevOps pipelines to enhance CPS trustworthiness; (3) improving CPS adaptability with static analysis, monitoring, and self-healing; (4) creating flexible architectures and frameworks for easy deployment and compatibility in DevOps and CPS toolchains; (5) validating solutions in real-world sectors like automotive, healthcare, and railways; and (6) discussing relevant open-source technologies to encourage further development. This chapter sets the context and highlights the research gaps in DevOps for CPS, focusing on continuous integration and delivery, automated testing, AI methods, and runtime verification.

S. Panichella (✉)
University of Bern, Bern, Switzerland
e-mail: spanichella@gmail.com

P. Arcaini
National Institute of Informatics, Tokyo, Japan

M. B. Cohen
Iowa State University, Ames, IA, USA

A. Arrieta
Mondragon University, Mondragón, Spain

S. Panichella et al. (eds.), *Roadmap for DevOps in Cyber-Physical Systems*,
https://doi.org/10.1007/978-981-95-1786-2_2

1 Context and Motivation of the Chapter

This chapter explores the limitations and challenges of applying DevOps and AI practices to CPS. While DevOps has successfully improved time-to-market for traditional systems, scaling these practices for large, complex CPS involving hardware-in-the-loop, software controllers, and firmware presents significant obstacles. This chapter aims to discuss these challenges and needs broadly, while the following chapters address them in more detail:

- Developing innovative DevOps automation solutions tailored for CPS (all chapters), focusing on integrating software and Hardware-in-the-Loop (HiL) testing, and leveraging machine learning for increased dependability.
- Establishing reference quality attributes and assessment methods for CPS, open source datasets, and benchmarks in different CPS domains.
- Automating verification, validation, and security assessment within DevOps pipelines to enhance CPS trustworthiness, including generating safe test cases and developing domain-specific languages for runtime verification.
- Enhancing CPS adaptability by monitoring and evolving their behavior in response to unexpected changes, incorporating static analysis, monitoring, and self-healing solutions.
- Creating flexible architectures, frameworks, and technologies, and integrating them into various DevOps and CPS toolchains to ensure ease of deployment and compatibility.
- Validating solutions in open source and industrial cases across different sectors (e.g., automotive, healthcare, and railways) to assess their effectiveness in real-world scenarios.
- Testing Generation and Monitoring for CPS (possibly with high-fidelity Digital Twins), standardization.
- Discussing relevant open source technologies to promote further adoption and development.

All the challenges and needs discussed in this book, and this chapter, concern continuous integration and delivery, automated testing, AI-based methods, and runtime verification to support comprehensive DevOps pipelines for CPS development and evolution.

2 Challenges, Automation Needs, and Objectives of CPS Development

In the challenging world of CPS, the integration of DevOps and AI practices faces a unique set of challenges and needs. While DevOps has transformed traditional software development, reducing time-to-market and enhancing product quality, its application to CPS—a field that intertwines hardware, firmware, and software—requires a comprehensive approach [13, 19, 24, 25, 36, 37].

To understand this more closely, let us consider the scenario where a company is developing an advanced autonomous vehicle. The integration of DevOps in this context is not merely about pushing code updates or automating deployment; it is about ensuring that every software update seamlessly integrates with the vehicle's sensors, actuators, and embedded systems, all while maintaining the highest safety standards. This chapter touches on these multifaceted challenges and related innovation needs, setting the stage for a detailed discussion in the subsequent chapters.

The various stages of DevOps require achieving specific automation objectives to meet the needs of CPS. We identified several such automation needs from the COSMOS[1] and Adeptness[2] EU projects [36, 37] and further expanded together with relevant experts who took part in the writing of this book. To complement the narrative of the problem identified before, we provide a comprehensive overview of the objectives we target(ed) to achieve in applying DevOps to CPS.

Challenges and Objectives of DevOps for CPS. The key challenge that this book discusses is the need *to realize DevOps pipelines entailing an efficient and cost-effective development of trustworthy and secure CPS capable of adapting their behavior to dynamic contexts and unexpected operating scenarios*. More specifically, the book discusses solutions that focus on (1) reducing the human effort and costs of the development, V&V, and evolution activities of CPS [3, 4, 7, 8, 13, 16, 18, 25, 28, 31–35]; (2) reducing the CPS fault proneness [5, 19, 25, 35, 36] to security threats, thus contributing to increased trustworthiness, and (3) making CPS capable to autonomously adapt (or react) to unexpected behavior [6, 25, 26]. This ambitious goal can be addressed through novel DevOps practices, automated infrastructure, and technologies for CPS [10–12, 26, 27], articulated around the following specific objectives.

Innovating DevOps Automation for CPS. One of the primary challenges is developing tailored DevOps automation solutions that operate specifically for CPS. Traditional DevOps tools and practices are often insufficient when it comes to handling the complexity of integrating software with Hardware-in-the-Loop (HiL) testing [1]. Imagine testing a drone's navigation system, which requires a combination of simulated and real-world environments to ensure reliability and safety [24–26]. Leveraging strategies to monitor the system and predict potential faults, while enhancing system dependability, becomes crucial in such scenarios [24, 27].
As a research community, we aim to provide novel DevOps practices and automated solutions. They are expected to address software and HiL testing through Infrastructure as Code solutions (e.g., emulation, simulation, automatic deployment, and upgrade of physical devices) enhanced by data from multiple sources (e.g., historical change data, failure data, runtime data), and machine learning techniques, to ultimately increase the dependability of the CPS [37]. Thus, while the aim is to increase

[1] https://www.cosmos-devops.org/.

[2] https://www.adeptness.eu.

automation in the CPS development directly, we also target the analysis of a large variety of CPS behaviors (that can be observed during the execution of test cases). This is to detect, predict, and fix an increasing number of bugs [19, 36], before the system changes are deployed to production. Previous work on traditional software systems demonstrated the existence of technical barriers and anti-patterns concerning CI and CD adoption when applying DevOps practices [37, 38]: such barriers are more difficult to detect and handle in CPS domains. For example, instantiating a CD pipeline for CPS that leverages self-healing solutions in case practitioners encounter CPS anti-patterns and obstacles.

Quality Assessment, Benchmarks, and Automated Verification and Validation. Quality attributes and their assessment are critical in evolving and testing CPS in the DevOps pipeline. This book will reflect on the importance of establishing reference quality attributes, open-source datasets, and benchmarks across various CPS domains [13, 16–18, 25, 26, 28]. For instance, let us consider the healthcare sector, where robotic surgery systems must adhere to stringent quality metrics to ensure patient safety. The development of standard benchmarks and datasets aids in the consistent evaluation of these systems, ensuring they meet the required standards.

Automating the verification, validation, and security assessments within DevOps pipelines is also a significant challenge. For CPS, this includes generating safe test cases [13, 16–18, 25, 28] and developing end-to-end runtime verification solutions. Let us consider an industrial robotic arm used in manufacturing: it must be continuously tested and validated to prevent malfunctions that could disrupt production or cause injuries. Automation in this context not only improves efficiency but also enhances the trustworthiness of the CPS. An important objective is to define *quality assurance* techniques, specifically *automated testing* [25] and *run-time verification*, tailored to CPS V&V in DevOps pipelines. For test automation, a key sub-goal is to efficiently derive test cases that *discover faults by leveraging* reliable *simulation/HiL environments* [13, 16–18, 25, 28]. Another is to *generate safe test cases* that minimize hardware damage risk in physical testing, including developing *hybrid solutions* with simulated components using *machine learning*.

For runtime verification, one goal is to define a *domain-specific language* for *specifying complex system-level properties* of CPS in DevOps environments. Another is to develop non-intrusive, scalable solutions for checking these properties during system execution and *diagnosing property violations* through informative verdicts. For security assessment, key objectives include defining methods to *model CPS-specific security requirements and threats* and developing solutions to *automatically assess the system against identified threats*. This involves (1) developing security auditing techniques supporting typical CPS programming languages and constructs, (2) ensuring *traceability and coverage* through automated test case generation from security requirements, and (3) defining strategies to *automatically and continuously generate test inputs* to identify vulnerabilities.

Enhancing Adaptability and Self-Healing. CPS must be adaptable, and capable of monitoring and evolving their behavior in response to unexpected changes [6, 19, 36]. This involves incorporating static analysis, continuous monitoring, and self-healing solutions. Let us consider a smart grid system that manages electricity distribution; it needs to dynamically adjust to changes in power demand and supply, requiring sophisticated monitoring and adaptive algorithms to maintain stability and efficiency.

To maximize CPS software quality, it is crucial to enhance the CPS ability to adapt to unprecedented events at runtime, such as unexpected inputs or rapidly changing operating contexts. The focus is to develop innovative maintenance and evolution techniques that trigger *static analysis*, *monitoring*, and *testing automation*, incorporating HiL and simulation activities and operational data and inputs of CPS [25, 28]. This assesses system behavior in unprecedented situations and failures. By *monitoring the impact* of *CPS behavioral changes* on non-functional (e.g., execution time, resource management) and functional properties (e.g., testability), we aim to create adaptive mechanisms to *identify sub-optimal CPS implementations/behaviors*. This will enhance CPS behavior and reliability with *self-learning* and *self-healing* solutions. An essential objective is ensuring quality and reliability in human-CPS interactions (e.g., via interactive dashboards), which is vital for improving CPS self-adaptability to operational scenarios.

Flexible Architectures and Integration. Creating flexible architectures and frameworks that can be seamlessly integrated into various DevOps and CPS toolchains is crucial for achieving scalable and useful automation for CPS [3, 10–12, 18, 26, 27]. The goal is to ensure ease of deployment and compatibility across different systems. For example, in the automotive industry, integrating a new AI-based driver and assistance module should not require a complete overhaul of the existing system, but should be a plug-and-play addition, previously assessed by cost-effective testing mechanisms. To maximize CPS software quality, the aim is to develop a *flexible architecture for DevOps* configuration, development, and V&V services using a microservice-based approach [15, 21, 29]. Each service will be testable in isolation and able to communicate with others within a highly modular architecture [15, 21, 26, 29].

Open Source Technologies and Real-World Validation. Most chapters of the book discuss (directly or indirectly) the relevance of open-source technologies in promoting further adoption and development of DevOps for CPS. Open-source tools and frameworks offer a collaborative platform for innovation, allowing for shared improvements and widespread adoption of best practices. Validating DevOps solutions for CPS in both open-source and industrial cases across different sectors–such as automotive, healthcare, and railways–is essential to assess their effectiveness in real-world scenarios. This real-world testing (or assessment) helps to identify unforeseen challenges and refine the solutions accordingly [25, 28]. For instance, testing an automated rail control system in a real-world setting can reveal unique operational issues that are not apparent in a controlled (or Digital Twin-based) environment.

High-Fidelity Digital Twins and Standardization. A digital twin is a virtual (or digital) representation of a real-world object, system, or process that continuously serves as a digital counterpart for purposes such as simulation, integration, testing, monitoring, and maintenance. Testing and monitoring CPS [24, 25] can be enhanced with the use of high-fidelity Digital Twins [14]. Specifically, a common strategy for system-level testing of CPS, such as unmanned aerial vehicles (UAVs) and self-driving cars (SDCs), relies on end-to-end simulations where the system under test operates within a virtual environment [13, 25, 30]. These digital replicas of physical systems enable extensive testing and monitoring without the risks of real-world deployment [24, 25]. However, the applicability of traditional software testing methods in these contexts remains uncertain. Simulation-based testing introduces unique challenges, including simulation realism, computational cost, simulator complexity, and the *Oracle Problem* [9, 14]. Recent research has addressed test generation in simulation environments for UAVs and SDCs [22–25], laying the groundwork for testing methodologies tailored to autonomous systems [16]. Search-based software testing has emerged as a key approach, contributing to test generation and supporting regression testing tasks such as test minimization, selection, and prioritization [10, 11, 13, 17, 18]. Still, broader generalization is needed, as challenges like the reality gap [2, 25], the oracle problem [9, 14], and the vast simulation input space remain open issues.

Standardization in this area ensures that Digital Twins–virtual representations of physical systems–can be reliably and consistently used across various domains [14, 20]. This is particularly important for complex and safety-critical systems such as CPS [20], which tightly integrate computational components with physical processes, including autonomous vehicles, industrial automation, and smart infrastructure. By adhering to standardized models, data formats, and interfaces, Digital Twins can serve as trustworthy tools for simulating, monitoring, and validating CPS behavior under diverse operating conditions. This standardization enhances interoperability between tools and platforms, reduces development effort, and provides a robust foundation for testing, analysis, and continuous improvement of CPS [14].

3 Conclusion

In conclusion, this chapter outlines the significant challenges of integrating DevOps and AI technologies into CPS development practices, emphasizing the complexity added by hardware-in-the-loop, software controllers, and CPS firmware. It sets the stage for the following chapters, which will present solutions such as CPS-specific DevOps automation, HiL testing, and machine learning for dependability. Other solutions include automating verification, validation, and security to enhance trustworthiness, improving adaptability through static analysis and self-healing, and developing flexible architectures for seamless deployment. Real-world applications in automotive, healthcare, and railways validate these solutions. By highlighting research gaps and contextualizing the current state of DevOps for CPS, this chapter lays the groundwork for further advancements and research in this field.

Competing Interests The authors have no conflicts of interest to declare that are relevant to the content of this chapter.

Acknowledgements We thank the Horizon 2020 (EU Commission) and the SERI (State Secretariat for Education, Research, and Innovation) support for the project InnoGuard, Marie Sktodowska-Curie Actions Doctoral Networks (HORIZON-MSCA-2023-DN), the Hasler Foundation for the project (Project No. 23064) entitled "Bridging the Reality Gap in Testing Unmanned Aerial Vehicles", and the SNSF for the project entitled "SwarmOps: Human-sensing based MLOps for Collaborative Cyber-physical systems" (Project No. 200021_219732). P. Arcaini is supported by the ASPIRE grant No. JPMJAP2301, JST; and also by Engineerable AI Techniques for Practical Applications of High-Quality Machine Learning-based Systems Project (Grant Number JPMJMI20B8), JST-Mirai.

References

1. S. Abbaspour Asadollah, R. Inam, H. Hansson, A survey on testing for cyber physical system, in *Proceedings of IFIP WG 6.1 International Conference on Testing Software and Systems*, vol. 9447 (Springer, 2015), pp. 194–207
2. A. Afzal, D.S. Katz, C. Le Goues, C.S. Timperley, Simulation for robotics test automation: developer perspectives, in *Conference on Software Testing, Verification and Validation* (IEEE, 2021), pp. 263–274
3. I. Aldalur, A. Arrieta, A. Agirre, G. Sagardui, M. Arratibel, A microservice-based framework for multi-level testing of cyber-physical systems. Softw. Qual. J. **32**(1), 193–223 (2024)
4. A. Arrieta, M. Otaegi, L. Han, G. Sagardui, S. Ali, M. Arratibel, Automating test oracle generation in devops for industrial elevators, in *2022 IEEE International Conference on Software Analysis, Evolution and Reengineering (SANER)* (IEEE, 2022), pp. 284–288
5. A. Arrieta, S. Wang, U. Markiegi, G. Sagardui, L. Etxeberria, Search-based test case generation for cyber-physical systems, in *2017 IEEE Congress on Evolutionary Computation (CEC)* (2017), pp. 688–697
6. J. Ayerdi, A. Iriarte, P. Valle, I. Roman, M. Illarramendi, A. Arrieta, Marmot: metamorphic runtime monitoring of autonomous driving systems. ACM Trans. Softw. Eng. Methodol. **34**(1), 1–35 (2024)
7. J. Ayerdi, S. Segura, A. Arrieta, G. Sagardui, M. Arratibel, Qos-aware metamorphic testing: an elevation case study, in *2020 IEEE 31st International Symposium on Software Reliability Engineering (ISSRE)* (IEEE, 2020), pp. 104–114
8. J. Ayerdi, V. Terragni, A. Arrieta, P. Tonella, G. Sagardui, M. Arratibel, Generating metamorphic relations for cyber-physical systems with genetic programming: an industrial case study, in *Proceedings of the 29th ACM Joint Meeting on European Software Engineering Conference and Symposium on the Foundations of Software Engineering* (2021), pp. 1264–1274
9. E.T. Barr, M. Harman, P. McMinn, M. Shahbaz, S. Yoo, The oracle problem in software testing: a survey. IEEE Trans. Softw. Eng. **41**(5), 507–525 (2015)
10. C. Birchler, N. Ganz, S. Khatiri, A. Gambi, S. Panichella, Cost-effective simulation-based test selection in self-driving cars software with SDC-Scissor, in *IEEE International Conference on Software Analysis, Evolution and Reengineering, SANER 2022, Honolulu, HI, USA, March 15-18, 2022* (IEEE, 2022), pp. 164–168
11. C. Birchler, N. Ganz, S. Khatiri, A. Gambi, S. Panichella, Cost-effective simulation-based test selection in self-driving cars software. Sci. Comput. Program. **226**, 102926 (2023)
12. C. Birchler, S. Khatiri, B. Bosshard, A. Gambi, S. Panichella, Machine learning-based test selection for simulation-based testing of self-driving cars software. Empir. Softw. Eng. **28**(3), 71 (2023)
13. C. Birchler, S. Khatiri, P. Derakhshanfar, S. Panichella, A. Panichella, Single and multi-objective test cases prioritization for self-driving cars in virtual environments. ACM Trans. Softw. Eng. Methodol. **32**(2), 28:1–28:30 (2023)

14. C. Birchler, S. Khatiri, P. Rani, T. Kehrer, S. Panichella, A roadmap for simulation-based testing of autonomous cyber-physical systems: challenges and future direction (2025)
15. C. Birchler, S. Klikovits, M. Fazzini, S. Panichella, ICST tool competition 2025—self-driving car testing track, in *IEEE/ACM International Conference on Software Testing, Verification and Validation*. (ICST, 2025)
16. C. Birchler, T.K. Mohammed, P. Rani, T. Nechita, T. Kehrer, S. Panichella, How does simulation-based testing for self-driving cars match human perception? in *ACM International Conference on the Foundations of Software Engineering* (2024)
17. C. Birchler, C. Rohrbach, T. Kehrer, S. Panichella, SensoDat: simulation-based sensor dataset of self-driving cars, in *21st IEEE/ACM International Conference on Mining Software Repositories, MSR 2024, Lisbon, Portugal, April 15-16, 2024*. ed. by D. Spinellis, A. Bacchelli, E. Constantinou (ACM, 2024), pp.510–514
18. C. Birchler, C. Rohrbach, H. Kim, A. Gambi, T. Liu, J. Horneber, T. Kehrer, S. Panichella, TEASER: simulation-based CAN bus regression testing for self-driving cars software, in *38th IEEE/ACM International Conference on Automated Software Engineering, ASE 2023, Luxembourg, September 11-15, 2023* (IEEE, 2023), pp. 2058–2061
19. A. Di Sorbo, F. Zampetti, A. Visaggio, M. Di Penta, S. Panichella, Automated identification and qualitative characterization of safety concerns reported in uav software platforms. ACM Trans. Softw. Eng. Methodol. **32**(3) (2023)
20. E. Ferko, A. Bucaioni, P. Pelliccione, M. Behnam, Standardisation in digital twin architectures in manufacturing, in *2023 IEEE 20th International Conference on Software Architecture (ICSA)* (2023), pp. 70–81
21. J. Fritzsch, J. Bogner, M. Haug, A.C. Franco da Silva, C. Rubner, M. Saft, H. Sauer, S. Wagner, Adopting microservices and devops in the cyber-physical systems domain: a rapid review and case study. Softw. Practice Exp. **53**(3), 790–810 (2023)
22. A. Gambi, M. Müller, G. Fraser, Automatically testing self-driving cars with search-based procedural content generation, in *Proceedings of the 28th ACM SIGSOFT International Symposium on Software Testing and Analysis, ISSTA 2019, Beijing, China, July 15-19, 2019*. ed. by D. Zhang, A. Møller (ACM, 2019), pp. 318–328
23. A. Gambi, V. Nguyen, J. Ahmed, G. Fraser, Generating critical driving scenarios from accident sketches, in *IEEE International Conference On Artificial Intelligence Testing, AITest 2022, Newark, CA, USA, August 15-18, 2022* (IEEE, 2022), pp. 95–102
24. S. Khatiri, F.M. Amin, S. Panichella, P. Tonella, When uncertainty leads to unsafety. empirical insights into the role of uncertainty in unmanned aerial vehicle safety. Empirical Softw. Eng. (2025)
25. S. Khatiri, S. Panichella, P. Tonella, Simulation-based test case generation for unmanned aerial vehicles in the neighborhood of real flights, in *International Conference on Software Testing, Verification and Validation* (IEEE, 2023), pp. 281–292
26. S. Khatiri, S. Panichella, P. Tonella, Simulation-based testing of unmanned aerial vehicles with aerialist, in *International Conference on Software Engineering (ICSE)* (2024)
27. S. Khatiri, P. Saurabh, T. Zimmermann, C. Munasinghe, C. Birchler, S. Panichella, SBFT tool competition 2024—cps-uav test case generation track, in *IEEE/ACM International Workshop on Search-Based and Fuzz Testing, SBFT@ICSE 2024* (2024)
28. S. Khatiri, A.D. Sorbo, F. Zampetti, C.A. Visaggio, M.D. Penta, S. Panichella, Identifying safety-critical concerns in unmanned aerial vehicle software platforms with SALIENT. SoftwareX **27**, 101748 (2024)
29. S. Khatiri, T. Zohdinasab, P. Saurabh, D. Humeniuk, S. Panichella, ICST tool competition 2025—CPS-UAV test case generation track, in *IEEE/ACM International Conference on Software Testing, Verification and Validation* (ICST, 2025)
30. T. Mancini, I. Melatti, E. Tronci, Optimizing highly-parallel simulation-based verification of cyber-physical systems. IEEE Trans. Softw. Eng. **49**(9), 4443–4455 (2023)
31. V. Riccio, G. Jahangirova, A. Stocco, N. Humbatova, M. Weiss, P. Tonella, Testing machine learning based systems: a systematic mapping. Empir. Softw. Eng. **25**, 5193–5254 (2020)

32. V. Riccio, P. Tonella, Model-based exploration of the frontier of behaviours for deep learning system testing, in *ESEC/FSE '20: 28th ACM Joint European Software Engineering Conference and Symposium on the Foundations of Software Engineering, Virtual Event, USA, November 8-13, 2020*. ed. by P. Devanbu, M.B. Cohen, T. Zimmermann (ACM, 2020), pp. 876–888
33. V. Riccio, P. Tonella, When and why test generators for deep learning produce invalid inputs: an empirical study, in *45th IEEE/ACM International Conference on Software Engineering, ICSE 2023, Melbourne, Australia, May 14-20, 2023* (IEEE, 2023), pp. 1161–1173
34. P. Valle, A. Arrieta, L. Han, S. Ali, T. Yue, Defining and generating multi-level and uncertainty-wise test oracles for cyber-physical systems. Softw. Syst. Model. 1–26 (2025)
35. P. Valle, V. Riccio, A. Arrieta, P. Tonella, M. Arratibel, An industrial experience report on applying search-based boundary input generation to cyber-physical systems. Empir. Softw. Eng. **30**(4), 1–34 (2025)
36. F. Zampetti, R. Kapur, M. Di Penta, S. Panichella, An empirical characterization of software bugs in open-source cyber–physical systems. J. Syst. Softw. **192**, 111425 (2022)
37. F. Zampetti, D.A. Tamburri, S. Panichella, A. Panichella, G. Canfora, M.D. Penta, Continuous integration and delivery practices for cyber-physical systems: an interview-based study. ACM Trans. Softw. Eng. Methodol. **32**(3), 73:1–73:44 (2023)
38. F. Zampetti, C. Vassallo, S. Panichella, G. Canfora, H. Gall, M Di Penta, An empirical characterization of bad practices in continuous integration. Empirical Softw. Eng. (2019)

Cross-Domain Traceability and Consistency Management in DevOps for Cyber-Physical Systems

Cosmina Cristina Raţiu, Antonio Cicchetti, Robbert Jongeling, Alexander Egyed, and Wesley K. G. Assunção

Abstract Cyber-physical systems (CPS) are developed in a collaborative manner by software engineers, engineers, mechanical engineers, physicists, and other specialists. However, a challenge when multiple engineers work concurrently is to keep artifacts synchronized and consistent, mainly in the context of constant and iterative cycles of DevOPS. This is even harder when the engineering process relies on a myriad of tools and domains (e.g., mechanic, electronic, and software). Previous approaches have addressed this challenge from various perspectives, such as establishing trace links between artifacts or computing change propagation paths. However, these methods primarily offer supplementary information to engineers, still requiring manual work for propagating changes. Moreover, existing tools often fall short in supporting traceability across domains and lack the efficiency and granularity required for developing software-intensive systems. This chapter introduces our solution, *reactive links*, which are fine-grained trace links that enable automatic change propagation between property values across artifacts from different domains, even when managed in separate tools. Unlike traditional passive links, reactive links actively synchronize artifacts in response to model modifications, ensuring consistency and alignment across engineering tools. The core contribution reactive links to improve the engineering of CPS in DevOPS by reducing the manual effort needed to

C. C. Raţiu (✉) · A. Egyed
Johannes Kepler University, Linz, Austria
e-mail: cosmina-cristina.ratiu@jku.at

A. Egyed
e-mail: alexander.egyed@jku.at

A. Cicchetti · R. Jongeling
Mälardalen University, Västerås, Sweden
e-mail: antonio.cicchetti@mdu.se

R. Jongeling
e-mail: robbert.jongeling@mdu.se

W. K. G. Assunção
North Carolina State University, Raleigh, USA
e-mail: wguezas@ncsu.edu

S. Panichella et al. (eds.), *Roadmap for DevOps in Cyber-Physical Systems*,
https://doi.org/10.1007/978-981-95-1786-2_3

maintain model synchronization and by minimizing inconsistencies that often arise in collaborative, multi-tool environments.

1 Introduction

As cyber-physical systems (CPS) grow in complexity, their development requires a complex collaboration between teams with various expertise [26, 47]. Software engineers, mechanical engineers, physicists, and other specialists must work together to design, implement, and validate the hardware and software components that must be integrated to provide the desired functionalities of the system [51]. The variety of expertise between these teams may lead to significant difficulties in their collaboration [23, 35]. While the software engineering team may focus on developing clean and efficient software components, they may struggle to compare and synchronize their software models with the complex calculations and simulations created by the physicists [41]. This collaboration becomes even more challenging due to the heterogeneous nature of the tools, methodologies, and abstraction levels used in each domain [42]. Each domain uses a suite of specialized tools specifically tailored for their needs and development focus. Data and tool integration remains a challenge even within one domain. For instance, imagine a software development environment in which each tool is perfectly integrated with every other tool. Thus, cross-domain integration is an even higher hurdle to cross [37].

A key difficulty in CPS development lies in maintaining consistency and traceability across these diverse components, tools, and teams [41]. The use of different, poorly integrated tools leads to fragmented data management, where similar information is scattered across multiple models and tools, with some duplication being necessary but hard to maintain [43]. For instance, physical parameters defined by mechanical engineers must align with control software developed by software engineers. As each team has a specific view of the system and may struggle to effectively communicate their view to teams that do not share their expertise, inconsistencies can be hard to identify and rectify before causing significant issues and safety risks [9, 52].

Consider, for example, the development of an industrial robotic arm [42].[1] The software controllers are created and maintained by a software engineering team, while physicists and mechanical engineers compute the physical parameters needed to achieve the desired functionality. The hardware components used may be acquired off-the-shelf from third-party vendors, providing additional fixed parameters and safety thresholds. For instance, the height of the robotic arm, which cannot be modified due to the off-the-shelf components used, is relevant both for the calculations of the robot's mechanical parameters and safety conditions, as well as for the controller code that provides its autonomous functionalities. Any inconsistency in this data could result in anything from minor malfunctions to significant safety concerns [18,

[1] A video with the demonstration of this scenario is available at: https://youtu.be/gdqROocDq30.

31, 52]. Without mechanisms for ensuring consistency, such discrepancies may go unnoticed until they cause failures in the final product.

Given the issues discussed so far, it becomes evident why putting into practice continuous development processes like DevOps can become very challenging for CPS [19, 34, 53]. In fact, DevOps demands smooth (largely automated) evolution management support such that each refinement cycle triggered from operations can rapidly be tracked back to needed modifications to the design, propagated to corresponding improvements, and checked again at operations time. Such a pipeline is critically dependent on consistency management, as the lead time for each change request and realization limits the rate of improvement cycles.

This chapter first illustrates the available techniques to develop CPS taking into account the related consistency issues together with some commonly adopted management patterns. Then, the chapter explores a selected approach devoted to consistency checking and traceability in CPS development. By implementing these mechanisms, teams can detect and resolve discrepancies early in the development lifecycle, improving collaboration and reducing risks.

The rest of this chapter is organized as follows. We first introduce a working example that further extends the hypothetical development of the robotic arm. We then discuss existing approaches which provide traceability, consistency checking, and automatic change propagation functionalities. After this, we present reactive links, an approach that combines fine-grained traceability, consistency checking, and change propagation to provide data integration in cross-domain collaboration.

2 Working Example

In order to elaborate further on the inherent challenges of CPS development, we examine the previously mentioned industrial robotic arm example in more detail (complete example in our previous work [42]). The main aim of this robot is to offer support in assembly tasks that require both precision and lifting power. It is expected to work autonomously, while strict safety criteria must still be met. As a result, the robotic arm requires a seamless integration between its mechanical parts and actuators, and the software controllers that coordinate its movements and actions. These components are developed by different teams with expertise in physics, or mechanical or software engineering. Each of these teams uses different tools, specific for their domain, and different models and modeling languages.

Let us consider, for the working example, that there are four collaborating teams. One team is responsible for client and supplier communication. They elicit the requirements in a textual requirements tool, and use a separate spreadsheet to fill in the parameters provided by the off-the-shelf component suppliers. Another team consists of mechanical engineers who model the robotic arm and ensure it fulfills the safety criteria. They use a highly specialized calculator, with pre-programmed complex physical formulas and models. A third team writes and maintains the software code for the controller in an IDE such as IntelliJ. Their software must take into consideration several parameters resulted from the modeled hardware of the robotic arm, such as component attributes and physical parameters. Lastly, a team of graphical designers use the CAD tool SolidWorks to obtain a graphical model of the robotic arm and enable simulations for safety checks.

Despite the variety of tools and domains, these teams must work together to develop each component of the robotic arm, resulting in duplicated data and fragmented information. But if each of these tools works in isolation, the consistency of the data developed must be maintained manually. However, this process requires constant and effective communication across different domains. For example, suppose that one of the off-the-shelf components of the arm is replaced with a new model. This model has different safety parameters, as well as a different height. These new parameters have to be communicated to all the teams, which may seem straightforward at first. The difficulty comes when these changes lead to new calculations for the mechanical engineering team, the results of which have to be communicated to the software engineering team and the graphical designers. Suppose that the new component height results in a different deflection value for the arm, making it less rigid when heavy items are lifted. This value would be an intermediary result in the mechanical engineering team's calculations, but it may influence the safety features of the controller. If this result is not communicated to the software engineering team, or worse yet, misunderstood during the change communication, the resulting robotic arm may become unsafe or even entirely unusable in some use cases.

In order to address these risks, the teams can implement DevOps practices to support the continuous integration and early validation of the data and changes across the different tools and teams. For this purpose, we need to facilitate the maintenance of traceability and the checking of consistency constraints across multiple tools and domains. Better still, providing a solution to integrate the tools could prevent some of these inconsistencies from occurring in the first place, by propagating value changes or solving inconsistencies automatically across the traceability links.

3 Modeling CPS and Consistency Management: Issues and Solutions

The complex nature of CPS implies that they are necessarily developed and maintained by multiple engineering teams, spanning domains of hardware, electronics, and software [34]. As a natural step in developing a complex system, these teams create models of various types to describe aspects of the system under development. Models are abstractions of the system, i.e., they leave out irrelevant details, and they have a particular focus. Modern CPS have become increasingly software-intensive, due to the increasing demand for more functionality and more interoperability with other CPS. Consequently, CPS development has adopted best practices from software engineering, one of which is DevOPS [19].

From the running example, we see that consistency management is considered essential to establish a DevOPS pipeline. This holds even for less extensive continuous development practices, such as CI/CD, because manual steps to check for and resolve inconsistencies inhibit rapid development cycles and at the same time these rapid development cycles may cause inconsistencies to be propagated through the development artefacts faster. In this section, we elaborate on the factors that make establishing consistency management so challenging. The challenges extend beyond tooling issues and the cross-domain nature of CPS development, and are fundamental to consistency management in DevOPS for CPS contexts. The remainder of this section contains our insights based on research in close collaboration with various industry partners [24, 25].

During the development and maintenance of CPS, inconsistencies are typically inevitable. Multiple models are created to design and document the system and an update to one of them cannot and typically should not be instantly propagated to all other places where it induces changes. Hence, there is almost always a temporary inconsistent state between models and almost never complete consistency. This is not a bad thing, on the contrary, complete consistency is often also not desired since it would interfere with development too much to have the need to immediately update related models. Therefore, to maintain the freedom of design iterations, inconsistencies must be tolerated to a certain extent.

However, from the running example, we also see a clear limit to this inconsistency tolerance. In practice, it is not at all straightforward to decide when an inconsistency shall no longer be tolerated. A reasonable starting point would be that inconsistencies shall be resolved before their effects ripple through the set of models describing the system. It is still difficult to pinpoint when problems would start due to, e.g., further development iterations on a model being based on assumptions that are no longer valid due to an inconsistency. Especially in a continuous development practice such as DevOPS, this may induce a high frequency of resolving inconsistencies. Manual checking and resolution of inconsistencies would then inhibit the DevOPS practice too much, which is why tooling to support consistency management is desperately needed.

Providing such tooling is not simply a matter of implementation, impediments may be caused by factors inherent to the distributed development of CPS. Different teams working on different components of the CPS may be modeling with different goals in mind; indeed, their models are created for different purposes. Commonly, the teams use the tooling suitable for their own domain to model their component of the CPS. For some teams in the CPS, this means using industry standard modeling tooling, whereas for others (especially software teams), these tools may commonly be of an informal nature. That is, they rely on drawing boxes and lines diagrams without established semantics in Office tools, rather than using modeling tools to create models that conform to the syntax and semantics of a modeling language. This informality is then a hurdle towards establishing automation for traceability and consistency management. For that automated support, there is a need for at least some alignment between teams and a minimum of established semantics within the models created by each team.

The second consequence of the cross-domain collaborative nature of CPS development is that the models from different teams are created at different levels of abstraction and semantic gaps appear between them. For example, a system engineering team may make choices about dividing the system in functions, components, defining their interfaces, and assigning them to particular software blocks. But this team would not further specify how the software shall be structured. Conversely, the software engineering team tasked with implementing specific function may create, e.g., sequence diagrams to understand the communication between several components, but is not concerned with the bigger picture of the system. These teams may moreover communicate using other means than by directly consulting the system model, since it is typically huge and contains many aspects irrelevant to a software engineering team. Also, the necessary tooling may not even be accessible to all teams that could benefit from viewing the model. Given these gaps, inconsistencies between the models is not trivially noticed nor repaired.

One of the challenges to consistency management in CPS is that each team is interpreting the design of the system with respect to their own components. Consistency is thus not limited to structure and behavior, but is related to the intention of the design of the system. When a change in the model of one team is made to change the intent of the system's behavior beyond the implementation of a specific component, then these types of changes must be propagated to other components and interpreted by other teams. Referring to the running example, consider that the length of the robotic arm is increased to ensure a longer reach. The underlying intent of this change may have been to increase throughput of the production line, in which case there are many other changes induced on the other components, apart from updating their components to deal with the longer arm. In the running example, the changed parameters can be shared across the teams, but it is then up to each team to appropriately interpret this information. Take the case of the mechanical engineering team needing to make new calculations and to communicate again those changes to the other teams. The key of this communication is not the value of the calculation, but rather the implications it has on other components of the CPS. In practice, teams developing a certain component do not always know how changes on their side affect others. The continuous integration of components in DevOPS may help to find out about unknown effects sooner. Still, avoiding unknown inconsistency issues require frequent communication between teams. Hence, traceability is about making sure that the intent of the changes is appropriately interpreted by each involved team and not only about creating links between model elements and ensure consistency when information appears in multiple places.

In practice, consistency checks are commonly run manually [25]. Automated resolution of consistency checks is sometimes possible but most often requires human in the loop [13], precisely because of the above reasons. In the DevOPS paradigm, consistency checks shall be kicked off automatically within the build pipeline, and we cannot wait too long for inconsistencies to be resolved either, because it would block the speed of development iterations. What can be done is to generate suggestions for resolutions that then are approved by humans in the loop [13].

The practical challenges of consistency management depend on the phase in development it is introduced. When introducing consistency checks in an already established project, challenges are encountered starting with defining consistency rules, then identifying all exceptions to those rules that the teams think should be acceptable, and lastly resolving the many (not uncommonly hundreds or thousands) of inconsistencies that will show up once automated checks are run.

In conclusion, the development of CPS inevitably brings inconsistencies between models, and they shall be tolerated to some extent but resolved eventually. Providing automated support for consistency management is challenging due to the nature of distributed development across multi-disciplinary teams and how and what they model.

4 Existing Solutions

A number of existing solutions proposed in the literature tackle these challenges from several different perspectives. Some solutions focus on enabling and ensuring traceability across tools from different domains, at various levels of granularity. Others extend these traceability links with consistency checking functionalities, allowing for inconsistencies to be automatically identified and flagged. In this section, we discuss these different approaches, their benefits for improving the development of CPS as well as the remaining limitations.

4.1 Traceability Management

The first aspect to be discussed is how to maintain connections between logically related artifacts from cross-domains. When information is duplicated across multiple locations and artifacts, it either demands time-consuming and error-prone manual updates or necessitates an automated solution that achieves the same outcome without adding to the engineers' workload. Klespitz et al. [33] propose a solution based on OSLC links for cross-tool traceability. OSLC protocol is supported by several tool suites used in practice.

Linsbauer et al. [36] introduced a trace-based approach for managing variability in product line systems. Their method involves capturing dependencies between procedures and the abstract syntax tree derived from variant executions. Trace links not only help maintain these relationships but can also store supplementary system information for further analysis. For instance, the Dapper platform [46] leverages trace links to monitor communication within distributed systems. Similarly, Asuncion et al. [5] propose using the Federated Information-based Design Environment to link system components and enrich these links with metadata about the system's architecture and operational state.

Several traceability approaches also address incremental management of trace links across artifacts in heterogeneous models [6, 45]. A critical requirement in managing such heterogeneous traceability is the use of a uniform or compatible representation for all involved artifacts. To this end, Heisig et al. [21] employ MOF as a common modeling foundation, while other solutions adopt Ecore [4] for similar purposes. Tools like Eclipse CAPRA[2] and YAKINDU[3] build on this principle, enabling traceability between any artifacts compatible with the EMF framework within the Eclipse ecosystem. Moreover, some approaches enhance traceability support through automatic maintenance of trace links [16, 40], as well as improved navigability for consistency checks [44] and trace analysis [38]. Ratiu et al. [43] propose a flexible, Eclipse CAPRA-like solution, offering additional runtime extensibility for traceability management.

These approaches highlight the value of trace links in preserving relationships between logically related artifacts across different models or tools. Nonetheless, a shared limitation among them is their relatively coarse granularity. While trace links effectively connect entire artifacts, they lack the ability to precisely associate specific properties within those artifacts, unless the underlying data model is extensively restructured or redundancy is introduced.

4.2 Maintaining Consistency Across Tools

Maintaining data consistency is a key challenge in the cross-domain context [14]. Although most development tools offer features to enforce consistency within a single model, ensuring coherence becomes significantly more difficult when multiple developers collaborate on the same project.

Alvaro et al. [3] propose a range of solutions to tackle this challenge at various levels of the system, including storage, runtime, and compile time, often utilizing language-encoded annotations. Some of these approaches integrate consistency checking with traceability to bridge the gaps between models and tools. For example, Adersberger and Philippsen [1] introduce a UML extension that automatically verifies consistency between architectural specifications and implementation code. Similarly, Tröls et al. [49] combine an artifact management platform with trace matrix representations and consistency rules encoded in Object Constraint Language to maintain consistency across different tools and models.

In the absence of trace links, maintaining consistency often requires limiting the set of tools and languages engineers can use. While incorporating traceability features can help mitigate this issue, it may also result in reduced granularity, as mentioned above. This method can be effective in some cases, such as using consistency rules to verify that all requirements are properly prioritized and categorized. When combined with traceability, these rules ensure that each requirement is implemented and tested.

[2] https://projects.eclipse.org/projects/modeling.capra.

[3] https://www.itemis.com/en/products/itemis-create/.

However, even with traces in place, the consistency checking methods outlined above remain too broad and general to adequately verify consistency across cross-domain artifacts.

4.3 Change Propagation

Consistency is a fundamental aspect for cross-domain artifacts, particularly in the context of CPS. Thus, propagating changes ensures that the system is in a consistent state. However, this is challenging task, with many change propagation solutions requiring extensive user involvement, which can increase the risk of failure and result in slower and less efficient propagation.

Determining the most effective change propagation path helps guide engineers in manually managing the effects of a change. Tang et al. [48] propose a solution that uses a dependency matrix to capture relationships between system components and reconstruct all possible propagation paths from a modified element. Their algorithm then recommends the shortest and most efficient path. Similarly, Ullah et al. [50] present a mathematical model that quantifies propagation impact and leverages it to analyze a design structure matrix, identifying the path that offers the most comprehensive risk coverage. Although these methods help reduce the likelihood of overlooked impacts, they can also introduce considerable overhead during each change propagation process.

Predicting the impact of change propagation has the advantage of not being triggered by every system modification. For example, Pasqual et al. [39] introduce a multi-layered network built from system history, which captures the organizational structure of the development team, the product architecture, and the change history, along with the interconnections between these layers. Similarly, Hamraz et al. [20] construct a network comprising the system's functional, behavioral, and structural elements. Ahmad et al. [2] also propose a network model that links requirements, functions, component structures, and detailed design processes. These structured representations serve as the basis for algorithms and heuristics used in change propagation analysis.

Change propagation techniques have valuable practical applications, especially for investigating various ways to link system components. However, they typically depend on significant user input to guarantee accurate propagation of changes.

5 Proposed Solution: Reactive Links

All the solutions previously described tackle the challenges of cross-domain development from different angles, while some limitations still remain. A possible way to reduce these limitations is to combine the features of these approaches into a single, unified artifact integration solution. For this purpose, we propose the use of reactive links [41, 42], which combine traceability, consistency checking and automatic change propagation to support the development of cross-domain projects.

Reactive links allow engineers to connect fine-granular data, represented as artifact property values, across tool boundaries. Once connected, the two property values associated with each link will be monitored for any changes. Depending on the setting of the link itself, a change to one of these properties can set the opposite property to the new value, or flag a possible inconsistency to be solved by the engineers.

5.1 *Working Assumptions*

Before selecting a solution to mitigate multi-domain development risks, the engineers need to ensure that their development environment is set up to support such solutions. Most existing solutions, including the reactive links solution we propose, make a number of assumptions about this environment, in the absence of which the solutions are not applicable. In the following, we discuss these assumptions and possible approaches to address them in practice.

To begin with, we assume that the integration solution can access and, where it is the case, modify the data maintained in the tools. This assumption is essential for DevOps-driven CPS development, where quick iteration cycles and automated validation depend on real-time data synchronization across heterogeneous tools. For example, if a mechanical component's properties change, the common environment must ensure that all related models, such as control algorithms, physics simulations, and digital twins, reflect the updated parameters without requiring manual intervention [7, 10, 15]. The ideal solution uses a single, shared environment where the data of each tool is stored in a uniform representation. Whenever a value is modified in a specialized tool, it is also automatically updated in the shared environment. If the integration, such as a change propagation solution, modifies a value in the shared environment, the equivalent value is also update in the tool that created the value. There is a variety of possible such environments, including:

- Federated data management systems or synchronized databases synchronized with the tools in use.
- Model repositories and artifact storage solutions that model the tool data.
- The use of a fully integrated tool suite, enhanced with background services that support integration solutions.

While the reactive links may support any of these approaches, their prototypical implementation is based on the DesignSpace artifact storage system [17, 22].[4] DesignSpace communicates with each tool through a customized adapters, that allow the synchronization between the data contained in the tools, and the data stored in the DesignSpace artifacts. As such, DesignSpace can create a synchronized copy of the

[4] More details available at: https://isse.jku.at/designspace.

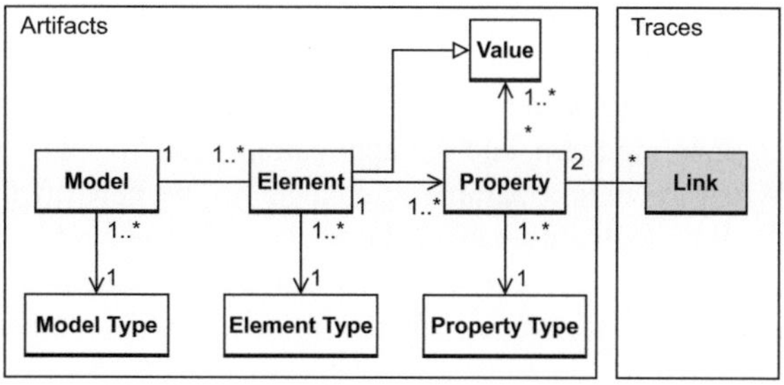

Fig. 1 Representation of multi-domain models and links

data available in the tools (or of a selection of this data), which can then be accessed, maintained and modified by the reactive links.

The representation format of the data is important to ensuring that the shared environment allows for automated traceability and consistency validation. Commonly, integration solutions require data represented in a property value schema, such as JSON formats or UML diagrams. This assumption is even more crucial when the solution targets fine-granular dependencies and automatic change propagation. Additionally, providing a uniform and stable metamodel significantly simplifies the implementation and use of integration solutions. For CPS development, the wide variety of tools and domains used require a balanced representation, that can both capture the data expressively, and not limit the types of tools that can be used.

For the reactive links solution, we define a generic artifacts representation, illustrated in Fig. 1, which accommodates a wide range of models and engineering artifacts. The metamodel consists of model elements, each characterized by a type, properties, and associated values. Notably, model elements themselves can serve as values, ensuring that hierarchical relationships between artifacts can be represented consistently. This design enables a highly adaptable and extensible representation, ensuring compatibility with diverse engineering tools and modeling approaches. Then, the artifacts are stored in the shared environment, and maintained in sync with their in-tool equivalent data throughout the development lifecycle.

Another aspect to be considered before deciding to add reactive links or other traceability and consistency support tools is identifying the granularity of the dependencies maintained. Most traceability and consistency checking solutions establish connections at model level, linking artifacts to each other. They can be used to document dependencies at a higher level, document the rationale or impact of changes, or identify when two artifact represent similar concepts in different views. However, the critical information these links reference is typically stored at the property level, within specific parameters or attributes of a model. This discrepancy can lead to unnecessary propagation or consistency checks, even when changes to unrelated properties have no actual impact on the linked data. If this type of information is targeted, using reactive links may be more effective. These links enable engineers to establish fine-grained links between specific corresponding properties rather than entire model elements. Going back to the working example, the engineers could use traceability links to document coarse dependencies between artifacts, such as between the controller section that lifts the arm and the graphical representation of the arm. Reactive links can then observe all the uses of the arm height in the project, as well as the dependencies between the results of calculations made by the mechanical engineering team, and the application points of these results in the controller code. When the height parameter changes to the new off-the-shelf component attribute, the links will automatically update this value everywhere the height is used. Then, when the calculations are applied again, the results are also propagated through the reactive links, reducing the risk of miscommunication between teams.

5.2 Reactive Link Attributes

Provided that the development environment matches our working assumptions, reactive links can be added to monitor constraints [27] and propagate changes between related property values. When creating a link, the engineers can select a variety of attributes that define the functionality fulfilled by the link. The implementation details of these attributes can enable more specialized or flexible reactive links to more accurately match the needs of the development teams.

5.2.1 Link Operators

The most important attribute to the functionality of a link is its associated operator. This operator defines the documented relation between the two property values connected. When creating a link, the engineers select the appropriate operator depending on specific use case for this link. Let us consider, for example, when linking the robotic arm height between the third party parameters spreadsheet to the calculator tool used by the mechanical engineers. If the engineers expect that an update on either side of this link is highlighted as an inconsistency, they would select an *Equals* (==) operator. Alternatively, if they prefer for the changes to automatically apply the same change to the connected property value, they would select an *Assignment* (=) operator.

The prototypical implementation of the reactive links provides a number of comparative operators and an assignment operator, as described in Table 1. Some of these operators are type-specific, such as the *"includes"* operator that requires both connected property values to be collections. On the other hand, the *Assignment* (=), *Equals* (==) and *Not equals* (!=) operators can be applied to property values of any type. This list of operators can be extended to cover additional use cases and property types for additional scenarios. This extension has to be applied during the implementation of the reactive links, at which point the developers can define the symbols used for any new operator, the logic to be applied when a connected property value is modified, and any additional constraint the property value must fulfill to be linked with the new operator.

Table 1 Full list of available operators for numerical, textual and collection data types

Operator	Description
=	*Assignment* propagates the change to the linked property value
==	*Equals* checks the equality of the linked values
!=	*Not equals* checks the inequality of the linked values
<	*Less than* checks that the value is less than its counterpart
<=	*Less than or Equal* checks that the value is less or equal to its counterpart
>	*Greater than* checks that the value is greater than its counterpart
>=	*Greater than or Equal* checks that the value is greater or equal to its counterpart
Includes	Checks that one set property value contains all the elements of another set property value
Contains	Checks that the set property value contains one specific property value
StartWith	Checks that a string property value begins with the characters of another string property value
EndsWith	Checks that a string property value ends with the characters of another string property value
SubString	Checks that a string property value contains another string property value

5.2.2 Propagation Direction

Automatically propagating a change in any direction may introduce unintended changes, which is a concern. For example, suppose that the mechanical engineering team wants to determine the edge case values that would result in safety concerns. To determine this, they edit the robotic arm height parameter in their calculator to an extreme value. But this height parameter is, as mentioned in the previous example, connected to the third party parameters spreadsheet that documents the off-the-shelf component characteristics. If the experiments of the mechanical engineering team alter this spreadsheet, the result may potentially be an extremely unsafe CPS design, or a design that cannot be applied to the actual components selected. As such, another important attribute of the reactive links is the direction in which their effect occurs. We provide three direction types, which can be selected case-by-case for each created link:

- *Bidirectional effect*: a change applied to any of the values connected has the same effect. If the operator chosen is assignment, the change will be propagated. Any other selected operator will trigger a consistency check.
- *Unidirectional effect*: a change only triggers the link if applied to one of the values, while a change to the other value does not result in a link evaluation.
- *Asymmetric effect*: a change to a value triggers a different effect depending on which value was modified. In this case, the link operator differs depending on the source of the change.

Our example assumes that the link is a bidirectional propagation, however, this does not have to be the case. Engineers can choose to use a unidirectional propagation link, which only propagates changes done to the parameter spreadsheet. If an off-the-shelf component parameter changes, this change will be mirrored in the mechanical engineering team's calculator. On the other hand, this team can experiment with edge case values or different settings without affecting the spreadsheet or triggering any links. However, what if they experiment with edge cases and forget to return to the correct parameter value? Or a small error occurs when they undo their changes and the calculator parameter is no longer accurate? If they use a unidirectional link, this may go unnoticed. In this case, they may prefer to opt for an asymmetrical link, with an assignment operator from the spreadsheet to the calculator, and an equals operator in the opposite direction. In this case, they can still experiment without affecting the spreadsheet data, but an inconsistency warning will remind them that the current parameter value does not match the chosen components for the project.

5.2.3 Propagation Trigger Types

Another possible solution to limit unwanted propagation is to create links that are manually triggered. In our prototype, all the reactive links are, by default, automatically triggered. In this case, whenever a property value is changed, all the links connected to it are automatically evaluated. During our discussions with industry partners, they expressed that, in some cases, the engineers may prefer to have more control over when the links are evaluated. For this, the implementation of the reactive links can introduce a manual signal to evaluate the affected links. As such, the mechanical engineering team could experiment with values in the calculator without triggering any reactive link, and then go back to the spreadsheet and trigger the links on that side, to set all the values back and return to a consistent state.

While manually triggered links offer more control to the engineers, they also involve a number of risks that should be considered. Firstly, if a property value is connected to a large number of links (e.g., this value is an input used in all the tools), ensuring that all these links are triggered can become quite overwhelming. Any link that is not triggered may introduce an inconsistency that goes unnoticed. Additionally, the evaluation of a link may introduce a cascade propagation that requires other links to be triggered. For example, suppose the engineers trigger the links to set the arm height to the value set in the spreadsheet. This may result in some calculator results changing, which need to be propagated further through other links that must also be manually triggered. On the other hand, automatic propagation solves this issue by triggering each link whenever a change has occurred, including when this change is the result of another link propagation. However, there are other risks to consider, as the lack of manual control can lead to the automatically triggered links becoming very intrusive. Consider that the mechanical engineering team is experimenting with corner cases and right then, a new off-the-shelf component is selected by another team. The new value in the parameter spreadsheet is propagated to the calculator, overwriting the changes made by the mechanical engineers. While obviously annoying, this may result in even more issues when this propagation does not come with a notification and goes unnoticed. Thus, both propagation trigger types have their own risks and benefits, which have to be weighed against the development process priorities and mitigated through additional safe-guards.

5.2.4 Transformations and Unit Conversions

While the attributes above define how the reactive links should react to changes, additional attributes and formulas can be used to define how the connected values are compared or propagated and to allow the definition of small data transformations. Consider, for example, that a link connects the deflection value in the mechanical engineering calculator to a static constant in the controller code that stores the same value. The adapter designed for the calculator stores all the value to the artifact store preserving the type, so the deflection would be a floating point number. The adapter provided for the software engineering team's IDE, on the other hand, only parses the code and stores it in textual form, so the value of this constant will be stored as a string. The reactive link between these two values can be enhanced with small transformations (e.g., `toString()` and `toFloat()` in the respective directions) to propagate or check the consistency between the values while maintaining the correct typing. Alternatively, suppose that the calculator computes a maximum weight value, representing the extreme limits of the robotic arm, but the requirements specify the off-the-shelf components should have a weight limit at least 25% higher for increased safety. A reactive link can connect the maximum weight parameter in the calculator and the actual weight limit in the parameters spreadsheet, and check that the first is at least 25% lower than the second.

Similarly, when the property values are stored with additional unit information, the reactive links can perform simple type conversions. For example, suppose this particular robotic arm is expected to pick up a package, lift it a few centimeters above the conveyor belt and transfer it to another conveyor belt. This would be represented in the requirements and the movement distance in each direction needs to be considered in the calculations and controller, as well as the simulations for testing [8, 10, 29]. However, these values may be represented in different measurement units depending on the specific expert team that maintains them [11, 12, 30, 32]. The software engineers and graphical designers would probably work with centimeter values, while the mechanical engineers would prefer values in meters, for easier use in other formulas. The reactive links can connect a property value containing a distance in meters to another in centimeters and maintain the consistency without requiring additional transformations. The links manage the consistency of the measurement units whenever the units are available.

5.2.5 Implementation Challenges

Aside from the risks involved in selecting the propagation trigger type, reactive links have a few other limitations that need to be considered and mitigated during the implementation.

The first such risk comes from the creation of circular link patterns. Imagine the collection of reactive links in a project as a directed graph. The nodes are the property values connected, while the links themselves are the edges. A change to one property value triggers a graph traversal, as the change gets propagated across the links according to the link direction and operator. Problems can, however, occur when this graph has a cycle. While the propagation only occurs when it would generate an impact (i.e., if the property value is already correct, it will not be set again to the same value), infinite cycles of propagation can still occur, for example, when the type conversion leads to slightly different results (e.g.,"0.1" and "0.10" are numerically the same value, but different string) or when transformations are applied. For this, the reactive link implementation must detect cycles and stop propagation before it generates issues. For this purpose, the reactive links implementation can choose one of three options:

- *Support engineers in identifying and maintaining these cycles*: graphical views of the link network, notifications when a cycle is created.
- *Prevent cycles from occurring in the first place*: identify when a cycle is about to be closed and prevent the creation of the last link.
- *Identify cycles and stop propagation when a cycle is traversed*: cycle detection algorithms, strong component identification and propagation based on strong component information.

The data types of the property values connected may also present added risks. For example, the mechanical calculator uses floating point values, as does the CAD tool used for graphical design and simulation. A challenge of floating point numbers is the supported level of precision. This defines, in easy terms, the number of decimal digits supported before the number is rounded. Suppose a calculation returns the value 1.(4), which in mathematics is a 1, followed by an infinite number of 4 decimals. The mechanical calculator works with high precision values, so it may represent this number as 1.4444445, for example. The graphical design tool accepts much lower precision, representing the same number as 1.45. Now, suppose these two values are linked with a bidirectional propagation reactive link. While in essence, the value represents the same number, the different precision levels of the tools lead to different rounding. As a result, the link may not detect that the propagation is complete, leading to infinite propagation loops. This, in combination with the presence of a link cycle, can easily lead to significant issues, or even completely freeze the development while the same value is propagated and rounded again and again. In order to prevent this occurrence, the links should be enhanced with precision limits and rounding sensitivity. During the implementation of the reactive linking mechanism, the developers must consider the data types that will be linked and the challenges generated by the data types.

5.3 Using Reactive Links in Practice

Having defined reactive links and their variety of attributes, the next question is how can they actually be used in practice for optimal support. In the following, we discuss a number of different perspectives.

5.3.1 Recommended Linking Process During Development

Firstly, for the reactive links to be available, they need to be created in the project. Currently, reactive links can only be created manually, although automation may be possible using similar approaches to traceability recovery, as we will discuss shortly.

Most development teams conduct an early-stage analysis to identify dependencies between the different models they are developing in each specialized tool, particularly in safety-critical applications where undetected dependencies can pose significant risks. This process typically begins when new client requirements are elicited and documented by the requirements engineering team. The system design is then modeled, followed by a preliminary requirements analysis during which dependencies and traceability links are identified. We propose that reactive links are also defined at this stage.

Once dependencies are identified, translating them into reactive links is a straightforward process. Engineers specify which property values are linked and define the behavior of the link using predefined properties. For example, in the development of an industrial robotic arm, a requirement specifying the maximum piston pressure would be linked to the corresponding property in a computational model used by mechanical engineers. Engineers could then define an asymmetric reactive link that propagates changes from the requirements to the model while simultaneously detecting inconsistencies in the opposite direction.

After the initial creation of reactive links, the development process proceeds as usual. Since CPS development following DevOPS is often iterative, new dependencies may emerge during later stages. We recommend capturing these as soon as they are identified to maintain consistency and prevent errors. Since new dependencies arise incrementally, adding new reactive links over time is less burdensome than the initial dependency analysis. If a link is no longer necessary or needs modification, engineers can adjust or delete it as needed. For manual propagation, inactive links can simply be ignored without requiring deletion. For automatic propagation, links must be explicitly modified or removed.

Identifying dependencies is often one of the most complex and crucial steps in ensuring traceability, consistency, and safety. While manual dependency analysis may be feasible for smaller projects, larger-scale projects require automated support to mitigate the risks of human error and inefficiency. Research shows that manually comparing all requirements in a project can take up to 12 hours, and this estimate would significantly increase when extended to model artifacts and their fine-grained properties.

To address this challenge, various automated solutions for dependency identification exist. Some leverage content analysis techniques to detect common concepts that imply dependencies. Others utilize syntax tree parsing, annotation-based methods, or engineer activity tracking to improve accuracy. However, most existing solutions focus on requirements or code dependencies, meaning that additional training or manual intervention may be required to adapt them for fine-grained property value dependencies. Even in cases where automated tools require some manual input, their use can significantly reduce the workload associated with establishing reactive links.

5.3.2 Reactive Links for DevOps in CPS

Most of our analysis of reactive links usage and benefits targets maintaining consistency in cross-tool and cross-domain contexts, with a focus on the development itself. However, these links can be useful in a wide array of other applications, both during the development and, potentially, during the autonomous operation and coordination of CPS. Some of the main applications include:

- Continuous integration and deployment for CPS, where reactive links can maintain the consistency of software and hardware configurations, similarly to our previous examples.
- Automated compliance checking for safety-critical domain CPS, which must adhere to strict regulation and safety standards, including safety limits for parameters across multiple tools.
- Digital twin synchronization, for which the reactive links could be used to synchronize real-world sensor data with digital models to maintain the quality and accuracy of the simulations [15, 28].
- Complex simulations, where the reactive links could be used to synchronize runtime data across multiple tools for more accurate and expressive simulations, such as including controller runtime data and updating calculator formulas with real-time inputs.

5.4 Collaboration with Reactive Links

The reactive links are developed to be individual instances stored in the same environment as the data they connect. As a result, they can be seamlessly integrated with the rest of the artifacts for smooth collaboration support.

In our prototype, the implementation is based on DesignSpace, which emphasizes multi-tool, multi-domain, and multi-user collaboration, providing various features to support different working styles and team preferences. In DesignSpace, each user operates within one or more workspaces, which serve as isolated environments for managing artifacts related to specific tools or domains. These workspaces follow a hierarchical inheritance structure, where each workspace has a parent and can have multiple child workspaces. Changes made within a workspace remain private until the user explicitly commits them, making them available in the parent workspace. Conversely, updates from a parent workspace can be pulled into a child workspace. These commit and update actions can be performed manually or automated based on user preferences.

Reactive links seamlessly integrate into this workspace model, ensuring that dependencies between properties are maintained across the hierarchy. Changes made in one workspace do not immediately affect others unless explicitly committed and pulled, allowing engineers to work in parallel while maintaining data integrity. This reduces disruptions while also ensuring that changes propagate in a controlled and traceable manner. Additionally, the engineers can customize the collaboration model to their preferred style, having the option to automatically commit or automatically pull any changes if they prefer.

6 Conclusion

This chapter presents a novel solution to ensure the traceability and consistency among artifacts in multi-tool and cross-domains development of CPS. For that, we propose the use of reactive links, which involves creating links that connect artifacts in a highly granular network of related property values, which react automatically to changes in any of their connected values. This reaction can be customized to either propagate the change throughout the network or alert the user of any constraint violations introduced.

While our solution offers a solid foundation for artifact linking, further development and customization are needed to support specific use cases. For instance, it currently does not address precision discrepancies, which are critical in complex engineering contexts. Additionally, improving the user interface to better handle cyclic links, by displaying more detailed information about detected cycles and the properties involved, would enhance the overall user experience. Addressing these limitations could significantly improve the solution's usability and applicability, offering valuable directions for future research.

Competing Interests The authors have no conflicts of interest to declare that are relevant to the content of this chapter.

References

1. J. Adersberger, M. Philippsen, Reflexml: Uml-based architecture-to-code traceability and consistency checking, in *Software Architecture*. ed. by I. Crnkovic, V. Gruhn, M. Book (Springer, Berlin, 2011), pp. 344–359
2. N. Ahmad, D.C. Wynn, P.J. Clarkson, Change impact on a product and its redesign process: a tool for knowledge capture and reuse. Res. Eng. Design **24**(3), 219–244 (2013)
3. P. Alvaro, P. Bailis, N. Conway, J.M. Hellerstein, Consistency without borders, in *4th Annual Symposium on Cloud Computing, SOCC '13* (Association for Computing Machinery, New York, NY, USA, 2013)
4. N. Anquetil, U. Kulesza, R. Mitschke, A. Moreira, J.-C. Royer, A. Rummler, A. Sousa, A model-driven traceability framework for software product lines. Softw. Syst. Model. **9**, 427–451 (2010)
5. H.U. Asuncion, R.N. Taylor, Capturing custom link semantics among heterogeneous artifacts and tools, in *2009 ICSE Workshop on Traceability in Emerging Forms of Software Engineering* (IEEE, 2009), pp. 1–5
6. T. Beyhl, R. Hebig, H. Giese, A model management framework for maintaining traceability links, in *Software Engineering 2013-Workshopband* (2013)
7. C. Birchler, N. Ganz, S. Khatiri, A. Gambi, S. Panichella, Cost-effective simulation-based test selection in self-driving cars software with SDC-Scissor, in *IEEE International Conference on Software Analysis, Evolution and Reengineering, SANER 2022, Honolulu, HI, USA, March 15-18, 2022* (IEEE, 2022), pp. 164–168
8. C. Birchler, S. Khatiri, B. Bosshard, A. Gambi, S. Panichella, Machine learning-based test selection for simulation-based testing of self-driving cars software. Empir. Softw. Eng. **28**(3), 71 (2023)
9. C. Birchler, S. Khatiri, P. Derakhshanfar, S. Panichella, A. Panichella, Single and multi-objective test cases prioritization for self-driving cars in virtual environments. ACM Trans. Softw. Eng. Methodol. **32**(2), 28:1–28:30 (2023)
10. C. Birchler, S. Khatiri, P. Rani, T. Kehrer, S. Panichella, A roadmap for simulation-based testing of autonomous cyber-physical systems: challenges and future direction (2025)
11. C. Birchler, S. Klikovits, M. Fazzini, S. Panichella, ICST tool competition 2025—self-driving car testing track, in *IEEE/ACM International Conference on Software Testing, Verification and Validation* (ICST, 2025)
12. C. Birchler, S. Klikovits, M. Fazzini, S. Panichella, SBFT tool competition 2025 - cps-sdc regression testing track, in *IEEE/ACM International Workshop on Search-Based and Fuzz Testing, SBFT@ICSE 2025* (2025)
13. C. Birchler, T.K. Mohammed, P. Rani, T. Nechita, T. Kehrer, S. Panichella, How does simulation-based testing for self-driving cars match human perception? 1(FSE) (2024)
14. C. Birchler, C. Rohrbach, T. Kehrer, S. Panichella, SensoDat: simulation-based sensor dataset of self-driving cars, in *21st IEEE/ACM International Conference on Mining Software Repositories, MSR 2024, Lisbon, Portugal, April 15-16, 2024*. ed. by D. Spinellis, A. Bacchelli, E. Constantinou (ACM, 2024), pp. 510–514
15. C. Birchler, C. Rohrbach, H. Kim, A. Gambi, T. Liu, J. Horneber, T. Kehrer, S. Panichella, TEASER: simulation-based CAN bus regression testing for self-driving cars software, in *38th IEEE/ACM International Conference on Automated Software Engineering, ASE 2023, Luxembourg, September 11-15, 2023* (IEEE, 2023), pp. 2058–2061
16. A. Bougdira, I. Akharraz, A. Ahaitouf, A traceability proposal for industry 4.0. J. Ambient Intell. Humanized Comput. **11**, 3355–3369 (2020)
17. A. Demuth, M. Riedl-Ehrenleitner, A. Nöhrer, P. Hehenberger, K. Zeman, A. Egyed, Designspace: an infrastructure for multi-user/multi-tool engineering, in *30th Annual ACM Symposium on Applied Computing* (ACM, New York, NY, USA, 2015), pp. 1486–1491
18. A. Di Sorbo, F. Zampetti, A. Visaggio, M. Di Penta, S. Panichella, Automated identification and qualitative characterization of safety concerns reported in uav software platforms. ACM Trans. Softw. Eng. Methodol. **32**(3) (2023)

19. J. Fritzsch, J. Bogner, M. Haug, A.C. Franco da Silva, C. Rubner, M. Saft, H. Sauer, S. Wagner, Adopting microservices and devops in the cyber-physical systems domain: a rapid review and case study. Softw. Practice Exp. **53**(3), 790–810 (2023)
20. B. Hamraz, N.H. Caldwell, T.W. Ridgman, P.J. Clarkson, Fbs linkage ontology and technique to support engineering change management. Res. Eng. Design **26**(1), 3–35 (2015)
21. P. Heisig, J.-P. Steghöfer, C. Brink, S. Sachweh, A generic traceability metamodel for enabling unified end-to-end traceability in software product lines, in *Proceedings of the 34th ACM/SIGAPP Symposium on Applied Computing* (2019), pp. 2344–2353
22. E. Herac, W. Assunçãao, L. Marchezan, R. Haas, A. Egyed, A flexible operation-based infrastructure for collaborative model-driven engineering. J. Object Technol. **22**(2), 1–14 (2023)
23. E. Herac, L. Marchezan, W.K. Assunção, A. Egyed, Conflict-based change awareness for collaborative model-driven software engineering. J. Object Technol. **23**(3) (2024)
24. R. Jongeling, J. Carlson, A. Cicchetti, Impediments to introducing continuous integration for model-based development in industry, in *2019 45th Euromicro Conference on Software Engineering and Advanced Applications (SEAA)* (IEEE, 2019), pp. 434–441
25. R. Jongeling, F. Ciccozzi, J. Carlson, A. Cicchetti, Consistency management in industrial continuous model-based development settings: a reality check. Softw. Syst. Model. **21**(4), 1511–1530 (2022)
26. A.K. Kamrani, E.S.A. Nasr, *Collaborative Engineering* (Springer, 2008)
27. S. Khatiri, F.M. Amin, S. Panichella, P. Tonella, When uncertainty leads to unsafety: empirical insights into the role of uncertainty in unmanned aerial vehicle safety. Empir. Softw. Eng. (2025)
28. S. Khatiri, S. Panichella, P. Tonella, Simulation-based test case generation for unmanned aerial vehicles in the neighborhood of real flights, in *International Conference on Software Testing, Verification and Validation* (IEEE, 2023), pp. 281–292
29. S. Khatiri, S. Panichella, P. Tonella, Simulation-based testing of unmanned aerial vehicles with aerialist, in *International Conference on Software Engineering (ICSE)* (2024)
30. S. Khatiri, P. Saurabh, T. Zimmermann, C. Munasinghe, C. Birchler, S. Panichella, SBFT tool competition 2024—cps-uav test case generation track, in *IEEE/ACM International Workshop on Search-Based and Fuzz Testing, SBFT@ICSE 2024* (2024)
31. S. Khatiri, A.D. Sorbo, F. Zampetti, C.A. Visaggio, M.D. Penta, S. Panichella, Identifying safety-critical concerns in unmanned aerial vehicle software platforms with SALIENT. SoftwareX **27**, 101748 (2024)
32. S. Khatiri, T. Zohdinasab, P. Saurabh, D. Humeniuk, S. Panichella, SBFT tool competition 2025—CPS-UAV test case generation track, in *IEEE/ACM International Workshop on Search-Based and Fuzz Testing, SBFT@ICSE 2025* (2025)
33. J. Klespitz, M. Bíró, L. Kovács, Enhanced traceability and consistency with augmented lifecycle space, in *2016 IEEE 20th Jubilee International Conference on Intelligent Engineering Systems (INES)* (IEEE, 2016), pp. 207–212
34. I. Koren, F. Rinker, K. Meixner, J. Matevska, J. Walter, Challenges and opportunities of devops in cyber-physical production systems engineering, in *2023 IEEE 6th International Conference on Industrial Cyber-Physical Systems (ICPS)* (IEEE, 2023), pp. 1–6
35. P. L. Li, A.J. Ko, A. Begel, Cross-disciplinary perspectives on collaborations with software engineers, in *2017 IEEE/ACM 10th International Workshop on Cooperative and Human Aspects of Software Engineering (CHASE)* (IEEE, 2017), pp. 2–8
36. L. Linsbauer, F. Angerer, P. Grünbacher, D. Lettner, H. Prähofer, R.E. Lopez-Herrejon, A. Egyed, Recovering feature-to-code mappings in mixed-variability software systems, in *2014 IEEE International Conference on Software Maintenance and Evolution* (2014), pp. 426–430
37. S. Nambisan, D. Wilemon, Software development and new product development: Potentials for cross-domain knowledge sharing. IEEE Trans. Eng. Manag. **47**(2), 211–220 (2000)
38. A. Noyer, P. Iyenghar, E. Pulvermueller, F. Pramme, G. Bikker, Traceability and interfacing between requirements engineering and uml domains using the standardized reqif format, in *2015 3rd International Conference on Model-Driven Engineering and Software Development (MODELSWARD)* (IEEE, 2015), pp. 1–6

39. M.C. Pasqual, O.L. de Weck, Multilayer network model for analysis and management of change propagation. Res. Eng. Design **23**(4), 305–328 (2012)
40. M. Rahimi, W. Goss, J. Cleland-Huang, Evolving requirements-to-code trace links across versions of a software system, in *2016 IEEE International Conference on Software Maintenance and Evolution (ICSME)* (2016), pp. 99–109
41. C.C. Raţiu, W.K. Assunção, R. Haas, A. Egyed, Reactive links across multi-domain engineering models, in *25th International Conference on Model Driven Engineering Languages and Systems* (2022), pp. 76–86
42. C.-C. Raţiu, W. K. Assunção, E. Herac, R. Haas, C. Lauwerys, A. Egyed, Using reactive links to propagate changes across engineering models. Softw. Syst. Model. 1–27 (2024)
43. C.C. Raţiu, C. Mayr-Dorn, W.K. Assunção, A. Egyed, Taming cross-tool traceability in the wild, in *2023 IEEE 31st International Requirements Engineering Conference (RE)* (IEEE, 2023), pp. 233–243
44. H. Schwarz, J. Ebert, A. Winter, Graph-based traceability: a comprehensive approach. Softw. Syst. Model. **9**, 473–492 (2010)
45. A. Seibel, R. Hebig, H. Giese, Traceability in model-driven engineering: Efficient and scalable traceability maintenance. Softw. Syst. Traceability 215–240 (2012)
46. B.H. Sigelman, L.A. Barroso, M. Burrows, P. Stephenson, M. Plakal, D. Beaver, S. Jaspan, C. Shanbhag, Dapper, a large-scale distributed systems tracing infrastructure. Technical report, Google, Inc., 2010
47. B. Song, N.S. Zurita, G. Zhang, G. Stump, C. Balon, S.W. Miller, M. Yukish, J. Cagan, C. McComb, Toward hybrid teams: A platform to understand human-computer collaboration during the design of complex engineered systems, in *Design Society Conference*, vol. 1 (Cambridge University Press, 2020), pp. 1551–1560
48. D.-B. Tang, L.-L. Yin, Q. Wang, I. Ullah, H.-H. Zhu, S. Leng, Workload-based change propagation analysis in engineering design. Concurr. Eng. **24**(1), 17–34 (2016)
49. M.A. Tröls, A. Mashkoor, A. Egyed, Collaboratively enhanced consistency checking in a cloud-based engineering environment, in *ACM SIGCHI Symposium on Engineering Interactive Computing Systems* (ACM, 2019)
50. I. Ullah, D. Tang, Q. Wang, L. Yin, Exploring effective change propagation in a product family design. J. Mech. Des. **139**(12), 121101 (2017)
51. B. Vogel-Heuser, M. Böhm, F. Brodeck, K. Kugler, S. Maasen, D. Pantförder, M. Zou, J. Buchholz, H. Bauer, F. Brandl et al., Interdisciplinary engineering of cyber-physical production systems: highlighting the benefits of a combined interdisciplinary modelling approach on the basis of an industrial case. Des. Sci. **6**, e5 (2020)
52. F. Zampetti, R. Kapur, M. Di Penta, S. Panichella, An empirical characterization of software bugs in open-source cyber–physical systems. J. Syst. Softw. **192**, 111425 (2022)
53. F. Zampetti, D.A. Tamburri, S. Panichella, A. Panichella, G. Canfora, M.D. Penta, Continuous integration and delivery practices for cyber-physical systems: an interview-based study. ACM Trans. Softw. Eng. Methodol. **32**(3), 73:1–73:44 (2023)

DevOps Testing for Cyber-Physical Systems

Mattia Fazzini, Alessio Gambi, Vincenzo Riccio, Annibale Panichella, and Stefan Klikovits

Abstract DevOps is driven by feedback signals that help developers identify issues and potential improvements. One of these signals comes from automated testing activities that stress the CPS under test at various levels during development and, potentially, at runtime, to verify its functional correctness and non-functional properties (e.g., timing and safety). After introducing the phases and levels of CPS testing, this chapter presents the unique challenges of applying automated testing to CPS within the DevOps lifecycle. Next, the chapter presents current automated testing solutions to address the most pressing issues of CPS Testing for DevOps, including addressing the reality gap via domain augmentation and simulation ensembles, improving automated test generation by generating valid and adequate test input and correct test oracles, and increasing testing efficiency by prioritizing and selecting test cases. The chapter concludes by presenting the path to achieve the DevOps vision of continuously evaluating CPS systems grounded in operational reliability and evolving environments. The proposed path forward includes defining effective methods for improving existing test suites using production data, as well as further enhancing testing efficiency through the optimized setup of the testing environment and reducing system tests.

M. Fazzini (✉)
University of Minnesota, Minneapolis, MN, USA
e-mail: mfazzini@umn.edu

A. Gambi
Austrian Institute of Technology, Vienna, Austria
e-mail: alessio.gambi@ait.ac.at

V. Riccio
University of Udine, Udine, Italy
e-mail: vincenzo.riccio@uniud.it

A. Panichella
Delft University of Technology, Delft, The Netherlands
e-mail: a.panichella@tudelft.nl

S. Klikovits
Johannes Kepler University, Linz, Austria
e-mail: stefan.klikovits@jku.at

S. Panichella et al. (eds.), *Roadmap for DevOps in Cyber-Physical Systems*,
https://doi.org/10.1007/978-981-95-1786-2_4

1 Introduction and Motivation

Cyber-Physical Systems (CPS) are software-intensive systems that integrate computational algorithms with physical processes [36] through tightly coupled sensors, actuators, and communication infrastructure. Prominent examples include self-driving vehicles [4, 28], medical devices [114], industrial automation systems [36], and autonomous drones [80, 134]. The increasing reliance of these systems on software for perception, decision-making, and control, and their use in safety-critical applications, has amplified the critical role of software quality assurance—especially *software testing* [9]—in ensuring their safety and correctness.

The correctness of a CPS cannot be assessed purely in terms of abstract logic, that is, at the software level; instead, it must account for the concrete, often safety-critical, impact of the system's actions in the physical world [34, 126]. In CPS domains such as autonomous driving, robotic surgery, and smart grids, software failures can lead to *catastrophic outcomes*, including loss of life [137], property damage [6], or disruption of essential services [68]. Unlike purely software systems, CPS operate in unpredictable and dynamic environments [34], where software faults can lead to failures in sensing, control, or timing, timing, each of which can pose safety constraints and regulatory requirements [4].

The tight coupling between software and the physical environment introduces *new classes of faults* that go beyond functional errors [149]. These include timing violations [92], control instabilities [77], and violations of physical invariants [96]. For example, a defect in an autonomous vehicle's lane detection algorithm may cause a subtle but persistent drift in steering, eventually leading to a collision. The consequences of such faults are compounded by the *real-time and safety-critical* nature of CPS operations, making rigorous and systematic testing indispensable.

Testing in the context of CPS serves several key purposes [34, 96]:

- *Verifying functional correctness and non-functional properties*, ensuring that the system behaves according to the specification in normal and edge-case scenarios.
- *Assessing reliability and robustness*, especially under varying environmental conditions such as noise, interference, or component degradation.
- *Ensuring performance and timing guarantees*, which are often critical for real-time control loops [143].
- *Validating safety properties*, ensuring that the system does not enter unsafe states or violate safety constraints during operation.

However, these goals are challenged by several intrinsic characteristics of CPS and their development processes, particularly in a DevOps context [4, 28, 110, 149]:

- *Multimodal Faults*: A CPS can fail due to software bugs, sensor inaccuracies, actuator misbehavior, or environmental uncertainty. These faults can be hard to isolate and reproduce, particularly in safety-critical domains [149].
- *Gap Between Simulation and Reality* [110]: Simulation environments offer safe and scalable ways to test CPS during early development (e.g., Model-in-the-Loop, Software-in-the-Loop, Hardware-in-the-Loop). However, simulations often

abstract or simplify real-world physics, sensor noise, and human interaction, creating a *semantic gap* between simulated correctness and field performance. In DevOps for CPS, this reality gap might also affect the quality and usefulness of the feedback signals from operations.

- *High Levels of Autonomy*: Many CPS, such as self-driving cars, are built from modular *features* that operate autonomously (e.g., adaptive cruise control, lane-keeping, emergency braking). These features may interact in unpredictable or undesirable ways, especially when they share control over physical actuators. For instance, conflicting braking commands from multiple features may compromise safety unless managed explicitly [4]. CPS are usually embedded in smart ecosystems; thus, they might interact and interfere, causing hard-to-predict emergent behaviors. For example, when autonomous vehicles share the road, they might cause disruptions and collisions [53]. Detecting such *undesired interactions* through testing is crucial but combinatorially complex.
- *Test Generation and Scalability*: Effective CPS testing often requires generating large suites of test scenarios—many of which must cover rare but safety-critical situations (e.g., unexpected pedestrian crossings, sensor spoofing, or degraded road conditions). Simulation-based tests are useful [], but their *long execution times and large input spaces* pose significant challenges for scalability, particularly in regression testing [26, 28].

Chapter Structure. The remainder of this chapter is structured as follows. Section 2 introduces the phases and levels of CPS testing, providing a foundation for understanding how testing fits into the DevOps lifecycle. Section 3 discusses the unique challenges of CPS testing in DevOps, including the reality gap, feature interactions, and test generation. Section 4 presents current solutions to address these challenges, such as simulation ensembles, automated test generation, and test prioritization. Finally, Sect. 5 outlines future directions for CPS testing in DevOps.

2 Phases and Levels of CPS Testing

The combination of systems engineering and software development practices for the construction of cyber-physical systems (CPS) also requires the adaptation and integration of a diverse set of testing techniques on various levels of abstraction, to assert correct-by-construction approaches.

Thereby, classical systems engineering techniques such as the well-known V-model [63] are still relevant for validating and verifying the physical components. However, in the context of Cyber-Physical Systems (CPS), these are increasingly complemented—or even replaced—by DevOps pipelines that support continuous integration, testing, and deployment for the *cyber* components, which include agile software development and artificial intelligence (AI) technologies.

The DevOps pipeline for CPS (see Fig. 1) provides a more iterative and feedback-driven workflow compared to traditional models. It emphasizes automation, early

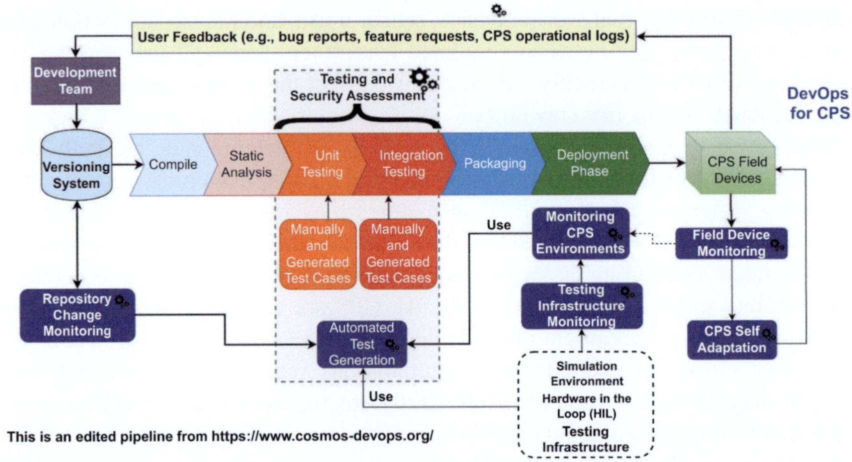

Fig. 1 DevOps pipeline for cyber-physical systems (from Chap. "Introduction")

testing, and the continuous integration of both hardware and software components. While physical validation may still follow structured plans, the software stack evolves continuously through rapid development cycles, supported by simulation environments and runtime monitoring.

In the rest of this section, we illustrate how the CPS-specific DevOps pipeline applies to different phases of system development, including practices such as model-based design, software-in-the-loop testing, and hardware–software co-integration (Sect. 2.1). Next, in Sect. 2.2, we relate these practices to the common "levels" of CPS testing.

2.1 *Phases of CPS Testing*

The engineering of trustworthy CPS requires the structured, consistent and comprehensive application of various testing methods throughout the entire system development cycle, starting from early designs meant to ensure the completeness of the deduced requirements, throughout various "X-in-the-loop techniques" [136] (where X stands model, software, hardware, or human) that progressively integrate more concrete system parts with the developed hard- and software and test their functionality.

2.1.1 Requirements-Based Testing

Requirements-based testing is a strategy that ensures that the derived functional and non-functional requirements capture and cover all aspects of the final application.

During this phase, test goals, test procedures and test cases for the final acceptance testing are defined, which can be checked against during the final CPS testing phases (system testing, deployment and operational testing). In many cases, formal modeling [83] and formal methods such as theorem proving are employed to assure requirement feasibility [86].

2.1.2 Conceptualization Phase (Model-in-the-Loop Testing)

During conceptualization, system components are developed—often as abstract implementations—so that they can be used as approximations of real-world implementations. These approximations are often based on simplified executable models [117] using mathematical models, system dynamics descriptions [51], differential equations, or, e.g., Simulink or Modelica models [144], and in many cases disregard important physical notions and "real-world aspects" such as friction, wind resistance, etc.

Nonetheless, they can be used as fast-executing stand-ins and enable the testing of conceptualized application stacks [119], and enable the early discovery of major design flaws. For instance, the kinematic bicycle model is an often-employed math-based approximation of a trajectory planner used in autonomous driving applications [118].

2.1.3 Development Phase (Software-in-the-Loop Testing)

Testing in the component development phase requires the functional (and non-functional) validation of the individually developed software and hardware. To reach beyond the scope of typical software testing, however, the software is integrated into simulated environments to enable Software-in-the-Loop setups [74]. This approach enables the verification and validation of a software's capabilities using realistic usage scenarios [43]. Such an approach is very common for the validation of software controller stacks in autonomous systems [20].

2.1.4 Integration Phase (Hardware-in-the-Loop Testing)

The correct integration of software and hardware requires the careful testing of all functionality. Before a complete assembly of the full CPS, however, it is often easier to test the integration of individual hardware components with the software stack and observe the behavior in experimental conditions [15]. Using such Hardware-in-the-Loop [34] approaches, for instance, the software stack might be connected to individual physical sensors or actuators, which are then run in a purpose-built testbed, where certain aspects (e.g., the real operation environment) may still be simulated [90].

This enables the calibration of both, the system's cyber [106] and physical parts [91], while still being able to pinpoint the causes of offsets. Similarly, timing effects [94], sensor fidelity and robustness of various components can be stress-tested, thereby creating benchmarks for the later assembled full system.

2.1.5 System Testing and Human-in-the-Loop Testing

Following the system's assembly, a complete testing procedure is needed under real-life conditions [21]. This includes the automated stress testing, identification of edge cases and assertion of safe operation conditions. In this critical phase, it is also needed to add human users into the testing loop [123], thus making sure that the CPS is usable, controllable and can also be safely paused or shut down in case of unexpected situations. Especially the safety validation [40] is of paramount importance, before releasing a CPS into circulation [93].

2.1.6 Deployment and Operational Testing

During deployment, CPS builders and operators are required to install monitoring and fault detection capabilities such that faults at runtime can be observed [78]. In many cases, the requirements that need to be observed are similar or equal to those in the requirements testing phase, such that automated runtime verification techniques such as formal monitoring [128] can deliver safety assurances on the one hand, and discover unsafe operation conditions on the other. Similarly, for large applications the model-based deployment of testing capabilities is part of the DevOps process [38].

2.2 Testing Levels

The complexity of CPS, including those incorporating learning-enabled components, requires a structured and multi-level approach to testing. Inspired by established software testing hierarchies [120], we distinguish between input, component, integration, and system-level testing. Each level targets specific sources of faults and provides opportunities for validation and monitoring throughout the system's lifecycle. In a DevOps pipeline, these testing stages are not confined to the development phase but extend into deployment and operation, allowing feedback-driven evolution and reliability tracking. The following taxonomy presents these testing levels, contextualized for CPS and aligned with continuous verification practices.

Figure 2 illustrates an example of a CPS, i.e., a self-driving car. Its inputs include real or simulated sensor data (e.g., camera, LiDAR, GPS) and control commands, while the outputs are actuator signals such as steering and brake commands.

Input Level: Input-level tests analyze both the training data used to develop learning-enabled components in CPS and the input data encountered during opera-

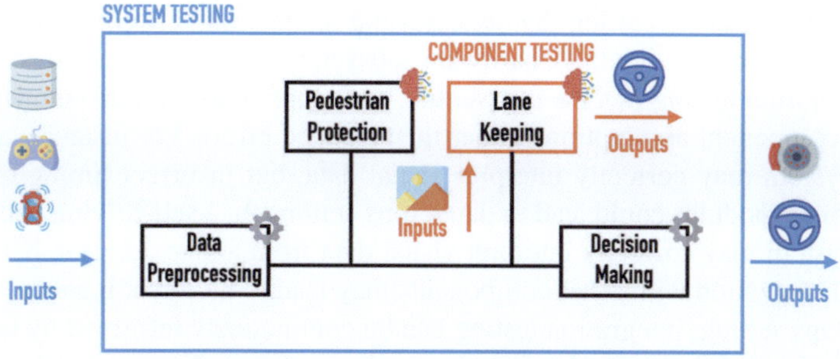

Fig. 2 Testing levels during CPS Testing: component-level versus system-level testing in an autonomous vehicle with rule-based and learning-enabled components. At the system level, tests interact with the entire CPS, providing inputs such as sensor readings or control commands (e.g., steering, braking) and observing the resulting vehicle behavior. At the component-level, individual modules (e.g., a lane-keeping component) are tested in isolation, with specific inputs like camera images and outputs such as the predicted steering angle

tion. Input-level tests do not directly target faults in the CPS or its embedded components. Instead, they aim to identify data-related issues that may compromise system behavior, such as insufficient representation of relevant operating conditions or the presence of misleading patterns in the data. These issues, if left unchecked, can result in unreliable predictions or unsafe decisions. In the context of CPS, input testing can be performed both offline—during system development—and online—during operation. Offline analysis may uncover biases or imbalances in training datasets (e.g., over-representation of nominal scenarios in an autonomous drone flight data or urban-only scenarios in a self-driving car dataset). Online input monitoring, a key DevOps activity, can identify out-of-distribution sensor readings or new environmental contexts (e.g., extreme weather conditions), enabling runtime risk mitigation through alerts, fallbacks, or adaptive retraining mechanisms.

Component Level: Component-level tests assess individual software or hardware components of a CPS in isolation, focusing on their correctness, performance, and robustness under expected inputs and operating conditions. For ML-based components, such testing may involve evaluating model architecture, training configuration, and predictive performance using metrics such as accuracy, precision, or task-specific indicators [69]. For traditional components (e.g., control algorithms or sensor drivers), it may include functional validation, timing analysis, or adherence to specified signal properties. In a CPS context, component testing corresponds to evaluating, for instance, the steering angle predictions of a lane-keeping model in a self-driving car [121] or the responsiveness of a PID controller managing drone altitude [79], independent of their integration within the full system. Within a DevOps pipeline, component tests can be continuously enriched using operational data and logs, enabling iterative refinement and fault detection throughout the system's lifecycle [132, 162].

Integration Level: Testing that assesses the interaction between software components (including ML models), hardware subsystems, and the cyber-physical interface. Integration testing in CPS is essential, as failures may stem from mismatches between component assumptions rather than isolated errors. For instance, a robot's control system may correctly interpret visual data, but incorrect timing or sensor fusion across modules could lead to dangerous actions. In a self-driving vehicle, the control system may correctly interpret visual data from a lane detector, but inaccurate synchronization with other components may lead to incorrect maneuvering [4]. In a DevOps setting, integration testing can be continuously informed by logs, system telemetry, and operational traces, supporting real-time diagnosis and regression prevention.

System Level: Testing conducted on a complete, integrated CPS to evaluate its compliance with functional and non-functional requirements in realistic conditions. System testing in CPS involves evaluating the entire system, including embedded ML components, actuation logic, sensing pipelines, and physical or virtual embodiment [157]. Such testing can occur in simulation or in the real world and aims to assess end-to-end behavior under conditions similar to or derived from operational environments. With DevOps principles, system testing extends beyond pre-deployment validation. It includes runtime monitoring, production data collection, and continuous assessment of system reliability, safety, and robustness [131]. This shift enables rapid feedback and adaptation, which are crucial in complex, dynamic CPS contexts such as autonomous vehicles or industrial robotics.

2.3 Access to the Tested Component in CPS

In a DevOps context, testing access to a CPS component can vary significantly depending on the level of integration, the nature of the component (e.g., ML-based, physical, or rule-based), and the phase in the pipeline. Inspired by prior work on ML-based systems [120], we extend the access-level taxonomy to the broader CPS landscape, considering three levels: *black-box*, *data-box*, and *white-box* testing (Fig. 3).

This taxonomy helps to structure the testing strategy across heterogeneous components, especially when components evolve independently or are updated based on operational feedback. The access level affects not only what can be observed or manipulated during testing but also which types of faults can be detected.

Black-Box Testing: A black-box test has access only to the system's or component's input and output interfaces [3, 22, 58, 121]. It is agnostic to internal implementation details, model structures, or training data. This form of testing is often used when the internal mechanics of a component (e.g., a proprietary control unit or a physical sensor) are unavailable. It supports regression, robustness, and functional validation using well-defined test cases or simulations.

Data-Box Testing: A data-box test has access to the same interfaces as black-box testing, plus internal datasets used by data-driven components (e.g., ML training

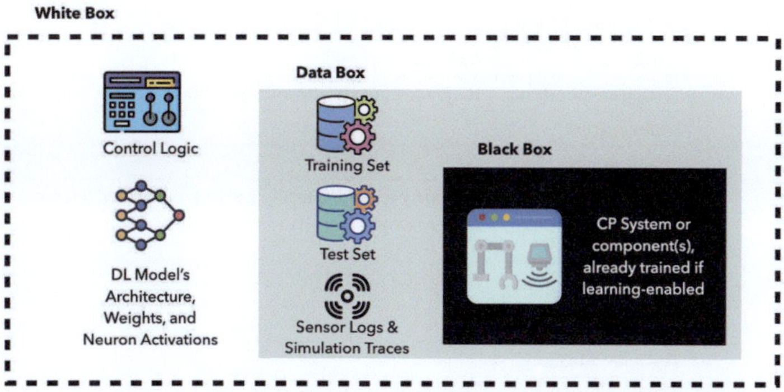

Fig. 3 Access levels during CPS testing

data, sensor logs, or simulation traces used for calibration. In CPS, data-box testing can be used to audit the representativeness of operational data, guide retraining of ML components, or validate decision-making under underrepresented physical conditions. This level assumes access to data artifacts but not to internal code or logic [37, 154].

White-Box Testing: A white-box test has full access to the internal implementation of each component, including its control logic, ML model architectures and weights, physical configuration parameters, and runtime states. White-box testing in CPS enables detailed fault injection and introspection of ML activations. It also supports mutation testing by altering internal structures (e.g., control strategies or network weights) to verify test sensitivity and coverage [70].

3 Challenges

Testing activities face significant challenges in DevOps workflows for CPS. Safety-critical CPS domains such as autonomous vehicles, unmanned aerial vehicles, and healthcare systems involve heterogeneous hardware and complex software dealing with real-time constraints and rich environments. Traditional testing techniques currently employed in DevOps workflows are not designed to handle such a complex setup. Thus, they might not be applicable in many CPS domains and incur execution overhead and maintenance costs incompatible with the DevOps paradigm [81]. Key challenges include choosing suitable test environments (simulation vs. real hardware), achieving seamless automation, meeting real-time performance constraints, ensuring safety and certification compliance, and integrating specialized toolchains into CI pipelines. Table 1 provide a summary of the main challenges in testing CPS under DevOps.

Table 1 Summary of the main challenges in testing CPS under DevOps

ID	Name	Summary description
1	Testing environments	Requirement to have a suitable infrastructure where to run tests
1.1	Reality gap	
1.2	Simulator ensembles	
2	Test generation	Necessity to automatically generate automated tests and verifying their adequacy
2.1	Test input generation	
2.2	Test oracle generation	
2.3	Test validation	
2.4	Test suite adequacy	
3	Testing efficiency	Need to efficiently run tests
4	Timing constraints	Requirement to consider timing constraints while testing
5	Safety and certification	Need to include verification of non-functional properties
6	Support for automated testing	Need for specific support to run tests

3.1 *Testing Environments*

One fundamental testing challenge is creating adequate test environments for CPS within a DevOps pipeline. Unlike in traditional software systems, CPS testing cannot be confined to software tests in isolation—hardware-in-the-loop and high-fidelity simulations are often required to model physical processes and device interactions [29]. For instance, Weber et al. [147] identify six layers that group all the configurations required to define testing scenarios in autonomous vehicle testing, ranging from road definitions (Layer 1) to communication (Layer 6) (see Fig. 4).

Engineers must combine model-in-the-loop, software-in-the-loop, and hardware-in-the-loop testing to validate CPS behavior, posing challenges in determining where and how to test each aspect [152]. For example, autonomous vehicles and unmanned aerial vehicles rely heavily on simulation environments to exercise perception and control software in virtual worlds, since real-world driving or flying tests are costly and dangerous [29].

Simulation-based testing is now a prevalent approach for validating these autonomous CPS. Yet, novel challenges arise: the realism of simulations (fidelity to the physical world), their complexity (which features they implement), and even the oracle problem (how to decide if an execution outcome is correct) complicate testing. Managing such complexity and ensuring that the capabilities of the testing environment match the requirements and assumptions of the test subjects requires a principled approach [82]. Additionally, discrepancies inevitably exist between simulation models and physical reality, so organizations need to have approaches for balancing simulated vs. physical testing [152]. Digital twins (synchronized, high-fidelity models of specific physical systems) are emerging to bridge this gap, but they introduce issues, such as integrating heterogeneous models [152], the automated flow of data

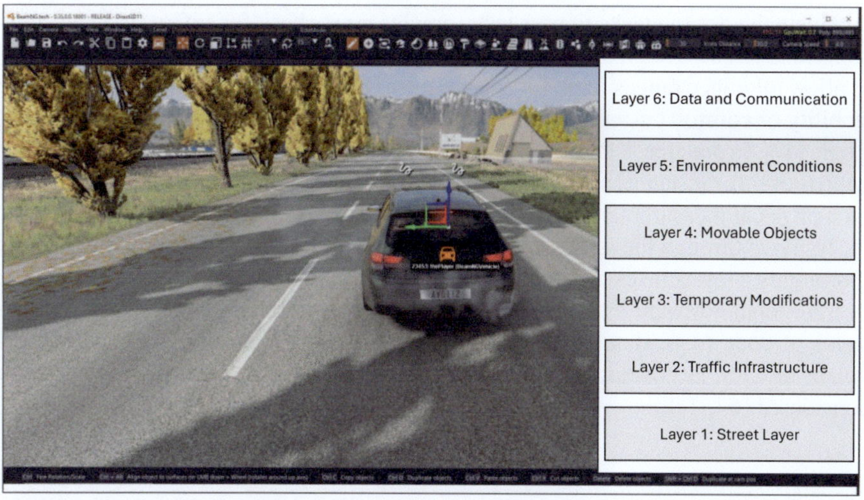

Fig. 4 A screenshot of the BeamNG's World Editor [113] (left panel) supporting the highlighted content from Weber et al.'s 6-layer model [147] (right panel)

and control between digital and physical twin [87], and the orchestrated evolution of digital twins and their purposes [103]. Surrogate models [5], often used as computationally efficient substitutes for high-fidelity simulations or physical systems, present both opportunities and challenges in CPS testing within DevOps workflows. While they enable rapid feedback by approximating complex physical behaviors, their use introduces uncertainty and potential inaccuracies that can undermine test validity. Moreover, maintaining surrogate model fidelity over time is difficult, especially when the underlying CPS evolves through frequent DevOps iterations.

3.2 *Test Generation*

Performing automated testing of CPS in DevOps workflows has several challenges.

CPS behaviors are influenced by a vast space of possible inputs and environmental conditions, making automated test input generation a necessity to keep pace with DevOps rapid releases [71]. Considering that CPS are also affected by a wide range of external stimuli (e.g., environmental states), effective testing requires generation of test inputs that also take into account the surrounding environment [124].

Designing oracles for CPS is also difficult due to the complexity of expected outcomes, especially when software outputs translate to physical effects. In a traditional software system, the oracle might be a simple assertion that checks an expected value. By contrast, a CPS often involves analog sensor values, continuous state changes, and time-dependent behaviors, making it hard to define precise pass/fail conditions [2]. For example, when testing autonomous driving systems, which must complete the driving tasks to pass tests, oracles must check for safety (e.g., no collisions) and liveness (e.g., timeout) properties [57]. Additionally, an oracle might need to allow tolerance ranges (e.g., for sensor noise) or evaluate complex properties (like stability or comfort) usually defined over temporal logics, such as Signal Temporal Logic [47]. In practice, CPS oracles often rely on human judgment or domain-specific heuristics—for instance, a developer inspecting logs or performing threshold checks on a physical measurement—which does not scale well in a DevOps environment.

To move through the stages of DevOps pipelines, it is necessary to evaluate how thoroughly a test suite exercises the system under test through test adequacy criteria. In traditional software, commonly used adequacy criteria are generally defined in terms of code (e.g., statement coverage). However, code coverage alone is insufficient in CPS, as coverage of the physical state space and scenarios must also be considered [67, 148].

3.3 Testing Efficiency

A key challenge in CPS's DevOps lifecycle is the lack of scalable, efficient, and targeted testing techniques. The vast space of possible inputs, configurations, environmental conditions, and operational modes can lead to a combinatorial explosion of test scenarios. For example, ensuring reliability in the autonomous vehicle domain requires testing millions of miles' worth of driving scenarios [76]. Even in simulation-based testing, generating and running many test scenarios is computationally expensive. This situation means that it is necessary to prioritize and intelligently select test cases for test execution [27, 28] to focus on the most critical or failure-prone scenarios while considering their diversity [160]. Continuous testing in a DevOps pipeline further emphasizes the need for effective test selection strategies and regression testing techniques to provide rapid feedback [29]. Organizations developing CPS often need to adopt a hybrid approach that combines continuous and periodic builds due to the lack of effective test selection approaches [29].

Another threat to automated testing is the build and test execution time of CPS [102]. Complex builds (cross-compiling large codebases, building firmware and software together, etc.) take a long time. Additionally, certain tests might require long observation periods [100]. Long feedback loops can discourage developers from running tests frequently, undermining DevOps's quick iteration principle. Similarly, flaky tests undermine the trust in automated test suites and can slow down deployments due to false alarms and the large effort to identify and resolve the source of flakiness [54]. CPS testing is particularly prone to flakiness because of the involvement of hardware, sensors, and asynchronous physical processes [8, 84, 85]. Unlike traditional software, where flakiness often arises from concurrency or order dependencies [95], in CPS, many flaky tests are caused by the external environment and hardware nondeterminism [152].

3.4 Timing Constraints

Many CPS are real-time systems that must satisfy strict timing and scheduling constraints. This requirement complicates testing in a DevOps workflow as it requires reliable execution environments and might introduce test flakiness [8, 135]. For instance, an autonomous vehicle's braking software must react in milliseconds, and test environments must reproduce these real-time conditions to perform testing effectively. Simulators often have limited capability to simulate real-time properties, such as exact timing, I/O latencies, or concurrency behavior [29], and their performance highly depends on the available hardware resources [143]. As a result, certain timing-dependent bugs might only manifest on actual hardware or hardware-in-the-loop setups, forcing engineers to include those in the pipeline despite the added complexity [29].

Continuous monitoring of performance is also necessary [62, 139]. In CPS, every code change could affect execution time, scheduling, or memory usage, making it essential to detect any performance regression as early as possible in the DevOps cycle [32]. For example, a change in an automated lane-keeping system's code might introduce a critical delay in the steering adjustment applied to the system—such an issue must be caught by specialized non-functional tests or runtime monitors in the DevOps pipeline. Ensuring temporal correctness under DevOps speed is difficult given the time-cost constraints—pipelines must remain fast, yet not skip essential timing tests [140].

3.5 Safety and Certification

Cyber-Physical Systems are often safety-critical systems and thus it is fundamental to minimize the possibility of harming humans or damaging properties [44]. This characteristic requires validation against standardization requirements (e.g., IEEE 2888.1-2023 [1]), which challenges the rapid, incremental nature of DevOps [100] since certification processes are traditionally slow and gated. For example, automating testing for medical device software faces significant challenges as it requires collecting extensive test execution data (e.g., software logs and coverage information) for compliance audits [98]. Traceability is also critical: test cases, results, and requirements must be linked to enable more effective and efficient bug fixing [112] and satisfy auditors that safety requirements are verified [114]. Another safety-related challenge is testing the system's response to hazardous conditions. Certain failure scenarios or stress tests cannot be freely executed on physical devices because they are disruptive, thus causing damage to hardware or endangering users. For example, intentionally corrupting an autonomous vehicle's sensors during field testing could have dreadful consequences on the passengers or nearby unprotected road users. To test those critical scenarios, developers currently either rely on simulations, which can be affected by a reality gap [130], or must design carefully controlled hardware-in-the-loop experiments [152], which is a manual and time-consuming task.

3.6 Support for Automated Testing

DevOps pipelines heavily rely on automation for test execution to increase efficiency and reproducibility. However, CPS development often involves specialized tools and hardware that are not readily built into standard continuous integration (CI) systems. Integrating the diverse toolchains for CPS development into an automated pipeline that effectively supports testing is an open challenge. Consequently, the lack of standards and automation-ready tools means that developers must find workarounds, e.g., custom scripts, to include compilation, flashing, and testing of CPS code in a CI pipeline [48]. Organizations have started to solve this by introducing specialized test frameworks that combine software and hardware. In the automotive domain, for instance, the Eclipse Foundation started the Eclipse Software Defined Vehicle working group to facilitate the development of in- and off-vehicle applications [52]. However, DevOps thrives on parallelization (running many tests concurrently), but multiplying specialized test systems is not always possible [104]. Virtual hardware and emulators can be a solution in certain cases; however, integrating these technologies into existing CD/CI pipelines and ensuring they accurately represent the real hardware remains an open challenge.

4 DevOps Testing Solutions for CPS

The research community started addressing the challenges of testing CPS within DevOps workflows by introducing new techniques and tools to facilitate testing activities. This section provides an overview of existing approaches. The presentation of the approaches is structured according to the challenges presented in Sect. 3. Table 2 provides a summary of the amount of focus that each challenge received based on current solutions.

4.1 Testing Environments

Existing work has focused on ensuring that CPS use adequate test environments. Significant efforts have been made to bridge the discrepancy between real-world and simulated behaviors by directly addressing the realism of simulation and creating co-simulation environments that leverage the capabilities of complementary simulators.

Table 2 Amount of focus on challenges based on relevant solutions

ID	Name	Amount of focus	Relevant solutions
1	Testing environments	Low	
1.1	Reality gap	Low	[17, 79]
	Simulator ensembles	Low	[23, 33, 127]
2	Test generation	Medium	
2.1	Test input generation	High	[4, 24, 31, 35, 49, 57–59, 121, 125, 129, 142]
2.2	Test oracle generation	Medium	[11, 12, 14, 99, 109, 111, 157]
2.3	Test validation	Medium	[46, 69, 122, 122, 162]
2.4	Test suite adequacy	Medium	[19, 39, 58, 89, 108, 115, 158]
3	Testing efficiency	Medium	[10, 13, 18, 25, 66, 97]
4	Timing constraints	Medium	[45, 75, 141, 152, 155]
5	Safety and certification	Low	[105, 145, 146, 153]
6	Support for automated testing	Low	[7, 16, 50]

4.1.1 Reality Gap

The discrepancy between simulated and real-world behaviors negatively affects the generalizability of simulation-based testing [29, 79]. Systems that appear robust in simulation may underperform or fail when deployed in the real world.

A promising direction to address this challenge is the use of Generative AI (GenAI) models [17], such as Variational Autoencoders (VAEs), Generative Adversarial Networks (GANs), and Diffusion Models. GenAI models learn from naturalistic data and can synthesize new data that match real-world distributions that can be used to augment or improve simulator-generated scenarios. Typical examples in the autonomous driving domain include generating photorealistic driving scenes, accurate Lidar cloud-points, and traffic. Consequently, GenAI can extend the diversity of conditions covered in simulation and improve their realism, thus positively impacting the quality of CPS simulation-based testing.

This domain augmentation techniques enable scalable and automated enhancement of simulator outputs, reducing the need for manual scene design or hardcoded scenario generation [17]. By enriching simulations with diverse conditions (e.g., variations in weather, lighting, or traffic), generative models help expose system weaknesses earlier in the development cycle, thus helping to extend the specific environmental and operational conditions, i.e., Operational Design Domain (ODD), under which the system under test is expected to operate.

As an example, a testing approach can leverage textual prompts in diffusion models for instruction-based editing, allowing high-level modifications to simulation scenes (e.g., changing a sunny setting to rainy using the prompt "make it rainy") [17]. Thanks to GenAI models, such modifications maintain semantic coherence while introducing controlled variation. This augmented testing pipeline improves system robustness by revealing failures previously undetected by simulators prior to deployment.

4.1.2 Simulator Ensembles

Suitably combining multiple simulators can also address the specific limitations of simulators, thus improving CPS simulation-based testing. Borg et al. [33] present a study investigating different simulators' capabilities for advanced driver-assistance systems. The study used search-based software testing to generate critical test scenarios. It revealed notable differences in test outputs between simulators, particularly regarding safety violations and simulated dynamics of vehicles and pedestrians. Borg and co-author suggested that future verification and validation plans should incorporate multiple simulators to enhance simulation-based testing of CPS and identify how test objectives relate to the internal workings of each simulator. Following the results of this work, Biagiola et al. [23] presented a multi-simulator approach called *digital siblings*, aimed at enhancing simulation-based testing for the lane-keeping component of autonomous vehicles. This approach involves generating road scenarios in two general-purpose simulators to better approximate the behavior of the lane-keeping model on a digital twin. It combines testing information conservatively, prioritizing agreements on potential failures, and improves the prediction of model failures compared to individual simulators. Sorokin et al. [127] presented an approach that leverages an ensemble of driving simulators to identify test cases that consistently fail across simulators and a machine learning component to label disagreements between test outcomes across different simulators before execution. Testing automated driving assistance systems with this approach showed that, compared to the standard single-simulator setup, simulator ensembles achieved a higher rate of simulator-agnostic failures, can mitigate simulator-specific failures, enhance efficiency, and reduce variability in valid failure identification.

4.2 Test Generation

This section presents techniques for generating tests for CPS. The section discusses approaches for test input generation, test oracle generation, test validation, and assessing test suite adequacy.

4.2.1 Test Input Generation

Existing solutions for test input generation aim to improve CPS testing effectiveness and efficiency [156]. These approaches are based on a wide variety of core techniques, such as search-based testing, model-based testing, and artificial intelligence. The techniques also span different domains, such as autonomous vehicles, unmanned aerial vehicles, health care, and elevator systems.

Search-based testing techniques have emerged as a powerful approach for generating test inputs in CPS. Gambi et al. [58] and Castellano et al. [35], for instance, propose approaches for systematically testing self-driving based on genetic algorithms that evolve realistic virtual roads to expose misbehavior in lane-keeping systems. Scheuer et al. [125] present an approach for generating realistic collision scenarios for testing collision avoidance systems based on multi-objective optimization. This approach generates realistic critical scenarios by exploiting existing pre-crash data and ensuring the generated scenarios maintain comparable criticality. Bartlett and Panichella [18] introduce a search-based approach that leverages dangerous real-world road maps sourced from Google Earth and evolves them to create more challenging driving scenarios for autonomous vehicles, with focus on testing the lane-keeping systems.

Abdessalem et al. [4] present a many-objective approach that generates test inputs for autonomous driving systems by evolving road scenarios that aims to identify feature interactions that leads to violations of safety properties. Compared to the other aforementioned studies, This approach therefore focuses on integration testing for different features of the autonomous driving system, such as lane-keeping, obstacle avoidance, and speed control.

Birkemeyer et al. [31] introduce a novel scenario generation technique that combines combinatorial testing and parameter sampling to create effective test suites for Advanced Driver Assistance Systems (ADAS) and Automated Driving Systems (ADS). The approach emphasizes the use of semi-concrete scenarios, which balance exploration of discrete parameters and exploitation of continuous parameters.

Existing work has also focused on generating boundary inputs. Riccio et al. [121] present a search-based approach to generate frontier inputs for deep learning systems in the context of autonomous driving. The evaluation of the tool reveals that a well-trained system's frontier predominantly consists of unrealistic scenarios, i.e., inputs outside ODD. On the contrary, poorly trained systems' frontier includes valid inputs, thus indicating significant deficiencies in their setup. Similarly, Biagiola and Tonella et al. [24] introduce a test generator that creates challenging driving conditions at the behavior boundary by mutating driving conditions collected from a failure-free environment.

Fahmy et al. [49] propose an approach using layer-wise relevance propagation to assess neuron relevance in deep neural networks. The approach highlights the generation of diverse safe and unsafe inputs through an evolutionary search algorithm, aiming to enhance the robustness of deep neural networks by characterizing the unsafe input space.

Valle et al. [142] present a search-based test generation approach designed to enhance the quality of elevator systems. The approach integrates test input minimization, boundary value detection, and automated system repair to improve the generation of valid test inputs.

Existing approaches also integrate AI-based techniques for generating test inputs. Gambi et al. [57] and [59] present approaches for generating efficient simulations that replicate real car crashes. The approach utilizes information extracted from police reports, such as crash descriptions in natural or visual languages, to recreate accurate critical scenarios, addressing the challenges posed by the scarcity of sensory data from actual accidents. Steininger et al. [129] propose an approach based on LLM to create focused test scenarios, i.e., three-dimensional virtual roads with given characteristics, from user descriptions in natural language.

4.2.2 Test Oracle Generation

Existing research on test oracle generation focuses on automating the correctness assessment of CPS while providing maintainable oracles that fit with DevOps's rapid and iterative workflow. Jahangirova et al. [72] investigate how to assess the driving performance of autonomous vehicles using various metrics in different driving environments. The paper also assesses the quality of autonomous vehicles driving by correlating metrics with human assessments of driving videos. Birchler et al. [30] conducted an empirical study to assess whether commonly used simulation test metrics align with human perceptions of realism and safety. The study identifies that traditional automated metrics may not capture nuanced human perceptions, highlighting the need for human-centered evaluations in simulation-based testing for autonomous driving. Arrieta et al. [12] presents a domain-specific language designed to specify test oracles and automate testing of industrial elevators. The domain-specific language allows users to define test oracles at a higher level of abstraction, independent of testing levels, and supports uncertainty-aware test oracles to accommodate various operational uncertainties.

Current work has also explored metamorphic testing to validate cyber-physical systems. Ayerdi et al. [14] presents an approach based on metamorphic testing to identify functional bugs in industrial elevator dispatchers. The approach addresses the test oracle problem by establishing metamorphic relation input patterns that relate multiple executions of the dispatcher under test. Later, Ayerdi et al. [14] extended this work by developing a tool to automatically generate metamorphic relations using genetic programming. Mandrioli et al. [99] proposed relying on control theory, specifically linear systems theory, to define metamorphic relations for testing the controller linearity assumptions. Being grounded in a general control-theoretical design, this approach is independent of the specific application domain of the CPS under test.

Existing solutions also leverage methods based on Machine Learning and Artificial Intelligence to define test oracles. Arrieta et al. [11] present a test oracle generation approach for testing elevator dispatching algorithms. The approach predicts the quality-of-service values of a system of elevators based on the passenger traffic data. The approach is also evaluated in an industrial case study by Gartziandia et al. [60]. Related work also focused on providing a better understanding of Machine Learning and Artificial Intelligence systems for defining test oracles of those systems. Zohdinasab et al. [157] propose a search-based approach to guide the users of the approach in identifying and quantifying the dimensions of the feature space of deep learning systems, allowing for a better understanding of how different features of generated inputs affect the system's behavior.

Additional solutions focus on domain-specific issues in the definition of test oracles. Nguyen [111] define an approach to generate quantifiably diverse and critical driving scenarios that can be instantiated on existing high-definition maps and implement them in an industrial driving simulator as executable test cases. Nesterini et al. [109] presents a technique for learning interpretable monitors (based on signal temporal logic formulas) that can predict safety property violations from the observable sensor data in CPS.

4.2.3 Test Validation

An open challenge in DevOps testing of CPS related to Test Generation is Test Validation, i.e., ensure that test inputs and execution are realistic, representative, and do not violate assumptions of the system under test.

Test validation becomes especially critical when test generation is automated and continuously executed as part of CI/CD pipelines, in which human supervision must be minimal. For instance, test inputs must be not only syntactically well-formed but also semantically meaningful with respect to the system's operational design domain.

In traditional software systems, input validity is often enforced through explicit preconditions or input contracts [116]. However, CPS operate in complex and dynamic environments (e.g., smart cities, autonomous vehicles, medical devices) where input validity depends on physical, environmental, or domain-specific constraints [156]. For example, a sequence of temperature sensor readings must conform to realistic thermal profiles depending on the given physical setting. Generating invalid test inputs in this context may lead to misleading test results or undetected failures, thus providing an unreliable quality assessment of the system under test.

The need for input validation becomes even more crucial when cyber-physical systems integrate Deep Learning (DL) components. Unlike traditional systems, DL models typically accept any input that matches their input shape [69], regardless of its semantic plausibility. For example, an image classifier embedded in a CPS drone may return a label even when presented with an input that is entirely unrelated to its intended domain (e.g., an underwater panoramic scene instead of an aerial landscape).

Recent solutions have proposed to assess input validity by learning the statistical distribution of valid operational data [133]. Such distribution-based models, trained on real-world datasets or production logs, can serve as real-time monitors to verify whether a generated test input aligns with the expected domain behavior. For example, autoencoders can be trained on valid domain data to detect anomalous inputs by looking at their reconstruction error, i.e., the discrepancy between the input and its reconstruction by the model. A high reconstruction error typically indicates an out-of-distribution or semantically invalid input [46, 122]. This approach enables automated and scalable filtering of invalid test inputs, helping ensure that testing focuses on semantically meaningful cases aligned with the system's real-world operational context.

However, the validity assessment returned by a distribution-aware AI model is essentially a proxy for the concept of input validity, as it measures the conformance to the training distribution, which may not fully capture the intended operational domain [61]. Consequently, distribution-based models may incorrectly flag rare—but valid—inputs as invalid, or vice versa, due to distributional mismatch. Human-in-the-loop approaches, such as expert annotation or crowd-sourced labeling, can better assess input validity and be used to train active learning classifiers that can progressively refine their understanding of validity through interaction with human feedback [61].

In conclusion, there is a trade-off between distribution-aware models, which offer scalable but potentially misaligned assessments, and actively trained models, which are more accurate but require costly human input. Current approaches aim to integrate these strategies to achieve more robust and reliable validity assessments. When integrated into the DevOps pipeline, these AI-based test validators can: (i) automatically filter semantically invalid test inputs before execution [122]; (ii) prioritize valid inputs more likely to trigger faults [162]; and (iii) reduce human effort in validating the relevance of test cases at scale [61].

4.2.4 Test Suite Adequacy

Understanding whether a test suite is adequate is a core need for successfully moving through the stages of the DevOps pipeline. Current solutions proposed approaches and methodologies to determine test suite adequacy based on domain-specific properties characterizing CPS.

Gambi et al. [58] propose an approach for improving the diversity of generated test scenario (and thus improving their adequacy) by considering and including mixed-traffic scenarios (i.e., AV and human drivers) in the context of AV testing. Bartocci et al. [19] propose signal feature coverage as a new coverage metric for systematically testing CPS dataflow models. Pei et al. [115] assess the adequacy of DL based systems by introducing the concept of neuron coverage for measuring the parts of a deep learning system exercised by test inputs. In particular, this criterion counts the number of neurons activated by a test input, where a neuron is considered activated if its output value is higher than a predefined threshold. Zohdinasab et al. [157–162], characterize and organize misbehavior-inducing test inputs through feature maps based on human-interpretable features. These maps define an N-dimensional input feature space where test inputs are positioned according to the values of test inputs' specific structural (e.g., road curvature in a driving scenario) or behavioral attributes (e.g., maximum value of the vehicle lateral position during the execution of the driving task). The count of the filled map cells (i.e., combinations of feature values within specific ranges) can be used to assess test adequacy. By further characterizing map regions according to the likelihood of misbehaviour, they act as misbehavior probability maps and help testers identify underexplored and high-risk areas of the feature space. For instance, in the context of a lane-keeping assist system, feature maps can expose dangerous combinations of road curvature and vehicle lateral position. As such, they support various tasks across the DevOps pipeline beyond adequacy assessment, including test selection and misbehavior explanation. Neelofar et al. [108] introduce a set of black-box test adequacy metrics called test suite instance space adequacy metrics, which can be used to identify the effectiveness of a test suite in artificial intelligence powered systems like AV. The metrics offer a way to assess both the diversity and coverage of the test suite and the range of bugs identified during testing. Neelofar et al. [107] also present follow-up work presenting a systematic technique that uses instance space analysis to detect features in test scenarios that affect the ability to reveal unsafe behavior of AVs. Laurent et al. [89] argue that the parameters of an AV system guide its decision process and propose the concept of parameter coverage to assess adequacy of AV systems. A parameter is covered when a change to its value in a test scenario leads to different simulation results, meaning that the parameter is relevant and central to the driving decisions made in the scenario. Cornejo et al. [39] enhance mutation analysis optimization techniques to enable their use in the context of CPS in the space domain.

4.3 Testing Efficiency

The task of improving testing efficiency in the context of DevOps for CPS has seen some preliminary solutions. Existing work has focused on regression test selection in the domain of self-driving cars.

Birchler et al. [25] present an approach for improving the efficiency of testing self-driving cars. The approach uses a machine-learning-based classifier that categorizes tests as likely or unlikely to expose faults before execution, thereby filtering out uninformative tests and reducing computational needs for testing. Malik and Khatiri [97] present a test case selection approach for self-driving cars that is based on an ensemble of several machine learning models to accurately predict if a test case is likely to fail. Arcaini and Cetinkaya [10] defined a test case selection technique for self-driving cars that first transforms road tests from a Cartesian representation to a curvature representation based on the Frenet frame. Based on the representation, the approach clusters tests according to their similarity and then selects non-executed tests that are closer to executed tests that are known to be failing. Bartlett et al. [18] propose an approach that combines a convolutional neural network with a greedy algorithm to select and prioritize the execution of diverse, failing roads during regression testing. Güllü et al. [66] present a technique that leverages a long short-term memory-based model for the classification of roads as safe and unsafe and selecting unsafe roads for testing. Aryan and Khatiri [13] proposed two approaches for test selection of self-driving cars, one based on road geometry and another one based on a graph neural network.

4.4 Timing Constraints

Researchers have proposed a variety of solutions to handle timing constraints and improve testing reliability for CPS in DevOps contexts.

One class of solutions uses simulation and virtual time to replicate real-time conditions in a controlled environment. Zheng et al. [155] propose real-time simulation architecture to generate and manage multiple real-time simulation environments based on existing simulation models in a manner that ensures sufficient accuracy for verifying a CPS application. Existing solutions have also used virtual clocks or time dilation in testing framework for handling timing constraints [152].

When software timing must be validated under realistic conditions, hardware-in-the-loop testing is indispensable. Johansson and Paulsson [75] developed a microservice-based test framework supporting simulation-in-loop, data replay, and hardware test levels in DevOps pipeline.

An emerging solution is the use of digital twins and runtime testing techniques to handle timing constraints. Researchers have proposed leveraging digital twins to perform A/B testing or shadow testing of new software versions under real operating conditions, which must comply with timing constraints. Dobaj and Riel [45] propose detailed design models for operation-critical digital twins that integrate CPS closed-loop control and architecture-based CPS adaptation.

Handling timing in tests is not only about execution but also about checking the results within acceptable temporal bounds. Valle et al. [141] emphasize that CPS test oracles should handle continuous behaviors and introduces a domain-specific language to define test oracles.

4.5 Safety and Certification

CPS failures can endanger lives. Consequently, their development is often constrained by strict certification standards that demand extensive verification and documented assurance of safety. This need for thorough, evidence-based validation clashes with DevOps practices, which emphasize rapid, incremental changes and continuous deployment. Recent work has begun proposing solutions to bridge this gap, enabling continuous development and compliance.

Warg et al. [146] advocate making safety assessments an integrated part of development, updated at every iteration alongside the software. By updating safety cases with each change developers can avoid the "big-bang" certification crunch where problems are discovered late.

To reconcile fast DevOps cycles with safety constraints, existing work stresses automation of safety verification. Vost and Wagner [145] propose an approach in which safety analyses and tests are treated as first-class artifacts in the continuous integration pipeline. Specifically, the authors envision that an advanced continuous delivery pipeline for safety-critical systems should include the safety analysis as an artifact under version control (just like source code) and integrate test cases generated from that analysis into every build.

Another key solution area is integrating model-based safety assessment into the DevOps pipeline. Zeller [153] outlines a continuous delivery pipeline realizing continuous safety assessment in software-intensive safety-critical systems based on model-based safety assessment methods.

To handle certification constraints, new methodologies have been formulated that blend safety engineering into agile/DevOps workflows. Munk and Schweize [105] advocate for a that generates required safety artifacts (e.g., test reports) as part of the pipeline. With proper management of this type of artifacts, each software increment has an associated, updated set of evidence for safety assurance.

Because testing on physical hardware or in live environments can be dangerous or slow for safety-critical CPS, a prominent solution is to use simulation and virtual testing environments within DevOps. Continuous integration for CPS often requires balancing fast automated tests with more exhaustive trials that involve hardware-in-the-loop or field testing. Studies have found that teams combine continuous and periodic builds, using simulators to rapidly test most changes and scheduling less frequent runs on actual hardware when needed [152].

DevOps extends into the operations phase, and for safety-critical CPS this opens an opportunity: monitoring deployed systems to collect safety-related feedback. Rather than viewing certification as a one-time gate, recent work suggests using runtime data to continually validate and improve the safety case of an evolving system. Existing work [105] proposes obtaining quick and systematic feedback of the quality of the safety concept from the deployed products, feeding that information back into the development cycle and testing.

4.6 Support for Automated Testing

CPS combine software with physical components, making automated testing in a DevOps pipeline particularly challenging. Unlike conventional software, CPS development involves heterogeneous toolchains (e.g., domain-specific modeling tools, hardware test rigs) and interactions with physical processes [150]. Setting up Continuous Integration/Continuous Delivery for CPS often requires simulating or mocking the physical environment "in vitro" (e.g., weather conditions for a drone's sensors) and interfacing with hardware-in-the-loop equipment [150]. Recent work has proposed a range of solutions for supporting automated testing of CPS in DevOps pipelines.

One key approach is to leverage simulation and virtual models (e.g., digital twins) to test CPS software without needing the physical hardware at all times (e.g., [16]). While simulation is powerful, eventually the software must be validated with real hardware. Vendors have started offering tools tailored for CPS continuous testing. For example, Vector's CANoe Server Edition is specifically designed to automate simulations and hardware-in-the-loop tests in a server-based CI environment [50].

Another line of solutions focuses on adapting the DevOps pipeline architecture to better support CPS testing. Researchers have proposed DevOps frameworks that incorporate the unique needs of CPS. One example is the work from Aldalur et al. [7] that proposes a microservice-based architecture for continuous testing across multiple levels of a CPS. Containerization strategies are another solution to support automated testing in DevOps of CPS [151]. Containerizing the CPS software and its test dependencies ensures that complex toolchains (e.g., compilers, simulators, and device drivers) can run in a reproducible environment on the CI server.

5 The Path Forward

Looking ahead, a critical direction for testing and evaluation of CPS (especially those integrating AI components) is the evolution from development-centric validation to a continuous DevOps-oriented approach grounded in operational reliability [64].

While traditional software engineering often emphasizes test-case coverage and oracle-based failure detection, these techniques become insufficient in the context of modern CPS, where components interact with uncertain environments, process continuously evolving data streams, and may adapt over time through learning-enabled components.

In production environments, CPS are exposed to dynamic operational contexts that can significantly differ from those observed during testing. Thus, correctness observed in development is no longer a sufficient proxy for trustworthy behavior in production.

This development-to-operation data shift [64] poses a major challenge to ensuring continued system dependability.

DevOps practices introduce a paradigm where testing becomes an ongoing activity integrated with system deployment, runtime monitoring, and post-deployment feedback, placing system reliability in real-world conditions at the center of evaluation. For this reason, we draw inspiration from a recent viewpoint expressed by Paolo Tonella [138] depicted in Fig. 5, which—although originally proposed in the context of deep learning—extends well to CPS at large: *the ultimate goal of testing should be to improve the reliability of systems as measured in production, not just in controlled test environments.*

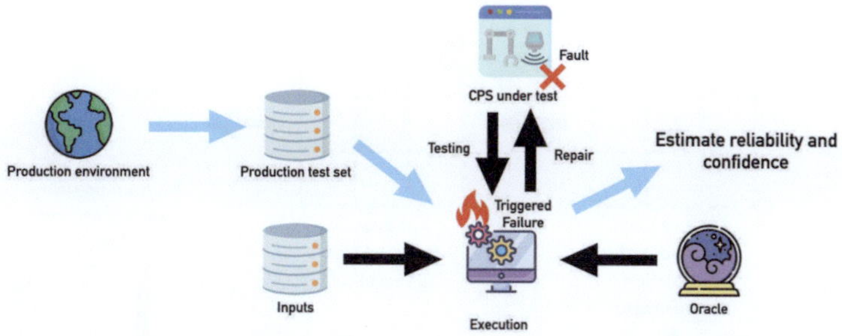

Fig. 5 Adaptation of the reliability-driven testing paradigm proposed by Tonella [138] to CPS

The introduction of this paradigm transforms testing into a continuous and adaptive activity, integrated throughout the DevOps pipeline and has several implications:

- Reliability estimates derived from test data may significantly overestimate real-world performance, due to deployment-time shifts such as sensor noise, human interaction patterns, or unforeseen environmental conditions [133].
- Testing frameworks must evolve to include mechanisms capable of capturing real usage patterns for collecting and analyzing production data, enabling reliability estimation grounded in actual usage [162].
- Given the high cost and potential risk of broad deployment, sample-efficient reliability estimation methods become essential especially for safety-critical CPS, without intrusive instrumentation or prohibitive costs [26, 65, 162].
- The effectiveness of testing strategies should increasingly be assessed not only in terms of fault detection or bug exposure, but in terms of their measurable impact on operational reliability [162].

This shift reframes the notion of a testing oracle: from static expectations of correctness to statistically supported confidence in system behavior (similarly to oracles developed for DL systems [73]), measured across realistic scenarios. It also underscores the importance of runtime monitoring and adaptation mechanisms as testing instruments, such as online retraining and anomaly detection [132].

One possible instance of this DevOps-oriented testing paradigm is illustrated in Fig. 6. The behavior of the CPS in the production environment is summarized through a feature map [158, 159, 161], which estimates the probability that specific combinations of input features lead to system misbehavior. A focused test generator (such as DeepAtash [160, 162]) can exploit this information to generate test inputs that target critical feature interactions. This includes generating diverse inputs exhibiting misbehaviors tied to critical features, inputs that trigger misbehaviors despite involving non-critical features, or inputs with previously unseen or rare feature combinations to probe generalization. Such inputs can be generated by leveraging perturbations in the input space [88], manipulations of domain-specific input models [121], or exploiting Generative AI models, such as Variational AutoEncoders, GANs, or Diffusion Models [101]. The generated test data can then be used to improve the system—for

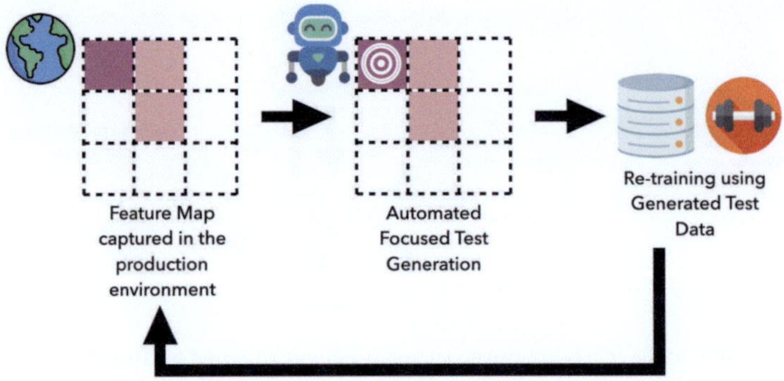

Fig. 6 Leveraging information captured in the production environment to improve the CPS under test

instance, through retraining or fine-tuning in the case of deep learning-based components. The updated CPS is subsequently redeployed in the production environment, closing the feedback loop and continuously improving reliability under real-world conditions.

To support this transformation, future research must address the following aspects:

- Modeling realistic operational conditions to generate test scenarios reflective of production;
- Incorporating runtime feedback into continuous testing loops;
- Defining and standardizing reliability-focused evaluation metrics for heterogeneous CPS;
- Ensuring transparency and traceability when adaptive or AI-based components modify their behavior post-deployment.

By moving toward production-centered reliability as a testing objective, we align CPS testing efforts more closely with their ultimate purpose: to ensure dependable, safe, and resilient operation in the real world.

Enabling the DevOps vision of making software testing an ongoing activity requires effective methods to identify relevant production data and make it actionable for improving existing test suites [41].

At the same time, as the existing test suites grow, methods to optimize them (e.g., removing broken or non-useful tests) are needed to maintain the DevOps cycle as efficiently as possible.

In the context of CPS, where system executions and end-to-end tests are the norm, we identify the following directions for future improvements: optimized simulation-based test deployment, test reduction, and test carving.

Testing CPS in simulations requires setting up "throw-away" (virtualized) testing environments so that each test can run predictably, repeatedly, and in complete isolation from other tests. Currently, CD/CI pipelines use container-based environments, such as those based on Docker, which are (re)built at every test execution by downloading and installing all the required packages, and can take several minutes to be ready. To improve test efficiency, it is essential to have a strategy for either safely reusing virtualized testing environments across test executions or reusing dependencies and components between tests. In the past, Gambi et al. [55] proposed O!SNAP, an approach to identify shared dependencies across tests deployed in the Cloud and automatically regenerate virtual machine snapshots optimized to reduce test setup time. We argue that similar approaches, augmented to verify the consistency of virtualized testing environments and their configurations [82], can be devised to enhance the CPS test deployment efficiency.

Another strategy to improve regression testing efficiency in CPS is test reduction. Test reduction complements standard techniques for regression testing optimization, such as test suite minimization, test selection, and prioritization, and it aims to identify (and remove) non-informative parts from the execution within each system-level test. For instance, in the context of autonomous driving, test reduction could be applied to identify segments of roads where simulated traffic and road geometry remain constant, thus becoming soon irrelevant for testing. Removing those segments from the simulation execution can be achieved by teleporting the ego vehicle or splitting long-running test cases into smaller ones, which improves test efficiency without significantly affecting test effectiveness.

A different strategy to improve regression test suites is using test carving [56], which generates integration and unit test cases from execution traces, to automatically generate new test cases.

Thanks to test carving, data and behavior observed in production can be automatically brought back to development in the form of understandable test cases [42], which developers can use *as-is* or, as the basis for writing new test cases, or as seed to feed automated test generation.

6 Conclusions

This chapter reviewed the current landscape of CPS testing and evaluation in DevOps contexts, highlighting the challenges and solutions proposed in the literature. Key challenges include the need for continuous testing, the complexity of CPS systems, and the need for effective test generation and validation techniques. Testing for CPS requires a shift from traditional software testing approaches to more dynamic and adaptive methods that can address timing constraints, safety and certification challenges, and the need for automated testing solutions.

To address these challenges, researchers have proposed various strategies, including advanced test generation and validation techniques, as well as methods designed to enhance testing efficiency. A key emphasis is placed on integrating testing seamlessly into the DevOps pipeline, particularly through automated solutions that support continuous validation of CPS. Simulation environments, virtual models, and digital twins play a crucial role in enabling such automation, while runtime testing techniques provide additional support for managing timing constraints and ensuring real-time behavior.

Finally, the chapter outlined key directions for advancing CPS testing within DevOps-oriented workflows. Future efforts should prioritize test generation and validation strategies that are not only efficient but also grounded in real-world operational conditions. This includes leveraging runtime feedback to guide test selection, incorporating simulation-based and digital twin environments for scalable automation, and adopting reliability-focused evaluation metrics. To sustain continuous testing, research must also address the optimization of growing test suites through techniques such as test reduction, test carving, and the efficient reuse of virtualized testing environments. Together, these directions aim to ensure that CPS testing evolves beyond development-time correctness toward a continuous, feedback-driven process that supports dependable, adaptive behavior in production.

Competing Interests The authors have no conflicts of interest to declare that are relevant to the content of this chapter.

Acknowledgements Mattia Fazzini is supported by the Facebook Testing and Verification award and a project funded by Medtronic. Alessio Gambi is supported by ShapeFuture, the Chips Joint Undertaking grant agreement No. 101139996-2, co-funded by the European Union. Vincenzo Riccio is supported by the M4C2 I1.3 "SEcurity and RIghts In the CyberSpace—SERICS" (PE00000014 - CUP H73C2200089001, D33C22001300002) projects, under the National Recovery and Resilience Plan (NRRP) funded by the European Union—NextGenerationEU. Annibale Panichella is supported by the European Union's Horizon 2020 Research and Innovation Programme under grant agreement No. 957254, project COSMOS (2021).

References

1. IEEE 2888.1-2023 IEEE Standard for Specification of Sensor Interface for Cyber and Physical Worlds (2023)
2. S. Abbaspour Asadollah, R. Inam, H. Hansson, A survey on testing for cyber physical system, in *Proceedings of IFIP WG 6.1 International Conference on Testing Software and Systems*, vol. 9447 (Springer, 2015), pp. 194–207
3. R.B. Abdessalem, S. Nejati, L.C. Briand, T. Stifter, Testing vision-based control systems using learnable evolutionary algorithms, in *International Conference on Software Engineering* (ACM, 2018), pp. 1016–1026
4. R.B. Abdessalem, A. Panichella, S. Nejati, L.C. Briand, T. Stifter, Testing autonomous cars for feature interaction failures using many-objective search, in *Proceedings of the 33rd ACM/IEEE International Conference on Automated Software Engineering, ASE 2018, Montpellier, France, September 3-7, 2018*. ed. by M. Huchard, C. Kästner, G. Fraser (ACM, 2018), pp. 143–154
5. H.B. Adeyemo, R. Bahsoon, P. Tiño, Surrogate-based digital twin for predictive fault modelling and testing of cyber physical systems, in *2022 IEEE/ACM International Conference on Big Data Computing, Applications and Technologies (BDCAT)* (IEEE, 2022), pp. 166–169
6. D. Albright, P. Brannan, C. Walrond, Did Stuxnet take out 1,000 centrifuges at the Natanz enrichment plant? (Institute for Science and International Security, 2010)
7. I. Aldalur, A. Arrieta, A. Agirre, G. Sagardui, M. Arratibel, A microservice-based framework for multi-level testing of cyber-physical systems. Softw. Qual. J. **32**(1), 193–223 (2024)
8. M.H. Amini, S. Naseri, S. Nejati, Evaluating the impact of flaky simulators on testing autonomous driving systems. Empir. Softw. Eng. **29**(2), 47 (2024)

9. P. Ammann, J. Offutt, *Introduction to Software Testing* (Cambridge University Press, 2017)
10. P. Arcaini, A. Cetinkaya, Detour at the icst 2025 tool competition—self-driving car testing track, in *2025 IEEE Conference on Software Testing, Verification and Validation (ICST)* (2015), pp. 805–806
11. A. Arrieta, J. Ayerdi, M. Illarramendi, A. Agirre, G. Sagardui, M. Arratibel, Using machine learning to build test oracles: an industrial case study on elevators dispatching algorithms, in *2021 IEEE/ACM International Conference on Automation of Software Test (AST)* (IEEE, 2021), pp. 30–39
12. A. Arrieta, M. Otaegi, L. Han, G. Sagardui, S. Ali, M. Arratibel, Automating test oracle generation in devops for industrial elevators, in *2022 IEEE International Conference on Software Analysis, Evolution and Reengineering (SANER)* (IEEE, 2022), pp. 284–288
13. P. Aryan, S. Khatiri, Nn-sdctest at the icst 2025 tool competition-self-driving car testing track, in *2025 IEEE Conference on Software Testing, Verification and Validation (ICST)* (IEEE, 2025), pp. 813–814
14. J. Ayerdi, S. Segura, A. Arrieta, G. Sagardui, M. Arratibel, Qos-aware metamorphic testing: An elevation case study, in *2020 IEEE 31st International Symposium on Software Reliability Engineering (ISSRE)* (IEEE, 2020), pp. 104–114
15. M. Bacic, On hardware-in-the-loop simulation, in *Proceedings of the 44th IEEE Conference on Decision and Control* (IEEE, 2005), pp. 3194–3198
16. A. Barbie, W. Hasselbring, M. Hansen, Digital twin prototypes for supporting automated integration testing of smart farming applications. Symmetry **16**(2), 221 (2024)
17. L. Baresi, D.Y.X. Hu, A. Stocco, P. Tonella, Efficient domain augmentation for autonomous driving testing using diffusion models, in *2025 IEEE/ACM 47th International Conference on Software Engineering (ICSE)* (IEEE Computer Society, Los Alamitos, CA, USA, 2025), pp. 743–743
18. A. Bartlett, C. Liem, A. Panichella, Drvn at the icst 2025 tool competition–self-driving car testing track, in *2025 IEEE Conference on Software Testing, Verification and Validation (ICST)* (IEEE, 2025), pp. 807–808
19. E. Bartocci, L. Mariani, D. Ničković, D. Yadav, Signal feature coverage and testing for CPS Dataflow Models. ACM Trans. Softw. Eng. Methodol. (2025)
20. A. Bayha, F. Grüneis, B. Schätz, Model-based software in-the-loop-test of autonomous systems, in *Proceedings of the 2012 Symposium on Theory of Modeling and Simulation-DEVS Integrative M&S Symposium* (Citeseer, 2012), pp. 1–6
21. B. Beizer. *Software System Testing and Quality Assurance* (Van Nostrand Reinhold Co., 1984)
22. R. Ben Abdessalem, S. Nejati, L.C. Briand, T. Stifter, Testing advanced driver assistance systems using multi-objective search and neural networks, in *Proceedings of the 31st IEEE/ACM International Conference on Automated Software Engineering* (2016), pp. 63–74
23. M. Biagiola, A. Stocco, V. Riccio, P. Tonella, Two is better than one: digital siblings to improve autonomous driving testing. Empir. Softw. Eng. **29**(4), 72 (2024)
24. M. Biagiola, P. Tonella, Boundary state generation for testing and improvement of autonomous driving systems. IEEE Trans. Softw. Eng. **50**(8), 2040–2053 (2024)
25. C. Birchler, N. Ganz, S. Khatiri, A. Gambi, S. Panichella, Cost-effective simulation-based test selection in self-driving cars software with SDC-Scissor, in *IEEE International Conference on Software Analysis, Evolution and Reengineering, SANER 2022, Honolulu, HI, USA, March 15-18, 2022* (IEEE, 2022), pp. 164–168
26. C. Birchler, N. Ganz, S. Khatiri, A. Gambi, S. Panichella, Cost-effective simulation-based test selection in self-driving cars software. Sci. Comput. Program. **226**, 102926 (2023)
27. C. Birchler, S. Khatiri, B. Bosshard, A. Gambi, S. Panichella, Machine learning-based test selection for simulation-based testing of self-driving cars software. Empir. Softw. Eng. **28**(3), 71 (2023)
28. C. Birchler, S. Khatiri, P. Derakhshanfar, S. Panichella, A. Panichella, Single and multi-objective test cases prioritization for self-driving cars in virtual environments. ACM Trans. Softw. Eng. Methodol. **32**(2), 28:1–28:30 (2023)

29. C. Birchler, S. Khatiri, P. Rani, T. Kehrer, S. Panichella, A roadmap for simulation-based testing of autonomous cyber-physical systems: challenges and future direction (2025)
30. C. Birchler, T.K. Mohammed, P. Rani, T. Nechita, T. Kehrer, S. Panichella, How does simulation-based testing for self-driving cars match human perception? in *ACM International Conference on the Foundations of Software Engineering* (2024)
31. L. Birkemeyer, J. Fuchs, A. Gambi, I. Schaefer, SOTIF-Compliant scenario generation using semi-concrete scenarios and parameter sampling, in *26th IEEE International Conference on Intelligent Transportation Systems, ITSC 2023, Bilbao, Spain, September 24-28, 2023* (IEEE, 2023), pp. 2139–2144
32. M. Böck, S. Habchi, M. Nayrolles, J. Cito, Performance prediction from source code is task and domain specific, in *31st IEEE/ACM International Conference on Program Comprehension, ICPC 2023, Melbourne, Australia, May 15-16, 2023* (IEEE, 2023), pp. 35–42
33. M. Borg, R.B. Abdessalem, S. Nejati, F. Jegeden, D. Shin, Digital twins are not monozygotic—cross-replicating ADAS testing in two industry-grade automotive simulators, in *14th IEEE Conference on Software Testing, Verification and Validation, ICST 2021, Porto de Galinhas, Brazil, April 12-16, 2021* (IEEE, 2021), pp. 383–393
34. D. Bullock, B. Johnson, R.B. Wells, M. Kyte, Z. Li, Hardware-in-the-loop simulation. Transp. Res. Part C: Emerg. Technol. **12**(1), 73–89 (2004)
35. E. Castellano, S. Klikovits, A. Cetinkaya, P. Arcaini, FreneticV at the SBST 2022 tool competition, in *2022 IEEE/ACM 15th International Workshop on Search-Based Software Testing (SBST)* (2022), pp. 47–48
36. H. Chen, Applications of cyber-physical system: a literature review. J. Ind. Integr. Manag. **02**(03), 1750012 (2017)
37. C.-H. Cheng, C.-H. Huang, H. Yasuoka, Quantitative projection coverage for testing ML-enabled autonomous systems, in *Automated Technology for Verification and Analysis: 16th International Symposium, ATVA 2018, Los Angeles, CA, USA, October 7-10, 2018, Proceedings 16* (Springer, 2018), pp. 126–142
38. B. Combemale, M. Wimmer, Towards a model-based devops for cyber-physical systems, in *International Workshop on Software Engineering Aspects of Continuous Development and New Paradigms of Software Production and Deployment* (Springer, 2019), pp. 84–94
39. O. Cornejo, F. Pastore, L.C. Briand, Mutation analysis for cyber-physical systems: scalable solutions and results in the space domain. IEEE Trans. Softw. Eng. **48**(10), 3913–3939 (2021)
40. L.F. Cranor, *A Framework for Reasoning About the Human in the Loop* (2008)
41. E. Cruciani, B. Miranda, R. Verdecchia, A. Bertolino, Scalable approaches for test suite reduction, in *2019 IEEE/ACM 41st International Conference on Software Engineering (ICSE)* (2019), pp. 419–429
42. A. Deljouyi, A. Zaidman, Generating understandable unit tests through end-to-end test scenario carving, in *23rd IEEE International Working Conference on Source Code Analysis and Manipulation, SCAM 2023, Bogotá, Colombia, October 2-3, 2023*. ed. by L. Moonen, C.D. Newman, A. Gorla (IEEE, 2023), pp. 107–118
43. S. Demers, P. Gopalakrishnan, L. Kant, A generic solution to software-in-the-loop, in *MILCOM 2007—IEEE Military Communications Conference* (2007), pp. 1–6
44. A. Di Sorbo, F. Zampetti, A. Visaggio, M. Di Penta, S. Panichella, Automated identification and qualitative characterization of safety concerns reported in uav software platforms. ACM Trans. Softw. Eng. Methodol. **32**(3) (2023)
45. J. Dobaj, A. Riel, T. Krug, M. Seidl, G. Macher, M. Egretzberger, Towards digital twin-enabled devops for cps providing architecture-based service adaptation and verification at runtime, in *Proceedings of the 17th Symposium on Software Engineering for Adaptive and Self-Managing Systems, SEAMS '22* (Association for Computing Machinery, New York, NY, USA, 2022), pp. 132–143
46. S. Dola, M.B. Dwyer, M.L. Soffa, Distribution-aware testing of neural networks using generative models, in *43rd IEEE/ACM International Conference on Software Engineering, ICSE 2021, Madrid, Spain, 22-30 May 2021* (IEEE, 2021), pp. 226–237

47. A. Donzé, T. Ferrère, O. Maler, Efficient robust monitoring for STL, in *Computer Aided Verification—25th International Conference, CAV 2013, Saint Petersburg, Russia, July 13-19, 2013. Proceedings*. ed. by N. Sharygina, H. Veith. Volume 8044 of Lecture Notes in Computer Science. (Springer, 2013), pp. 264–279
48. eSol, Overcoming major challenges of continuous integration (ci) in embedded software development, 2023. [Online; accessed 20-May-2025]
49. H. Fahmy, F. Pastore, L. Briand, T. Stifter, Simulator-based explanation and debugging of hazard-triggering events in DNN-based safety-critical systems. ACM Trans. Softw. Eng. Methodol. **32**(4), 1–47 (2023)
50. A. for Standardization of Automation and M. Systems. Vector informatik. https://www.asam.net/members/detail/vector-informatik. Accessed 30 May 2025
51. J.W. Forrester, Lessons from system dynamics modeling. Syst. Dyn. Rev. **3**(2), 136–149 (1987)
52. T.E. Foundation, The Eclipse software defined vehicle (SDV) working group. https://sdv.eclipse.org/what-is-sdv/. Accessed 22 May 2025
53. A. Gambi, P. Arcaini, D. Nickovic, Generation of critical interactive scenarios for trajectory planning, in *IEEE Intelligent Vehicles Symposium, IV 2025* (IEEE, 2025) to appear
54. A. Gambi, J. Bell, A. Zeller, Practical test dependency detection, in *11th IEEE International Conference on Software Testing, Verification and Validation, ICST 2018, Västerås, Sweden, April 9-13, 2018* (IEEE Computer Society, 2018), pp. 1–11
55. A. Gambi, A. Gorla, A. Zeller, O!Snap: cost-efficient testing in the cloud, in *2017 IEEE International Conference on Software Testing, Verification and Validation, ICST 2017, Tokyo, Japan, March 13-17, 2017* (IEEE Computer Society, 2017), pp. 454–459
56. A. Gambi, H. Gouni, D. Berreiter, V. Tymofyeyev, M. Fazzini, Action-based test carving for Android apps, in *IEEE International Conference on Software Testing, Verification and Validation, ICST 2023—Workshops, Dublin, Ireland, April 16-20, 2023* (IEEE, 2023), pp. 107–116
57. A. Gambi, T. Huynh, G. Fraser, Generating effective test cases for self-driving cars from police reports, in *Proceedings of the ACM Joint Meeting on European Software Engineering Conference and Symposium on the Foundations of Software Engineering, ESEC/SIGSOFT FSE 2019, Tallinn, Estonia, August 26-30, 2019*. ed. by M. Dumas, D. Pfahl, S. Apel, A. Russo (ACM, 2019), pp. 257–267
58. A. Gambi, M. Müller, G. Fraser, Automatically testing self-driving cars with search-based procedural content generation, in *Proceedings of the 28th ACM SIGSOFT International Symposium on Software Testing and Analysis, ISSTA 2019, Beijing, China, July 15-19, 2019*. ed. by D. Zhang, A. Møller (ACM, 2019), pp. 318–328
59. A. Gambi, V. Nguyen, J. Ahmed, G. Fraser, Generating critical driving scenarios from accident sketches, in *IEEE International Conference On Artificial Intelligence Testing, AITest 2022, Newark, CA, USA, August 15-18, 2022* (IEEE, 2022), pp. 95–102
60. A. Gartziandia, A. Arrieta, J. Ayerdi, M. Illarramendi, A. Agirre, G. Sagardui, M. Arratibel, Machine learning-based test oracles for performance testing of cyber-physical systems: an industrial case study on elevators dispatching algorithms. J. Softw. Evol. Process **34**(11), e2465 (2022)
61. D. Ghobari, M.H. Amini, D.Q. Tran, S. Park, S. Nejati, M. Sabetzadeh, Test input validation for vision-based DL systems: An active learning approach. CoRR (2015). arxiv:abs/2501.01606
62. L. Giamattei, A. Guerriero, R. Pietrantuono, S. Russo, I. Malavolta, T. Islam, M. Dînga, A. Koziolek, S. Singh, M. Armbruster et al., Monitoring tools for devops and microservices: a systematic grey literature review. J. Syst. Softw. **208**, 111906 (2024)
63. I. Graessler, D. Wiechel, D. Roesmann, H. Thiele, V-model based development of cyber-physical systems and cyber-physical production systems. Procedia CIRP **100**, 253–258 (2021); 31st CIRP Design Conference 2021 (CIRP Design 2021)
64. A. Guerriero, R. Pietrantuono, S. Russo, Operation is the hardest teacher: estimating DNN accuracy looking for mispredictions, in *2021 IEEE/ACM 43rd International Conference on Software Engineering (ICSE)* (IEEE, 2021), pp. 348–358

65. A. Guerriero, R. Pietrantuono, S. Russo, DeepSample: DNN sampling-based testing for operational accuracy assessment, in *Proceedings of the IEEE/ACM 46th International Conference on Software Engineering* (2024), pp. 1–12
66. A. Güllü, F. A. Shah, D. Pfahl, Its4sdc at the icst 2025 tool competition-self-driving car testing track, in *2025 IEEE Conference on Software Testing, Verification and Validation (ICST)* (IEEE, 2025), pp. 809–810
67. C. Hildebrandt, M. von Stein, S.G. Elbaum, PhysCov: physical test coverage for autonomous vehicles, in *Proceedings of the 32nd ACM SIGSOFT International Symposium on Software Testing and Analysis, ISSTA 2023, Seattle, WA, USA, July 17-21, 2023*. ed. by R. Just, G. Fraser (ACM, 2023), pp. 449–461
68. A. Humayed, J. Lin, F. Li, B. Luo, Cyber-physical systems security-a survey. IEEE Internet Things J. **4**(6), 1802–1831 (2017)
69. N. Humbatova, G. Jahangirova, G. Bavota, V. Riccio, A. Stocco, P. Tonella, Taxonomy of real faults in deep learning systems, in *ICSE '20: 42nd International Conference on Software Engineering, Seoul, South Korea, 27 June - 19 July, 2020*. ed. by G. Rothermel, D. Bae (ACM, 2020), pp. 1110–1121
70. N. Humbatova, G. Jahangirova, P. Tonella, Deepcrime: mutation testing of deep learning systems based on real faults, in *Proceedings of the 30th ACM SIGSOFT International Symposium on Software Testing and Analysis* (2021), pp. 67–78
71. D. Humeniuk, F. Khomh, G. Antoniol, A search-based framework for automatic generation of testing environments for cyber-physical systems. Inf. Softw. Technol. **149**, 106936 (2022)
72. G. Jahangirova, A. Stocco, P. Tonella, Quality metrics and oracles for autonomous vehicles testing, in *2021 14th IEEE Conference on Software Testing, Verification and Validation (ICST)* (IEEE, 2021), pp. 194–204
73. G. Jahangirova, P. Tonella, An empirical evaluation of mutation operators for deep learning systems, in *2020 IEEE 13th International Conference on Software Testing, Validation and Verification (ICST)* (IEEE, 2020), pp. 74–84
74. S. Jeong, Y. Kwak, W.J. Lee, Software-in-the-loop simulation for early-stage testing of autosar software component, in *2016 Eighth International Conference on Ubiquitous and Future Networks (ICUFN)* (IEEE, 2016), pp. 59–63
75. A. Johansson, S. Paulsson, *Microservice integration testing with hardware-in-the-loop in ci/cd pipelines* (Chalmers University of Technology, Thesis, 2024)
76. N. Kalra, S.M. Paddock, Driving to safety: how many miles of driving would it take to demonstrate autonomous vehicle reliability? Transp. Res. Part A: Policy Practice **94**, 182–193 (2016)
77. Z. Kazemi, A.A. Safavi, M.M. Arefi, F. Naseri, Finite-time secure dynamic state estimation for cyber-physical systems under unknown inputs and sensor attacks. IEEE Trans. Syst. Man Cybern. Syst. **52**(8), 4950–4959 (2021)
78. S. Khatiri, F.M. Amin, S. Panichella, P. Tonella, When uncertainty leads to unsafety: empirical insights into the role of uncertainty in unmanned aerial vehicle safety. Empir. Softw. Eng. (2025)
79. S. Khatiri, S. Panichella, P. Tonella, Simulation-based test case generation for unmanned aerial vehicles in the neighborhood of real flights, in *International Conference on Software Testing, Verification and Validation* (IEEE, 2023), pp. 281–292
80. S. Khatiri, P. Saurabh, T. Zimmermann, C. Munasinghe, C. Birchler, S. Panichella, SBFT tool competition 2024—cps-uav test case generation track, in *IEEE/ACM International Workshop on Search-Based and Fuzz Testing, SBFT@ICSE 2024* (2024)
81. G. Kim, P. Debois, J. Willis, J. Humble, *The DevOps Handbook: How to Create World-Class Agility, Reliability, and Security in Technology Organizations* (IT Revolution Press, 2016)
82. S. Klikovits, A. Gambi, D. Dhungana, R. Rabiser, Leveraging software product lines for testing autonomous vehicles, in *Proceedings of the 18th International Working Conference on Variability Modelling of Software-Intensive Systems, VaMoS 2024, Bern, Switzerland, February 7-9, 2024*. ed. by T. Kehrer, M. Huchard, L. Teixeira, C. Birchler (ACM, 2024), pp. 56–60

83. S. Klikovits, F. Ishikawa, T. Kobayashi, Formal modelling, in *Safety Assurance under Uncertainties: From Software to Cyber-Physical/Machine Learning Systems*, Chapter 8. ed. by I. Hasuo, F. Ishikawa (CRC Press, 2025)
84. S. Klikovits, C.H. Thanh, A. Cetinkaya, P. Arcaini, Trust your neighbours: Handling noise in multi-objective optimisation using kNN-averaging. Appl. Soft Comput. **146**, 110631 (2023)
85. S. Klikovits, C.H. Thanh, A. Cetinkaya, P. Arcaini, Trust your neighbours: Handling noise in multi-objective optimisation using kNN-Averaging (GECCO'24 Hot off the Press), in *Proceedings of the Genetic and Evolutionary Computation Conference Companion, GECCO 2024, Melbourne, VIC, Australia, July 14-18, 2024*. ed. by X. Li, J. Handl (ACM, 2024), pp. 39–40
86. T. Kobayashi, S. Klikovits, R. Bohrer, A. Yamada, I. Hasuo, Theorem proving at work, in *Safety Assurance under Uncertainties: From Software to Cyber-Physical/Machine Learning Systems*, Chapter 9. ed. by I. Hasuo, F. Ishikawa (CRC Press, 2025)
87. W. Kritzinger, M. Karner, G. Traar, J. Henjes, W. Sihn, Digital twin in manufacturing: a categorical literature review and classification. Ifac-PapersOnline **51**(11), 1016–1022 (2018)
88. S.C. Lambertenghi, H. Leonhard, A. Stocco, Benchmarking image perturbations for testing automated driving assistance systems, in *2025 IEEE Conference on Software Testing, Verification and Validation (ICST)* (IEEE, 2025), pp. 150–161
89. T. Laurent, S. Klikovits, P. Arcaini, F. Ishikawa, A. Ventresque, Parameter coverage for testing of autonomous driving systems under uncertainty. ACM Trans. Softw. Eng. Methodol. **32**(3), 58:1–58:31 (2023)
90. J.A. Ledin, Hardware-in-the-loop simulation. Embed. Syst. Program. **12**, 42–62 (1999)
91. S.-Y. Lee, J. Andert, D. Neumann, C. Querel, T. Scheel, S. Aktas, M. Miccio, J. Schaub, M. Koetter, M. Ehrly, Hardware-in-the-loop-based virtual calibration approach to meet real driving emissions requirements. SAE Int. J. Engines **11**(2018-01-0869), 1479–1504 (2018)
92. A. Li, J. Wang, S. Baruah, B. Sinopoli, N. Zhang, An empirical study of performance interference: timing violation patterns and impacts, in *2024 IEEE 30th Real-Time and Embedded Technology and Applications Symposium (RTAS)* (IEEE, 2024), pp. 320–333
93. W. Li, D. Sadigh, S.S. Sastry, and S. A. Seshia, Synthesis for human-in-the-loop control systems, in *Tools and Algorithms for the Construction and Analysis of Systems: 20th International Conference, TACAS 2014, Held as Part of the European Joint Conferences on Theory and Practice of Software, ETAPS 2014, Grenoble, France, April 5-13, 2014. Proceedings 20* (Springer, 2014), pp. 470–484
94. B. Lu, X. Wu, H. Figueroa, A. Monti, A low-cost real-time hardware-in-the-loop testing approach of power electronics controls. IEEE Trans. Ind. Electron. **54**(2), 919–931 (2007)
95. Q. Luo, F. Hariri, L. Eloussi, D. Marinov, An empirical analysis of flaky tests, in *Proceedings of the 22nd ACM SIGSOFT International Symposium on Foundations of Software Engineering, (FSE-22), Hong Kong, China, November 16-22, 2014*. ed. by S. Cheung, A. Orso, M.D. Storey (ACM, 2014), pp. 643–653
96. R.R. Maiti, C.H. Yoong, V.R. Palleti, A. Silva, C.M. Poskitt, Mitigating adversarial attacks on data-driven invariant checkers for cyber-physical systems. IEEE Trans. Dependable Secure Comput. **20**(4), 3378–3391 (2022)
97. F.M. Malik, S.M. Khatiri, Certifail at the icst 2025 tool competition—self-driving car testing track, in *2025 IEEE Conference on Software Testing, Verification and Validation (ICST)* (2025), pp. 811–812
98. G. Mallardi, F. Calefato, L. Quaranta, F. Lanubile, An mlops approach for deploying machine learning models in healthcare systems, in *IEEE International Conference on Bioinformatics and Biomedicine, BIBM 2024, Lisbon, Portugal, December 3-6, 2024*. ed. by M. Cannataro, H.J. Zheng, L. Gao, J. Cheng, J.L. de Miranda, E. Zumpano, X. Hu, Y. Cho, T. Park (IEEE, 2024), pp. 6832–6837
99. C. Mandrioli, S.Y. Shin, D. Bianculli, L. Briand, Testing cps with design assumptions-based metamorphic relations and genetic programming. IEEE Trans. Softw. Eng. (2025)
100. T. Mårtensson, D. Ståhl, J. Bosch, Continuous integration applied to software-intensive embedded systems–problems and experiences, in *Product-Focused Software Process*

Improvement: 17th International Conference, PROFES 2016, Trondheim, Norway, November 22-24, 2016, Proceedings 17 (Springer, 2016), pp. 448–457
101. M. Maryam, M. Biagiola, A. Stocco, V. Riccio, Benchmarking generative AI models for deep learning test input generation, in *2025 IEEE Conference on Software Testing, Verification and Validation (ICST)* (IEEE, 2025), pp. 174–185
102. C. Menghi, S. Nejati, L. Briand, Y.I. Parache, Approximation-refinement testing of compute-intensive cyber-physical models: an approach based on system identification, in *Proceedings of the ACM/IEEE 42nd International Conference on Software Engineering, ICSE '20* (Association for Computing Machinery, New York, NY, USA, 2020), pp. 372–384
103. J. Mertens, S. Klikovits, F. Bordeleau, J. Denil, Ø. Haugen, Continuous evolution of digital twins using the DarTwin notation. Softw. Syst. Model. (2024)
104. M. Mossige, A. Gotlieb, H. Spieker, H. Meling, M. Carlsson, Time-aware test case execution scheduling for cyber-physical systems, in *Principles and Practice of Constraint Programming: 23rd International Conference, CP 2017, Melbourne, VIC, Australia, August 28–September 1, 2017, Proceedings 23* (Springer, 2017), pp. 387–404
105. P. Munk, M. Schweizer, Devops and safety? safeops! towards ensuring safety in feature-driven development with frequent releases, in *International Conference on Computer Safety, Reliability, and Security* (Springer, Berlin, 2022), pp. 145–157
106. S. Nabi, M. Balike, J. Allen, K. Rzemien, An overview of hardware-in-the-loop testing systems at Visteon (2004)
107. N. Neelofar, A. Aleti, Identifying and explaining safety-critical scenarios for autonomous vehicles via key features. ACM Trans. Softw. Eng. Methodol. **33**(4), 1–32 (2024)
108. N. Neelofar, A. Aleti, Towards reliable ai: adequacy metrics for ensuring the quality of system-level testing of autonomous vehicles, in *Proceedings of the 46th IEEE/ACM International Conference on Software Engineering* (2024), pp. 1–12
109. E. Nesterini, E. Bartocci, A. Gambi, D. Nickovic, S.A. Seshia, H. Torfah, Mining specifications for predictive safety monitoring, in *Proceedings of the ACM/IEEE 16th International Conference on Cyber-Physical Systems, ICCPS 2025, (with CPS-IoT Week 2025), Irvine, CA, USA, May 6-9, 2025* (ACM, 2025), pp. 6:1–6:11
110. A. Ngo, M.P. Bauer, M. Resch, A multi-layered approach for measuring the simulation-to-reality gap of radar perception for autonomous driving, in *24th IEEE International Intelligent Transportation Systems Conference, ITSC 2021, Indianapolis, IN, USA, September 19-22, 2021* (IEEE, 2021), pp. 4008–4014
111. V. Nguyen, S. Huber, A. Gambi, SALVO: automated generation of diversified tests for self-driving cars from existing maps, in *International Conference on Artificial Intelligence Testing* (IEEE, 2021), pp. 128–135
112. F. Niu, W.K.G. Assunção, L. Huang, C. Mayr-Dorn, J. Ge, B. Luo, A. Egyed, RAT: a refactoring-aware traceability model for bug localization. In *45th IEEE/ACM International Conference on Software Engineering, ICSE 2023, Melbourne, Australia, May 14-20, 2023* (IEEE, 2023), pp. 196–207
113. C. Papamichail, D. Stark, A. Gambi, Scenario-based testing with beamng.tech (hands-on training), in *IEEE Conference on Software Testing, Verification and Validation, ICST 2025, Napoli, Italy, March 31 - April 4, 2025* (IEEE, 2025), pp. 767–768
114. Parasoft. Guide to CI/CD for Medical Device Software DevOps (2022)
115. K. Pei, Y. Cao, J. Yang, S. Jana, Deepxplore: Automated whitebox testing of deep learning systems, in *proceedings of the 26th Symposium on Operating Systems Principles* (2017), pp. 1–18
116. M. Pezze, M. Young, Testing object-oriented software, in *Proceedings. 26th International Conference on Software Engineering* (IEEE, 2004), pp. 739–740
117. A.R. Plummer, Model-in-the-loop testing. Proc Inst Mech Eng, Part I: J Syst Control Eng **220**(3), 183–199 (2006)
118. P. Polack, F. Altché, B. d'Andréa Novel, A. de La Fortelle, The kinematic bicycle model: a consistent model for planning feasible trajectories for autonomous vehicles? in *2017 IEEE Intelligent Vehicles Symposium (IV)* (2017), pp. 812–818

119. P. Polack, F. Altché, B. d'Andréa Novel, A. de La Fortelle, The kinematic bicycle model: a consistent model for planning feasible trajectories for autonomous vehicles? in *2017 IEEE intelligent vehicles symposium (IV)* (IEEE, 2017), pp. 812–818
120. V. Riccio, G. Jahangirova, A. Stocco, N. Humbatova, M. Weiss, P. Tonella, Testing machine learning based systems: a systematic mapping. Empir. Softw. Eng. **25**, 5193–5254 (2020)
121. V. Riccio, P. Tonella, Model-based exploration of the frontier of behaviours for deep learning system testing, in *ESEC/FSE '20: 28th ACM Joint European Software Engineering Conference and Symposium on the Foundations of Software Engineering, Virtual Event, USA, November 8-13, 2020*. ed. by P. Devanbu, M.B. Cohen, T. Zimmermann (ACM, 2020), pp. 876–888
122. V. Riccio, P. Tonella, When and why test generators for deep learning produce invalid inputs: an empirical study. In *45th IEEE/ACM International Conference on Software Engineering, ICSE 2023, Melbourne, Australia, May 14-20, 2023* (IEEE, 2023), pp. 1161–1173
123. L. Rothrock, S. Narayanan, *Human-in-the-Loop Simulations* (Springer, 2011)
124. Z. Sadri-Moshkenani, J. Bradley, G. Rothermel, Survey on test case generation, selection and prioritization for cyber-physical systems. Softw. Test. Verification and Reliab. **32**(1), e1794 (2022)
125. F. Scheuer, A. Gambi, P. Arcaini, STRETCH: generating challenging scenarios for testing collision avoidance systems, in *IEEE Intelligent Vehicles Symposium, IV 2023, Anchorage, AK, USA, June 4-7, 2023* (IEEE, 2023), pp. 1–6
126. S.Y. Shin, K. Chaouch, S. Nejati, M. Sabetzadeh, L.C. Briand, F. Zimmer, Uncertainty-aware specification and analysis for hardware-in-the-loop testing of cyber-physical systems. J. Syst. Softw. **171**, 110813 (2021)
127. L. Sorokin, M. Biagiola, A. Stocco, Simulator ensembles for trustworthy autonomous driving testing (2025). arXiv:2503.08936
128. M. Stadler, M. Vierhauser, A. Garmendia, M. Wimmer, J. Cleland-Huang, Flexible model-driven runtime monitoring support for cyber-physical systems, in *Proceedings of the ACM/IEEE 44th International Conference on Software Engineering: Companion Proceedings, ICSE '22* (Association for Computing Machinery, New York, NY, USA, 2022), pp. 350–351
129. B. Steininger, C. Papamichail, D. Stark, D. Nickovic, A. Gambi, Automatically generating content for testing autonomous vehicles from user descriptions, in *Proceedings of the 2025 ACM/IEEE 47th International Conference on Software Engineering: New Ideas and Emerging Results, NIER@ICSE 2025* (2025) to appear
130. A. Stocco, B. Pulfer, P. Tonella, Mind the gap! A study on the transferability of virtual versus physical-world testing of autonomous driving systems. IEEE Trans. Softw. Eng. **49**(4), 1928–1940 (2023)
131. A. Stocco, P. Tonella, Towards anomaly detectors that learn continuously, in *2020 IEEE international symposium on software reliability engineering workshops (ISSREW)* (IEEE, 2020), pp. 201–208
132. A. Stocco, P. Tonella, Confidence-driven weighted retraining for predicting safety-critical failures in autonomous driving systems. J. Softw. Evol. Process **34**(10), e2386 (2022)
133. A. Stocco, M. Weiss, M. Calzana, P. Tonella, Misbehaviour prediction for autonomous driving systems, in *Proceedings of the ACM/IEEE 42nd International Conference on Software Engineering*. ed. by G. Rothermel, D. Bae (ACM, 2020), pp. 359–371
134. Swissinfo, swiss post drone crashes in zurich—again (2019)
135. V. Terragni, P. Salza, F. Ferrucci, A container-based infrastructure for fuzzy-driven root causing of flaky tests, in *ICSE-NIER 2020: 42nd International Conference on Software Engineering, New Ideas and Emerging Results, Seoul, South Korea, 27 June-19 July, 2020*. ed. by G. Rothermel, D. Bae (ACM, 2020), pp. 69–72
136. G. Tibba, C. Malz, C. Stoermer, N. Nagarajan, L. Zhang, S. Chakraborty, Testing automotive embedded systems under X-in-the-loop setups, in *2016 IEEE/ACM International Conference on Computer-Aided Design (ICCAD)* (IEEE, 2016), pp. 1–8

137. T.N.Y. Times, Are there problems with the boeing 737 max? a second deadly crash raises new questions (2019)
138. P. Tonella, The road toward dependable ai based systems, in *2023 IEEE/ACM 45th International Conference on Software Engineering (ICSE)* (IEEE, 2023), p. 2
139. C. Trubiani, P. Jamshidi, J. Cito, W. Shang, Z.M. Jiang, M. Borg, Performance issues? Hey DevOps, mind the uncertainty. IEEE Softw. **36**(2), 110–117 (2019)
140. University of Luxembourg. Addressing the challenges of devops for cyber-physical systems, 2023. [Online; accessed 20-May-2025]
141. P. Valle, A. Arrieta, L. Han, S. Ali, T. Yue, Defining and generating multi-level and uncertainty-wise test oracles for cyber-physical systems. Softw. Syst. Model. 1–26 (2025)
142. P. Valle, V. Riccio, A. Arrieta, P. Tonella, M. Arratibel, An industrial experience report on applying search-based boundary input generation to cyber-physical systems. Empir. Softw. Eng. **30**(4), 1–34 (2025)
143. I. van Dinten, P. Derakhshanfar, A. Panichella, A. Zaidman, The slow and the furious? performance antipattern detection in cyber-physical systems. J. Syst. Softw. **210**, 111904 (2024)
144. T. Vepsäläinen, S. Kuikka, Integrating model-in-the-loop simulations to model-driven development in industrial control. Simulation **90**(12), 1295–1311 (2014)
145. S. Vost, S. Wagner, Keeping continuous deliveries safe, in *2017 IEEE/ACM 39th International Conference on Software Engineering Companion (ICSE-C)* (2017), pp. 259–261
146. F. Warg, H. Blom, J. Borg, R. Johansson, Continuous deployment for dependable systems with continuous assurance cases, in *2019 IEEE International Symposium on Software Reliability Engineering Workshops (ISSREW)* (IEEE, 2019), pp. 318–325
147. H. Weber, J. Bock, J. Klimke, C. Roesener, J. Hiller, R. Krajewski, A. Zlocki, L.E., A framework for definition of logical scenarios for safety assurance of automated driving. Traffic Injury Prev. **20**(sup1), S65–S70 (2019)
148. T. Woodlief, F. Toledo, S.G. Elbaum, M.B. Dwyer, S3C: spatial semantic scene coverage for autonomous vehicles, in *Proceedings of the 46th IEEE/ACM International Conference on Software Engineering, ICSE 2024, Lisbon, Portugal, April 14-20, 2024* (ACM, 2024), pp. 141:1–141:13
149. F. Zampetti, R. Kapur, M. Di Penta, S. Panichella, An empirical characterization of software bugs in open-source cyber–physical systems. J. Syst. Softw. **192**, 111425 (2022)
150. F. Zampetti, V. Nardone, M. Di Penta, Problems and solutions in applying continuous integration and delivery to 20 open-source cyber-physical systems, in *Proceedings of the 19th International Conference on Mining Software Repositories, MSR '22* (Association for Computing Machinery, New York, NY, USA, 2022), pp. 646–657
151. F. Zampetti, D. Tamburri, S. Panichella, A. Panichella, G. Canfora, M. Di Penta, Continuous integration and delivery practices for cyber-physical systems: an interview-based study. ACM Trans. Softw. Eng. Methodol. **32**(3), 1–44 (2023)
152. F. Zampetti, D.A. Tamburri, S. Panichella, A. Panichella, G. Canfora, M.D. Penta, Continuous integration and delivery practices for cyber-physical systems: an interview-based study. ACM Trans. Softw. Eng. Methodol. **32**(3), 73:1–73:44 (2023)
153. M. Zeller, Towards continuous safety assessment in context of devops, in *Computer Safety, Reliability, and Security. SAFECOMP 2021 Workshops: DECSoS, MAPSOD, DepDevOps, USDAI, and WAISE, York, UK, September 7, 2021, Proceedings 40* (Springer, 2021), pp. 145–157
154. M. Zhang, Y. Zhang, L. Zhang, C. Liu, S. Khurshid, Deeproad: Gan-based metamorphic testing and input validation framework for autonomous driving systems, in *Proceedings of the 33rd ACM/IEEE international conference on automated software engineering* (2018), pp. 132–142
155. X. Zheng, C. Julien, H. Chen, R. Podorozhny, F. Cassez, Real-time simulation support for runtime verification of cyber-physical systems. ACM Trans. Embed. Comput. Syst. (TECS) **16**(4), 1–24 (2017)
156. X. Zhou, X. Gou, T. Huang, S. Yang, Review on testing of cyber physical systems: methods and testbeds. IEEE Access **6**, 52179–52194 (2018)

157. T. Zohdinasab, V. Riccio, A. Gambi, P. Tonella, DeepHyperion: exploring the feature space of deep learning-based systems through illumination search, in *ISSTA '21: 30th ACM SIGSOFT International Symposium on Software Testing and Analysis, Virtual Event, Denmark, July 11-17, 2021*. ed. by C. Cadar, X. Zhang (ACM, 2021), pp. 79–90
158. T. Zohdinasab, V. Riccio, A. Gambi, P. Tonella, Deephyperion: exploring the feature space of deep learning-based systems through illumination search, in *Software Engineering 2023, Fachtagung des GI-Fachbereichs Softwaretechnik, 20.-24. Februar 2023, Paderborn*. ed. by G. Engels, R. Hebig, M. Tichy. Volume P-332 of LNI. (Gesellschaft für Informatik e.V., 2023), pp. 131–132
159. T. Zohdinasab, V. Riccio, A. Gambi, P. Tonella, Efficient and effective feature space exploration for testing deep learning systems. ACM Trans. Softw. Eng. Methodol. **32**(2), 49:1–49:38 (2023)
160. T. Zohdinasab, V. Riccio, P. Tonella, DeepAtash: focused test generation for deep learning systems, in *Proceedings of the 32nd ACM SIGSOFT International Symposium on Software Testing and Analysis, ISSTA 2023, Seattle, WA, USA, July 17-21, 2023*. ed. by R. Just, G. Fraser (ACM, 2023), pp. 954–966
161. T. Zohdinasab, V. Riccio, P. Tonella, An empirical study on low-and high-level explanations of deep learning misbehaviours, in *2023 ACM/IEEE International Symposium on Empirical Software Engineering and Measurement (ESEM)* (IEEE, 2023), pp. 1–11
162. T. Zohdinasab, V. Riccio, P. Tonella, Focused test generation for autonomous driving systems. ACM Trans. Softw. Eng. Methodol. **33**(6), 1–32 (2024)

Uncertainty-Aware DevOps for Cyber-Physical Systems and Runtime Verification

Shaukat Ali, Domenico Bianculli, Antonio Cicchetti, Robbert Jongeling, Violet Ka I Pun, Volker Stolz, and Catia Trubiani

Abstract This chapter raises the attention on possible sources of uncertainties (e.g., workload of requests, software and/or hardware availabilities) that may arise at both development and operational stages (DevOps) in cyber-physical systems (CPS). Given that such uncertainties are unavoidable, a possible solution is to devise an uncertainty-aware methodology to model, analyze, and test these systems, thus anticipating glitches, if any. This way, we aim to monitor and verify the stated requirements at runtime, with the goal of guaranteeing that systems behave as expected. Our main contribution is to shed the light on the most relevant uncertainties (and to foresee their smooth handling) when applying the DevOps paradigm for CPS.

S. Ali (✉)
Simula Research Laboratory, Oslo, Norway
e-mail: shaukat@simula.no

D. Bianculli
University of Luxembourg, Luxembourg, Luxembourg
e-mail: domenico.bianculli@uni.lu

A. Cicchetti · R. Jongeling
Malardalen University, Vasteras, Sweden
e-mail: antonio.cicchetti@mdu.se

R. Jongeling
e-mail: robbert.jongeling@mdu.se

V. K. I Pun · V. Stolz
Western Norway University of Applied Sciences, Bergen, Norway
e-mail: violet.ka.i.pun@hvl.no

V. Stolz
e-mail: volker.stolz@hvl.no

C. Trubiani
Gran Sasso Science Institute, L'Aquila, Italy
e-mail: catia.trubiani@gssi.it

S. Panichella et al. (eds.), *Roadmap for DevOps in Cyber-Physical Systems*,
https://doi.org/10.1007/978-981-95-1786-2_5

1 Introduction and Motivation

Uncertainties in the operation of CPS are unavoidable due to many factors, such as an unpredictable environment, issues in communication networks, and the increasing use of machine learning algorithms in CPS, which are also inherently uncertain [6, 15, 28, 30]. It is important to recognize the fact that uncertainties are thus unavoidable, and therefore methods are needed to identify, quantify, and model such uncertainties to enable CPS to deal with them.

During a CPS design, we do not have complete knowledge about the uncertainties a CPS may experience during its operation due to a lack of knowledge about the CPS's possible operating environments and their characteristics, as well as the existence of emergent behaviors. Therefore, it is crucial to continuously gain knowledge about the CPS's possible uncertainties during its operation to enable it to deal with them.

We argue that CPS DevOps shall be uncertainty-aware, in the sense that knowledge from design time about uncertainties shall be used during operation time to enable a CPS to deal with known uncertainties identified and quantified during design time. At the same time, knowledge gained during operation about uncertainties shall be fed back to the design to further improve existing knowledge about uncertainties, resulting in enhanced modeling and quantification of these uncertainties.

We identify a set of core aspects that call for attention from both researchers and practitioners. First, a key activity is represented by gathering the sources of uncertainty since CPS span in multiple application domains. It is indeed relevant to specify what the uncertainties are that may more frequently occur and their possible impact on quality-of-service (QoS) characteristics [15, 40]. Second, the design of these systems has to reflect such uncertainties so that software developers are aware of possible design alternatives to handle potential quality glitches, e.g., a high peak of workload requests can benefit from the mirroring of software components. Third, model-based analysis can support this stage of making decisions for a future implementation, in fact, quantitative results are derived to compare the design alternatives (subject to uncertainties), and there are metrics intentionally calculated for this scope, such as the robustness. Fourth, at the operational stage, the challenge is to verify if there are violations invalidating the previous analysis; the monitoring of CPS is aimed to verify if requirements are fulfilled, otherwise refactoring actions are required to fix issues, if any.

This chapter focuses on uncertainties in the DevOps of CPS. First, it begins by discussing some core aspects related to uncertainties in Sect. 2 that are various sources of uncertainty affecting quality-of-service properties (see Sect. 2.1); design-time modeling of uncertainties and various analyses (see Sect. 2.2); uncertainties during operation time, including techniques such as runtime verification (see Sect. 2.3). Based on the discussions of design-time and operation-time uncertainties in CPS DevOps, we present a path forward in Sect. 3 and conclude the chapter in Sect. 4.

2 Core Aspects

2.1 *Sources of Uncertainty for Quality-of-Service (QoS)*

In the software development of cyber-physical systems (CPS) there is a high interest in the early validation of Quality-of-Service (QoS) requirements because this avoids late and expensive repairs to consolidated software artifacts [34]. One of the proper ways to manage software quality is to systematically predict the non-functional properties of CPS throughout the development process. It is thus possible to make informed choices among different design alternatives, and know in advance if the CPS will meet the stated non-functional objectives [22] at the later operational stage.

Model-Driven Engineering (MDE) techniques have successfully been used to introduce automation in software quality modeling and analysis [21]. Nevertheless, the problem of interpreting non functional results is still quite challenging. A large gap exists between the representation of analysis results and the software design alternatives provided by the software engineers. In fact, the former usually contains functions, numbers, and trends, even over time (e.g., throughput variance, runtime evolution of failures, etc.), whereas the latter embeds design choices (e.g., software components, interaction among components, deployment choices).

QoS estimations at the early stages of software development are challenging, as there are many aspects that may be unknown or uncertain, such as the design decisions, code, and execution environment. Besides, the quality evaluation of CPS is also affected by external factors, such as the interplay between software and physical components, as well as increasingly fluctuating workloads and changing scenarios. As a result, software engineers need to make decisions under uncertainty (i.e., related to the design or refactoring of the system), without knowing the exact impact of those decisions on the QoS [36].

We devise two main challenges in this context: (i) how to explicitly specify the possible system uncertainties at the design level, and (ii) how to recognize, model and manage those uncertainties to mitigate their potentially QoS negative effects at runtime. Given that DevOps aims to bridge the gap between software development and operation teams, support for these challenges can be provided by (1) identifying the main sources of uncertainty that may be responsible for QoS-based issues, (2) elaborating on how these uncertainties manifest in input data, design models, and operational results, and (3) performing a sensitivity analysis that quantifies the impact of these sources of uncertainty for QoS results interpretation. It is therefore valuable to put in place a set of methodologies that model and analyze these uncertainties so that violations of QoS requirements can be anticipated, thereby linking the operational issues to the decisions made during the software design process. For instance, an experience on performance-related issues raising from different system uncertainties has been reported in reference [39].

Possible sources of uncertainties that may affect the quality of service of CPS are listed in the following:

- `Workload`, i.e., the number of users' requests to services, as well as how often these requests are generated.
- `Operational profile`, i.e., the way users interact with the system, the operations that the software system is required to perform, as well the operations' probabilities to be invoked.
- `Resource demand of software resources`, i.e., the processor and/or the disk units of computation needed to accomplish a certain software service.
- `Service time of hardware resources`, i.e., the processor and/or the disk latency in terms of the time needed to execute a service, or the network latency expressed in terms of exchanged data rates, e.g., number of megabits per second.
- `Interplay between software and hardware components`, i.e., software requests that trigger decisions at the physical level but may involve multiple hardware components that need coordination, e.g., wheels in a self-driving car scenario.

The outcome of uncertainties specification can be used to explicitly define the lower and upper bounds in input parameters during the quality evaluation process [1, 3]. This allows for approximations of quality indicators in cases where the system behaviour can not be determined or precisely evaluated in advance. Still, this constitutes a valid approximation at the development stage and it can be used as an oracle for the subsequent operational stage. For instance, model-based testing can exploit the uncertainty specification to drive the testing process itself in identifying the most critical parts of the software system under test, as proposed in [9]. When the system is in execution, some decisions need to be taken, and they can be motivated by tracing back to the knowledge collected during the design stage.

2.2 *Design Stage*

2.2.1 Design-Time Modeling Under Uncertainty

The development of subsystems that comprise a CPS cannot proceed completely in sync due to mutual dependencies and the constant needs to adopt domain-specific priorities and make design trade-off decisions. Simply, not everything can be done at the same time. Moreover, the development of CPS involves several engineering disciplines, each adopting its own tools, formalisms and modeling levels of abstraction. Hence, the design of CPS inherently combines prescriptive and descriptive models; the former specify blueprints of to-be-realized systems whereas the latter capture aspects of an existing system [24]. Prescriptive models inherently contain more uncertainty, given the type of information they are derived from: design decisions and assumptions early in development, rather than having an underlying ground truth such as descriptive models do. For example, a descriptive CAD model can be a quite precise reflection of the real system whereas a model prescribing a network topology configuration may be expressed at a higher level of abstraction and may be subject to significant changes over time to accurately reflect the latest knowledge on how the system shall be built. These practices result in development processes devoted to shrink the "cone of uncertainty" for the CPS under study by taking design decisions rather than selecting a single alternative from the beginning [4].

In this chapter, we refer to uncertainties (or unknowns) in CPS development as those situations where relevant information is subject to error margins and/or is not completely known [35]. Uncertainty is classified as aleatory or ontological when is related to the inherent randomness of a scenario: the noise affecting the signal and measures of a sensor, the variation and amount of workload generated by users, the delay of a network communication, are all examples of aleatory unknowns. Epistemic uncertainty instead is due to lack of knowledge: how many requests a system might be able to serve is unknown or grossly estimated in early stages of the development and becomes progressively more precise (less uncertain) as the system takes form in terms of software and hardware [12, 26].

Uncertainties need to be carefully handled in order to avoid design errors as well as the propagation of erroneous assumptions. A well-known situation is a tank sensor and the handling of different levels of fuel: from an algorithmic perspective it might seem straightforward that reaching a certain level triggers corresponding actions in the system. However, in reality the sensor values will start oscillating around the target level once sufficiently close, and this aspect needs to be managed appropriately in order to avoid, e.g., the system bouncing between different operation modes. Another common situation is the parameterization of software components of a vehicle based on physical characteristics: a braking force and the timing for its application might be dependent on several factors like the range of weight for produced vehicles, the kind of wheels used, and so forth. In this scenario, implicit assumptions on vehicle characteristics could result in braking ranges considerably out of allowed boundaries in case of configuration changes (e.g., the addition of a heavy third-party component). The problem of uncertainty handling is even more relevant in DevOps contexts, since continuous refinements exacerbate the issue of keeping track of the underlying design assumptions [11].

In the following, we illustrate an approach to document uncertainties at design time; this documentation becomes valuable when evaluating and propagating inconsistencies across subsequent development stages. Details can be found in previously published work [26].

Documenting Design-Time Uncertainty. During the development and maintenance of CPS, multiple models are created to represent the system and inevitably inconsistencies arise between them. It is well-established that these inconsistencies must be tolerated to some extent, but as development progresses and uncertainty is reduced, inconsistencies must at some point be resolved. The right time to stop tolerating an inconsistency is not easily determined. In [26], inconsistencies are related to the uncertainty associated with design elements. Higher uncertainty is postulated to imply a higher tolerance for inconsistency, since elements with high uncertainty associated to them are expected to change in the future, whereas elements with low uncertainty associated to them are expected to be stable and be built upon further. An approach is presented to document uncertainty and show a mechanism by which this information can be used to provide insight into prioritization and resolution of inconsistencies.

Practical applications of consistency management demand for lightweightness [25]. That is, inconsistency management tasks shall be to such an extent integrated in the development process that they do not present an additional burden and are therefore forsaken. Instead, approaches shall be able to deal with the reality of having a combination of formal and rather informal artefacts, allow definition of consistency rules in a simple way, allow expression of uncertainty in a simple way, and be able to be supported by automation.

This approach relies on annotating *doubts* to indicate design uncertainty about particular model elements. Various types of doubts may be raised: (i) *Occurrence* doubts question the existence of an element in a model, for example if a particular component shall be or shall not be part of a configuration; (ii) *Availability* doubts question if a particular element is available in a particular configuration, for example a component may not be available under certain conditions; (iii) *Content* doubts question the completeness of model elements inside containers, for example SysML blocks that may be missing elements; (iv) *Property* doubts question the correctness of values of syntactic or semantic attributes of model elements. Doubts of each type can be raised at four degrees of severity (each denoted by specific characters): very uncertain (??), uncertain (?), somewhat uncertain (∼), and instead very certain (!). A lightweight textual notation is proposed to express doubts: ⟨Agent⟩⟨Degree of Doubt⟩⟨Type⟩(⟨Element⟩) : ⟨Rationale⟩. The absence of doubt can be represented too in later stages of this approach, using an underscore (_). Absence of doubt can be due to uncommitted opinion, or not having given an opinion. This is distinct from certainty (!) which requires an explicit statement of opinion with a rationale.

Doubts are a simplified notation to denote an opinion. These opinions are formalized using subjective logic [27]. Subjective logic opinions comprise a degree of belief the statement is true, a degree disbelief of the statement, a degree of uncertainty in terms of uncommitted belief nor disbelief, and a base probability of the statement to be true without prior evidence. All factors are expressed as real numbers in the range between 0 and 1, and the first three factors describing the subjective opinion shall sum to 1.

In the proposed approach, an assertion maps the notations of doubts to pre-established values for belief, disbelief, and uncertainty. The approach uses the following quadruples for belief, disbelief, uncertainty and base rate for each degree of doubt: very certain (!), (1.0, 0.0, 0.0, 0.5); somewhat uncertain (∼), (0.95, 0.025, 0.025, 0.5); uncertain (?) (0.8, 0.1, 0.1, 0.5); very uncertain (??) (0.5, 0.25, 0.25, 0.5). Notice that the remainder of the calculations all follow from applying established subjective logic rules based on these underlying values. Indeed, this underlying formalism enables calculations with the doubts that can provide insight into the doubts on other models and on inconsistencies between linked models

Once doubts are annotated, they may need to be propagated to related models. For example, in development settings where product instance models are derived from previously established reference architecture model, a doubt about the occurrence of a component in the reference architecture shall be propagated to denote the same doubt on the occurrence of that component in the product instance model. Propagation rules are directed and not symmetric; an occurrence doubt on a component in the product instance model does not necessarily imply the same doubt on the level of the reference architecture. The specific propagation rules to apply depend on the development setting and on how the models are related to each other. Only expressions of doubt (∼, ?, ??) are propagated, while certainties (!) and the absence of doubt (_) are not, but will be used later for inconsistency prioritization. Doubts are also not propagated if the target element already has the same degree of doubt annotated to it. Lastly, doubts are only propagated between models that have a dependency due to one being derived from the other. Propagating doubts is not necessary between models that are not derived from each other and instead are independently created to describe the system under development, for example a SysML block diagram and a Simulink model both describing the same system under development.

Once doubts are propagated, a model element may be annotated with multiple doubts (e.g., d_1 and d_2) expressed by the same agent. These are merged into a single expression of doubt by relying on the *AND* operator of subjective logic. The final doubt d is thus given by $d = d_1 \wedge d_2$. When multiple agents have expressed doubts on the same model element (e.g., d_a and d_b), these are averaged by using the weighted belief fusion operator of subjective logic: $d = \mathit{WBF}(d_a, d_b)$. As with the propagation, combination and averaging of doubts only concerns expressions of doubt (∼, ?, ??) and excludes certainty (!).

Inconsistencies between models involve model elements that through the previous steps in the proposed approach may be associated with doubts. These doubts can be used for prioritization of the inconsistencies. Three cases are distinguished: (i) when an inconsistency involves elements neither of which has an associated doubt, it is then marked with the absence of doubt (_); (ii) an inconsistency involving one or more elements with an annotated certainty (!) is marked with also a degree of certainty (!); and (iii) an inconsistency involving one or more elements with an associated degree of doubt is marked with a combination of these doubts. The way to combine doubts depends on the directionality of the inconsistency: when one element implies the presence of another, the implication operator is used; when elements shall be equivalent, the bi-implication operator is used.

The resulting degrees of doubt on the inconsistency can be used to obtain a prioritized list of inconsistencies. Recall the starting assumption: more uncertainty implies less priority for inconsistency resolution. Thus, detected inconsistencies can be sorted in order from highest to lowest priority to resolve: !, _, ∼, ?, ??. Moreover, a side-effect of this approach is that we may uncover inconsistencies due to a difference in annotated degrees of doubts. These concern cases where the model elements themselves are consistent, but their annotated doubts differ. For example, the occurrence of a state in a SysML state machine diagram might be required to have an equivalent class in C++ code. Consider a case when they both exist, a doubt is raised on the need to have it in the state machine, but a certainty is expressed on its need in the code. Resolving these doubts may cause an inconsistency when it is decided to remove the state from the state machine and to keep it in the code. Thus, this forms an uncovered inconsistency, which was previously unknown prior to making doubts explicit.

The proposed approach is a mechanism that may be used to express doubts in a lightweight way and benefit from these expressions also for managing consistency between various models in the development of CPS. In general, the problem of prioritization of inconsistencies is multifaceted and requires considering many variables in addition to the one presented here. This approach is conceived to be applicable in realistic settings with models of various levels of abstraction and formalism. Annotating doubts is thus the lightweight means to access the underlying well-defined operators as defined in subjective logic and obtain insight into uncertainty and inconsistency, thereby allowing them both to be reduced during the development process.

2.2.2 Analysis Under Uncertainty

Modeled uncertainties can support various analyses during the CPS design, such as robustness analyses, verification, and testing. To explain the ideas, this section will use the example of an industrial elevator case study used in previous works [23]. This case study is from Orona,[1] a company based in the Basque Country, Spain. They are well known for building elevators of many different types. Their elevators have been deployed worldwide, and they have thousands of installations. During the development phase of elevators, Orona employs a wide range of methods for development, testing, and maintenance. For instance, it is common to perform testing under various simulation configurations [29], such as software in the loop (SiL) and hardware in the loop (HiL). In the former case, part of the elevator software is real, whereas the rest of the elevators' aspects are simulated (e.g., hardware, passengers). In the latter case, hardware components are incrementally included in the simulation. At the SiL level, Orona uses commercial software for simulation called Elevate.[2] This is one of the advanced industrial elevator simulation software capable of simulating various aspects of elevators, such as passengers using the elevator with different known patterns, hardware components, and building configurations. In the context of elevators, in addition to safety, it is also important to ensure that the elevators meet the required QoS. The QoS level is measured using different quantitative metrics in the industry. One of the industry standard metrics used to assess the QoS of elevator is the average waiting time (AWT), which measures the average time passengers have to wait since the passenger pressed the button to call the elevator and until the elevator arrives for a given time frame.

In the presence of uncertainties, elevators shall not compromise safety and try to maintain acceptable QoS as much as possible. Safety, indeed, takes priority over QoS. Uncertainties can arise from different sources in the context of CPS. For example,

[1] https://www.orona-group.com/.

[2] https://www.peters-research.com/elevate.

uncertainties can originate from various reasons inside the CPS, such as software errors. In the context of elevators, such software errors could cause the elevator to behave poorly regarding QoS, leading to a prolonged AWT. Uncertainties can arise from multiple sources outside of the elevator's environment, e.g., due to human interaction with the CPS [7], communication network problems, and sensor errors. In the context of elevators, an example is how humans interact with elevators, e.g., a person rushing toward the closing elevator and forcefully stopping the elevator door from closing so that the person can enter the elevator. This could potentially affect the QoS of the elevator and, in the worst-case scenario, cause hardware problems in the elevator door.

Below, the section discusses two applications of design-time analyses under uncertainty in the context of industrial elevators, i.e., robustness analysis and testing.

Data-Driven Robustness Analysis under Uncertainty. Robustness analysis helps assess how robust a given CPS is against various uncertainties. This robustness can be evaluated from functional correctness as well as from non-functional aspects (e.g., performance). An example of the latter is how much CPS performance deviates from the normal expected performance with and without specific types of uncertainties in its operation. There are different ways to assess the robustness of a CPS under uncertainties; however, this section focuses on data-driven methods, where a CPS is executed under various known uncertainties, under various testing setups, i.e., SiL or HiL. Alternatively, the data could be obtained from real operational data. On the one hand, data obtained from the operation represents more realistic situations. On the other hand, the uncertainties are not controlled in the operational data, allowing more controlled and detailed analyses with respect to uncertainties. With collected data (either from simulation or real operation), relevant statistical methods and frameworks can be applied to assess robustness.

This section will now explain how to assess the robustness of industrial elevator software in the context of SiL configuration. In particular, it will show the application of the Cynefin framework [31] in this industrial context to assess elevator software robustness under uncertainties [23]. The Cynefin framework was initially designed to help decision-making under various situations with different uncertainties [31]. In general, the framework defines five different contexts: simple, complicated, complex, chaotic, and disorder, where the degree of uncertainty increases from simple, complicated, complex to chaotic context, whereas the fifth context, i.e., disorder context, does not belong to any of the four contexts. Further information is needed so that the appropriate context in one of the first four can be determined for the scenario in the chaotic context. In this context, the four contexts are used as the baseline to assess the robustness of industrial elevator software. Such an assessment is based on classifying the impact of uncertainties on the robustness of elevator software. The robustness is then measured in terms of QoS, e.g., using the AWT metric. At a higher level, the higher the impact an uncertainty has on robustness, the higher the likelihood that it will be classified within a context with a high degree of uncertainty. The approach has three generic phases that can be applied to different systems (Fig. 1).

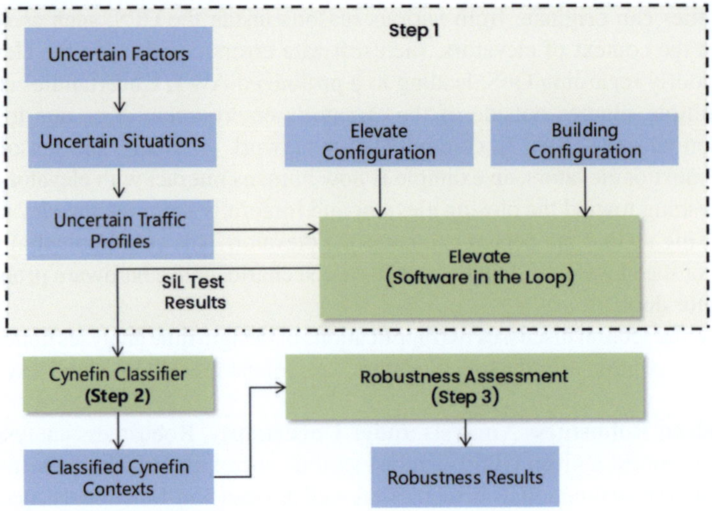

Fig. 1 Overview of design time uncertainty-aware robustness analysis solution

Phase 1: Uncertain Data Generation. During this phase, data is generated considering uncertainties that are subsequently used to classify uncertain situations into Cynefin contexts. There are multiple options. First, one could exercise the CPS in the SiL or HiL setting based on known uncertainties to generate data representing the system's behavior under simulated uncertainties. This way, the classification and robustness analysis can be more systematic since the uncertainties are controlled. Second, one can obtain real operational data of the CPS, where the CPS experienced various uncertainties and system performance was observed. Consider the example of elevator software. In this context, the focus is on passenger uncertainties, though the approach can be applied to other types of uncertainties as well, e.g., hardware. There are several uncertain factors in the context of passengers. For example, it is not known when the passenger will come and call for the elevator (arrival time), which floor the passenger would like to go to, and how much the passenger will weigh. An uncertain situation involves a combination of one or more uncertain factors. Based on these uncertain situations, traffic for elevators is generated, i.e., passengers coming and taking elevators at different times through a building. This passenger traffic and a building configuration are fed into Elevate for simulation. As a result, Elevate simulates the traffic in the building and produces various QoS metrics.

Phase 2: Cynefin Classifications. Based on the generated data, this phase involves classifying uncertain situations into one of the four contexts. Such a classification is performed by comparing an uncertain situation with running the same simulation without uncertainty. For example, one can fix a passenger's mass to a standard recommendation (e.g., 75 kg for a European) representing no uncertainty in the passenger's mass and perform a simulation to obtain QoS with respect to it. Next, the simulation results with uncertain passengers are compared with those without uncertainty with relevant statistical tests (e.g., the Wilcoxon test). Depending on the significance of the impact an uncertain situation has on the elevator's QoS, it is classified into one of the four contexts. For instance, if no significant difference is observed, an uncertain situation shall be classified into a Simple context. A detailed algorithm can be found in reference [23].

Phase 3: Robustness Classification. Once uncertain situations have been classified into the four contexts for a given software, the next step is to quantify the software's robustness based on the classification result. Simply put, the more situations are classified into higher uncertain contexts, the less robust the software. Details can be found in reference [23].

Phases 1 to 3 have been applied on 90 elevator software versions from Orona to assess their robustness and the applicability of the proposed approach in reference [23]. The results helped identify various situations under which some software versions were not robust. Moreover, Orona found the approach to be useful in their context.

Testing under Uncertainty with Software in the Loop Setup. During the design of CPS, testing under uncertainty can also be performed with different simulation setups (e.g., SiL or HiL) with different approaches. This case shows how a genetic algorithm (GA) can be applied to test elevator software under uncertain passenger traffic within the SiL setup. Since testing focuses on finding faults in the software, the focus is on finding uncertain passengers that lead to bad QoS (i.e., high AWT).

Figure 2 shows the process of the GA-based approach.

In this context, the GA-based approach is embedded inside the Elevate simulator [19]. The input to Elevate is an elevator configuration, e.g., a building configuration and a traffic profile with fixed values of passenger attributes (i.e., no uncertainties). In contrast, the timing of passengers in the profile follows a known pattern. An example of this pattern includes a morning profile, where everyone comes to the office and takes the elevator to the top floor, i.e., most of the traffic is going upward (often called the UpPeak profile). The main idea is to keep the traffic pattern the same while only introducing uncertainties in some passenger attributes so that the

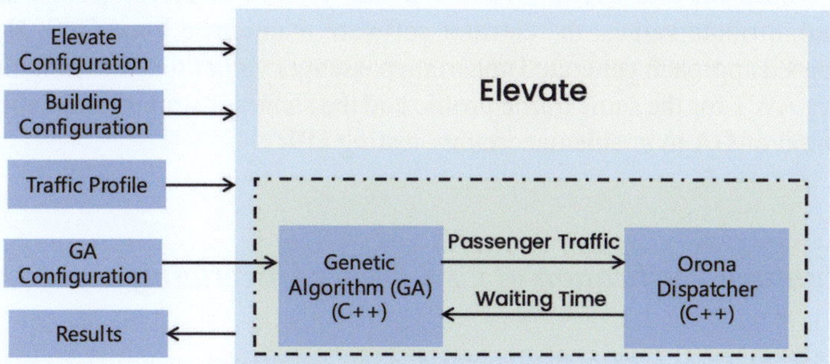

Fig. 2 Overview of uncertainty-aware testing solution

elevator software's QoS is degraded. GA-based approach achieves this by introducing the passengers with uncertain values during the simulation and calculating the waiting time. The fitness function maximizes the AWT, representing the degraded QoS. Once the simulation is complete for a given traffic profile, the SiL results are produced. The results include whether GA was successful in degrading QoS. If so, it means that the elevator software needs to be optimized; otherwise, it is robust against uncertainties.

Uncertainties are studied in the following four attributes of a passenger, i.e., mass, capacity factor, loading time, and unloading time. Mass represents the weight of a passenger. The capacity factor is a percentage of the elevator filled with passengers, based on which a passenger decides whether to take an elevator. For instance, if it is set to 90%, a passenger will not take the elevator if the passenger sees that the elevator is 90% full. Loading and unloading time represents the time taken by a passenger to get in or out of the elevator. In a typical setup, the values of these attributes are fixed, i.e., there is no uncertainty. The values of the rest of the attributes, i.e., the arrival floor, arrival time, and destination floor, are the same as those of the original traffic profile. This way, the traffic pattern remains the same as the original, i.e., realistic, whereas uncertainties only in the relevant attributes of passengers can be studied.

GA generates uncertain attribute values for the four attributes for each passenger during the simulation. When the simulation of the passenger is complete, it records the waiting time, i.e., the time the passenger had to wait. To keep the values of each attribute within reasonable limits, the range was set around each attribute within which the GA was configured to generate values. This ensures that uncertain but realistic attribute values are generated. Since AWT is calculated based on the waiting time of a set of passengers (e.g., n), uncertain attributes are generated for n passengers over time. Next, the AWT is calculated based on the waiting times of these n passengers. The AWT is then used as the GA's fitness function to guide the search and generate the next generation of passengers. The GA continues until the whole traffic profile is executed and the results are produced. The results are then analyzed to see if the GA generated passengers with uncertain attributes that lead to high AWT.

The GA-based approach is evaluated with a standard simulation with fixed attribute values for one traffic profile and one version of elevator software [19]. With fixed attribute values, the elevator software maintained good QoS. However, the GA-based approach generated uncertain passenger values that led to significantly increasing AWT for the same traffic profile and the same software version, indicating the potential of GA to enable uncertainty testing [19].

2.3 Runtime Verification of CPS Under Uncertainty

This section discusses the application of general monitoring techniques for DevOps in CPS. This applies on two different levels: firstly, on the level of *monitoring the pipeline* itself, and, more interestingly, of *deploying monitors as part of CI/CD* for the product, including possibly actions and dashboards. The section first surveys the state-of-practice by looking at current commercial and open-source offerings. After that, it examines if and how monitors are generated, maintained, and deployed via CI/CD pipelines.

Runtime Monitoring for DevOps: Frameworks and Metrics (State-of-Practice)

Monitoring the DevOps pipeline itself is independent of the output/product of the pipeline: any pipeline consumes computing resources (for executing the pipeline steps), storage (for the build environment as well as the intermediate and final output artifacts, including logs) and bandwidth (for updating resources for a build, pulling in dependencies, connecting to external services e.g., as part of testing, and deployment). Depending on the type of hosting, it is in the interest of both the owner of the CI/CD platform and the user building a product on the platform itself that system health and costs are monitored. The provider needs to make adequate resources available to the users and monitor their use (e.g., to detect jobs executing cryptocurrency-mining tasks [33]), and the users would want to optimise their costs. For example, storage costs can be optimised by reducing the number of historic versions that are kept within the CI; similarly, computing costs can be optimized by eliminating redundant steps in the pipeline, scheduling certain resource-intensive tasks only periodically (e.g., not for every push), or making use of incremental builds and rerun tests or analyses only for the affected parts of the product.

Table 1 summarizes the off-the-shelf possibilities given by common platforms. Note that results are essentially published in dashboards, and can be used as triggers for automation through APIs, and hence require customization. In fact, several 3rd party-services exist (e.g., Splunk, Datadog and Elastic) that generally work along the lines of ingesting CI-events as time series and producing analytics from this stream, or taking the log files as input [10]. While there is already a reference set of pipeline-based metrics for project management (the DevOps Research and Assessment metrics, DORA [18]), metrics that would refer to inherent uncertainty could not be identified.

Table 1 Off-the-shelf monitoring capabilities, as per product web-sites

Platform	Duration/History	Frequency	Lead/Recovery time	Resource usage
Gitlab	X	X	X	
Github	X			
Octopus	X	X	X	
Bitbucket	X	X	X	
CircleCI	X		X	
AWS CodePipeline				Event-API
Jenkins				Event-API
Forgejo				Event-API

Observability of DevOps Pipelines: State-of-the-Art

The above tooling also already gives insights into the performance of the built product: CI/CD systems run included tests, and hence the overall performance of the pipeline becomes a proxy for the product (assuming adequate coverage). Especially large changes in duration/build-time of the pipeline are bound to attract attention.

An open problem is still the non-uniform nature of the available log output that can be used for metrics. While each of the above services provides a predefined set of observables (that may evolve through new versions over time), often the output of the product both under testing in the pipeline and during runtime is designed ad-hoc [8]. While Bosch and Bosch [8] observed this primarily from the perspective of applying machine-learning techniques to log files, this can be generalized for any consumer of generated output in the DevOps cycle. The full integration of managing monitoring with a CI/CD-pipeline has been termed "Monitoring as Code" by Díaz et al. [16].

DevOps Monitoring for CPS

Runtime monitoring can feed back into the DevOps cycle. De Sanctis et al. [14] propose observing an IoT-system, and distinguishing between adaptation of the running system (e.g., to improve some quality metric) versus triggering a new development phase when the running system discovers e.g., a new class of device that needs support. Dawes and Bianculli [13] report on the adoption of a runtime verification framework (including the extension of an existing formal specification language) in DevOps pipelines for CPS in the automotive and embedded systems (acoustics) domains. They recommend (1) the provision of high-level specification languages for describing properties of interest and (2) the development of informative verdicts within the RV framework, as two viable strategies towards the adoption of RV approaches within DevOps pipeline, in particular for automated testing of CPS. Filaseta et al. [17] discuss the integration of simulation techniques in DevOps pipelines when developing distributed autonomous systems, as a way to test a system against different kinds of perturbations. They propose an architecture for monitoring distributed simulations of distributed systems, focusing on efficient mechanisms for retrieving (and aggregating) real-time simulation data, so that instantaneous feedback can be provided to developers. Gautham et al. [20] deal with dependable development in DevOps environments (i.e., "DepDevOps"), focusing on the need for defining *what to monitor*. They propose a DepDevOps workflow that connects high-level hazard analysis information (based on STPA—system-theoretic process analysis) with low-level monitoring, so that multi-level monitors (at the data, network, and functional level) can be generated from hazard analysis, using loss scenarios and causal factors as driving factors for the generation. Laxman et al. [32] discuss safety assurance in DevOps environments (i.e., "SafetyDevOps"), as traditional safe assurance cases built at design time cannot longer considered valid at run time due to environmental uncertainties, operational anomalies, and system evolution. They advocate for the development of automated solutions for integrating field monitoring and runtime verification approaches for safety performance monitoring and operational safety, to achieve the so-called "Cumulative Operational Safety Assurance" vision.

Another way to perform runtime verification throughout the DevOps cycle is by means of *digital twins*. Betzet et al. [5] discuss the integration of an executable digital twin as a way to enable runtime verification of autonomous robots in uncertain contexts. Such an integration, powered by the MQTT protocol, avoids running a resource-intensive RV framework directly on the resource-constrained hardware of the robots. In the proposed architecture, the digital twin receives the robot state (including sensor data and computed actuation) via the MQTT protocol, performs the actual consistency checking and, if the outcome of the latter is positive, sends a validation outcome to the robot, which can then execute the actuation command. Sarath et al. [37] focus on the integration of DevOps environments in industrial operations ("Industry 4.0") settings, highlighting the need to reconcile design data with operational data. This leads to the definition of semantic data models and traceability information as key aspects of the intermediate data representation used between the design/development model and the digital twin, and between the latter and the DevOps environment (including continuous testing and real-time monitoring).

3 The Path Forward

Uncertainties in the operation of CPS are unavoidable; it is therefore imperative that methods for CPS design, operation, and V&V deal with them by identifying, quantifying, modeling, detecting, and reacting to them. Consequently, DevOps cycles should be enriched to become *uncertainty-aware*. The main idea underpinning this concept is, starting from an initial model of the CPS uncertainties at design time, to gain knowledge about them during the CPS operations through suitable monitoring mechanisms, which can further inform revisions of the design. In this way, on the one hand, the information about uncertainties available at design time, though possibly incomplete or imprecise, can enable adaptation mechanisms when anomalies (resulting from uncertainties) are detected by run-time verification techniques (e.g., through the violation of an assertion); on the other hand, knowledge collected on the field (through monitoring of DevOps pipelines and of the actual system) can lead to refinement and improvement of the modeling and quantification of the uncertainties in the design, starting a new iteration of the DevOps cycle.

Achieving an uncertainty-aware DevOps cycle requires synergies between the design- and run-time phases. As seen in Sect. 2.2, at design time there is the need for specifying the possible system uncertainties, modeling them, quantifying them (through sensitivity analysis), and incorporating them into V&V techniques. However, moving forward, it is of utmost importance to devise data representation and traceability information methods for exchanging these data with representations of the system (and its environment) used at run time (e.g., digital twins) for monitoring the system, detecting violations of systems requirements and design assumptions, and for deciding on remediation actions. Moreover, as DevOps approaches are more and more adopted in mission-critical CPS, such approaches should not only be uncertainty-aware but should broaden their scope (from design time to run time) to include specific aspects such as dependability, security, and safety assurance.

In terms of runtime aspects, monitoring DevOps pipelines, just like monitoring deployed systems, has already been achieved with off-the-shelf tools. In both cases, domain experts can use these tools to deploy monitors that provide insights into system performance. However, there is limited existing work that in particular addresses making monitoring of the deployed system part of the DevOps cycle [28]. On the one hand, at least in open source repositories, there is little evidence that monitoring solutions are maintained and deployed as part of the code base. This is possibly due to the necessary adaptations of monitors for the specific environment in which a system is deployed (e.g., heterogeneous devices or operating systems). On the other hand, recent surveys [2, 38] suggest that, even though monitoring is featured prominently as feedback from operations into development, so far any observed metric informs primarily the design process, and not any particular automated development process.

Therefore, there is the need to make any outcome from the monitors (e.g., metrics from monitoring infrastructures and verdicts yielded by runtime verification frameworks) *interpretable and actionable* to trigger (and feed) an automated revision in the development process. This calls for research on mining software repositories to obtain reliable numbers on how far monitoring concerns are addressed in pipelines (e.g., deployment and evolution of logging, monitors and dashboards), and on investigating which development tasks could be automated based on the feedback from monitors (as opposed to only informing human decisions [7]).

4 Conclusion

This chapter has discussed how to deal with uncertainties in the context of DevOps for CPS, leading to the definition of the building blocks for achieving the vision of "Uncertainty-aware DevOps". First, at design time, it is important to identify the sources of uncertainty and model them by incorporating them as part of the core design elements. Second, uncertainties should become first-class citizens when it comes to analyzing the CPS design, e.g., by means of robustness analysis, verification, and testing techniques that take uncertainties into account. Third, the presence of uncertainties requires to use monitoring techniques for the DevOps pipeline itself and to deploy monitors as part of the CI/CD of the final product. In this way, the system can both gain knowledge about the uncertainties during the CPS operations (through suitable monitoring mechanisms) and inform the design, by refining and improving the modeling and quantification of the uncertainties in the design itself.

The chapter reflects on the path forward for devising uncertainty-aware DevOps, which calls for further research on (1) suitable mechanisms for representing, tracing, and exchanging information among the main elements of uncertainty-aware DevOps cycles, (2) broadening the scope to include fundamental aspects pertaining to mission-critical CPS (e.g., dependability, security, and safety assurance), and

(3) making any outcome from runtime monitors interpretable and actionable by autonomous agents.

Competing Interests The authors have no conflicts of interest to declare that are relevant to the content of this chapter.

Acknowledgements Shaukat Ali is supported by the Co-tester project (Project# 314544), funded by the Research Council of Norway. Violet Ka I Pun is supported by the project "Enabling Highly Automated Cross-Organisational Workflow Planning" (CROFLOW, Project# 326249), funded by the Research Council of Norway. Catia Trubiani is supported by the MUR PRIN project 20228FT78M DREAM, MUR Department of Excellence 2023–2027 for GSSI, and PNRR ECS00000041 VITALITY.

References

1. A. Aleti, C. Trubiani, A. van Hoorn, P. Jamshidi, An efficient method for uncertainty propagation in robust software performance estimation. J. Syst. Softw. **138**, 222–235 (2018)
2. R. Amaro, R. Pereira, M.M. da Silva, Capabilities and practices in devops: a multivocal literature review. IEEE Trans. Softw. Eng. **49**(2), 883–901 (2023)
3. P. Arcaini, O. Inverso, C. Trubiani, Automated model-based performance analysis of software product lines under uncertainty. Inf. Softw. Technol. **127**, 106371 (2020)
4. P. Aroonvatanaporn, C. Sinthop, B. Boehm, Reducing estimation uncertainty with continuous assessment: tracking the cone of uncertainty, in *Proceedings of the 25th IEEE/ACM International Conference on Automated Software Engineering* (2010), pp. 337–340
5. J.S. Betzer, J. Boudjadar, M. Frasheri, P. Talasila, Digital twin enabled runtime verification for autonomous mobile robots under uncertainty, in *2024 28th International Symposium on Distributed Simulation and Real Time Applications (DS-RT)* (2024), pp. 10–17
6. C. Birchler, S. Khatiri, P. Rani, T. Kehrer, S. Panichella, A roadmap for simulation-based testing of autonomous cyber-physical systems: challenges and future direction (2025)
7. C. Birchler, T.K. Mohammed, P. Rani, T. Nechita, T. Kehrer, S. Panichella, How does simulation-based testing for self-driving cars match human perception? in *ACM International Conference on the Foundations of Software Engineering* (2024)
8. N. Bosch, J. Bosch, Software logs for machine learning in a devops environment, in *46th Euromicro Conference on Software Engineering and Advanced Applications, SEAA 2020* (IEEE, 2020), pp. 29–33
9. M. Camilli, A. Gargantini, P. Scandurra, C. Trubiani, Uncertainty-aware exploration in model-based testing, in *Proceedings of the International Conference on Software Testing, Verification and Validation (ICST)* (2021), pp. 71–81
10. A. Capizzi, S. Distefano, L.J.P. Araújo, M. Mazzara, M. Ahmad, E. Bobrov, Anomaly detection in DevOps toolchain, in *Software Engineering Aspects of Continuous Development and New Paradigms of Software Production and Deployment*. ed. by J.-M. Bruel, M. Mazzara, B. Meyer (Springer International Publishing, Cham, 2020), pp. 37–51
11. J. Cederbladh, A. Cicchetti, J. Suryadevara, Early validation and verification of system behaviour in model-based systems engineering: a systematic literature review. ACM Trans. Softw. Eng. Methodol. (2023)
12. B. Combemale, J. Gray, J.-M. Jézéquel, B. Rumpe, How does your model represent the system? a note on model fidelity, underspecification, and uncertainty. Softw. Syst. Model. **23**(5), 1053–1054 (2024)
13. J. Dawes, D. Bianculli, Checking complex source code-level constraints using runtime verification, in *Companion Proceedings of the 32nd ACM International Conference on the Foundations of Software Engineering (FSE Companion '24)* (ACM, 2024), pp. 255–265

14. M. De Sanctis, A. Bucchiarone, C. Trubiani, A DevOps perspective for QoS-aware adaptive applications, in *Software Engineering Aspects of Continuous Development and New Paradigms of Software Production and Deployment*. ed. by J.-M. Bruel, M. Mazzara, B. Meyer (Springer International Publishing, Cham, 2020), pp. 95–111
15. A. Di Sorbo, F. Zampetti, A. Visaggio, M. Di Penta, S. Panichella, Automated identification and qualitative characterization of safety concerns reported in uav software platforms. ACM Trans. Softw. Eng. Methodol. **32**(3) (2023)
16. J. Díaz, J.E. Pérez, M.A.L. Peña, G.A. Mena, A. Yagüe, Self-service cybersecurity monitoring as enabler for DevSecOps. IEEE Access **7**, 100283–100295 (2019)
17. A. Filaseta, D. Pianini, A. Cortecchia, An architecture and prototype for monitoring distributed simulations of distributed systems, in *2024 28th International Symposium on Distributed Simulation and Real Time Applications (DS-RT)* (2024), pp. 158–165
18. N. Forsgren, M.C. Tremblay, D.E. VanderMeer, J. Humble, DORA platform: Devops assessment and benchmarking, in *Designing the Digital Transformation, DESRIST 2017*. ed. by A. Maedche, J. vom Brocke, A.R. Hevner. Volume 10243 of Lecture Notes in Computer Science. (Springer, Berlin, 2017), pp. 436–440
19. J. Galarraga, A. Arrieta, S. Ali, G. Sagardui, M. Arratibel. Genetic algorithm-based testing of industrial elevators under passenger uncertainty, in *2021 IEEE International Symposium on Software Reliability Engineering Workshops (ISSREW)* (2021), pp. 353–358
20. S. Gautham, G. Bakirtzis, A. Will, A.V. Jayakumar, C.R. Elks, Stpa-driven multilevel runtime monitoring for in-time hazard detection, in *Computer Safety, Reliability, and Security* (Springer International Publishing, Cham, 2022), pp. 158–172
21. M. Goulão, V. Amaral, M. Mernik, Quality in model-driven engineering: a tertiary study. Softw. Qual. J. **24**, 601–633 (2016)
22. P. Haindl, R. Plösch, Focus areas, themes, and objectives of non-functional requirements in devops: A systematic mapping study, in *Euromicro Conference on Software Engineering and Advanced Applications (SEAA)* (2020), pp. 394–403
23. L. Han, T. Yue, S. Ali, A. Arrieta, M. Arratibel, Are elevator software robust against uncertainties? results and experiences from an industrial case study. In *Proceedings of the 30th ACM Joint European Software Engineering Conference and Symposium on the Foundations of Software Engineering* (ESEC/FSE 2022, Association for Computing Machinery, New York, NY, USA, 2022), pp. 1331–1342
24. R. Heldal, P. Pelliccione, U. Eliasson, J. Lantz, J. Derehag, J. Whittle, Descriptive vs prescriptive models in industry, in *Proceedings of the ACM/IEEE 19th International Conference on Model Driven Engineering Languages and Systems, MODELS '16* (Association for Computing Machinery, New York, NY, USA, 2016), pp. 216–226
25. R. Jongeling, F. Ciccozzi, J. Carlson, A. Cicchetti, Consistency management in industrial continuous model-based development settings: a reality check. Softw. Syst. Model. **21**(4), 1511–1530 (2022)
26. R. Jongeling, A. Vallecillo, Uncertainty-aware consistency checking in industrial settings, in*2023 ACM/IEEE 26th International Conference on Model Driven Engineering Languages and Systems (MODELS)* (2023), pp. 73–83
27. A. Jøsang, D. Wang, J. Zhang, Multi-source fusion in subjective logic, in *Proceedings of FUSION'17* (IEEE, 2017), pp. 1–8
28. S. Khatiri, F.M. Amin, S. Panichella, P. Tonella, When uncertainty leads to unsafety. empirical insights into the role of uncertainty in unmanned aerial vehicle safety. Empirical Softw. Eng. (2025)
29. S. Khatiri, S. Panichella, P. Tonella, Simulation-based test case generation for unmanned aerial vehicles in the neighborhood of real flights, in *International Conference on Software Testing, Verification and Validation* (IEEE, 2023), pp. 281–292
30. S. Khatiri, A.D. Sorbo, F. Zampetti, C.A. Visaggio, M.D. Penta, S. Panichella, Identifying safety-critical concerns in unmanned aerial vehicle software platforms with SALIENT. SoftwareX **27**, 101748 (2024)

31. C.F. Kurtz, D.J. Snowden, The new dynamics of strategy: sense-making in a complex and complicated world. IBM Syst. J. **42**(3), 462–483 (2003)
32. N. Laxman, M. Schweizer, J. Reich, Employing field monitoring and runtime safety verification for cumulative operational safety assurance in a safetydevops process, in *2024 8th International Conference on System Reliability and Safety (ICSRS)* (2024), pp. 545–549
33. Z. Li, W. Liu, H. Chen, X. Wang, X. Liao, L. Xing, M. Zha, H. Jin, D. Zou, Robbery on devops: Understanding and mitigating illicit cryptomining on continuous integration service platforms, in *43rd IEEE Symposium on Security and Privacy, SP 2022* (IEEE, 2022), pp. 2397–2412
34. T. Menzies, W. Nichols, F. Shull, L. Layman, Are delayed issues harder to resolve? Revisiting cost-to-fix of defects throughout the lifecycle. Empir. Softw. Eng. **22**, 1903–1935 (2017)
35. W.L. Oberkampf, S.M. DeLand, B.M. Rutherford, K.V. Diegert, K.F. Alvin, Error and uncertainty in modeling and simulation. Reliab. Eng. Syst. Saf. **75**(3), 333–357 (2002)
36. R. Pinciroli, R. Mirandola, C. Trubiani, Modular quality-of-service analysis of software design models for cyber-physical systems, in *Proceedings of International Conference of Advanced Information Systems Engineering (CAiSE)*, vol. 13901, ed. by M. Indulska, I. Reinhartz-Berger, C. Cetina, O. Pastor (2023), pp. 88–104
37. S.D.C. Saratha, C. Grimm, F. Wawrzik, A digital twin with runtime-verification for industrial development-operation integration, in *2021 IEEE International Conference on Engineering, Technology and Innovation (ICE/ITMC)* (2021), pp. 1–9
38. D. Teixeira, R. Pereira, T. Henriques, M.M.D. Silva, J.A. Faustino, M. Silva, A maturity model for DevOps. Int. J. Agile Syst. Manag. **13**(4), 464–511 (2020)
39. C. Trubiani, P. Jamshidi, J. Cito, W. Shang, Z.M. Jiang, M. Borg, Performance issues? Hey DevOps, mind the uncertainty. IEEE Softw. **36**(2), 110–117 (2019)
40. F. Zampetti, R. Kapur, M. Di Penta, S. Panichella, An empirical characterization of software bugs in open-source cyber–physical systems. J. Syst. Softw. **192**, 111425 (2022)

Deployment for Cyber-Physical Systems: The Relations Between the Testing and Monitoring DevOps Phases

Sebastiano Panichella, Sajad Khatiri, and Christian Birchler

Abstract While DevOps has improved time-to-market for traditional systems, ensuring cyber-physical systems (CPS) trustworthiness in an operational environment poses several important challenges. This chapter focuses on field testing, and operational, and deployment challenges (or issues) of CPS and autonomous cyber-physical systems (ACPS). The chapter comprehensively addresses such topics, starting by discussing relevant testing, operational, and deployment challenges as well as solutions to address them. ACPS, such as unmanned aerial vehicles (UAVs) and self-driving cars (SDCs), are considered key use cases since the safety and reliability issues for these systems are of primary importance in both academia and industry. While providing concrete definitions of test cases within simulation environments and real-world testing, relevant to the discussion in this chapter, we also focus on the need to create new benchmark assets and the development of automated tools tailored explicitly for autonomous systems in the software engineering and robotics communities. Complementary, the chapter discusses approaches (1) for improving CPS adaptability with static analysis, monitoring, AI-based, and self-healing techniques; (2) reports already established architectures, toolchains, and frameworks supporting cost-effective testing and addressing deployment challenges for ACPS; (3) discusses the validation of solutions in real-world sectors such as automotive and aviation; (4) discusses relevant open-source technologies to encourage further development (e.g., a framework developed and shared in international contexts such as tool competitions). Finally, the book chapter provides a path forward on pressing issues the software engineering community should focus on (in terms of practices, expected automation, and paradigms), outlining ways to tackle them.

S. Panichella (✉) · C. Birchler
University of Bern, Bern, Switzerland
e-mail: spanichella@gmail.com

C. Birchler
e-mail: christian.birchler@unibe.ch

S. Khatiri
Università della Svizzera italiana–University of Bern, Bern, Switzerland
e-mail: sajad.khatiri@unibe.ch

S. Panichella et al. (eds.), *Roadmap for DevOps in Cyber-Physical Systems*,
https://doi.org/10.1007/978-981-95-1786-2_6

1 Context and Motivation of the Chapter

In earlier chapters, we explored key DevOps phrases and concepts (Chapter *Introduction*). This chapter is centered on the field testing and operational and deployment challenges associated with CPS and autonomous cyber-physical systems (ACPS). Unmanned aerial vehicles (UAVs) and self-driving cars (SDCs) are highlighted as key use cases due to their significant safety and reliability concerns, which are of paramount importance to both academia and industry [13, 31]. Hence, this chapter reflects on the need for DevOps to ensure the trustworthiness of CPS in real-world environments (after deployment), which presents several critical challenges. As follows, we provide a comprehensive examination of these issues, starting with an exploration of simulation-based testing, testing in operation, and deployment and operational challenges, and discuss current solutions addressing them.

Simulation-based Testing Challenges & Operational Automation Needs (Reality Gap Problem). Previous studies have characterized the software bugs in autonomous systems including UAV Autopilot platforms [22, 23, 66] and investigated the challenges associated with testing these systems in realistic environments [2, 16, 24, 31, 32, 64]. Wang et al. [2] focused on testing challenges in robotic systems, emphasizing the complexity of test environments.

A prevalent approach to system-level testing of CPS, such as UAVs and SDCs, involves end-to-end simulation environments where the system under test operates within a simulated physical world [12, 32, 41]. However, the applicability and transferability of traditional software testing techniques in these contexts remain uncertain. As a result, automated CPS testing continues to be a significant research challenge [22, 66]. Simulation-based testing offers a promising approach for improving testing practices in safety-critical systems [11, 12, 18, 47, 52] and supporting test automation [2, 5, 63]. Previous research has focused on monitoring CPS and predicting unsafe system states [22] using simulations [18, 65], as well as programmatic scenario generation [51]. Recent studies [1, 9, 11, 18] proposed approaches to test self-driving cars by creating (simulation) scenarios that induce failures in the driving process [12].

Reality gap. New challenges arise in simulation-based testing and operation and deployment of CPS, including simulation realism, computational costs, simulator complexity, and the *Oracle Problem*. Related to this, the *Reality Gap* [2, 32, 46] poses a critical concern: Simulated contexts often fail to faithfully mirror real-world situations due to simplifications necessary for computational feasibility. This trade-off between accuracy and computational time determines the extent to which simulations reflect reality [20, 31]. Robotics simulations particularly struggle with accurately replicating phenomena such as actuators (e.g., torque characteristics, gear backlash), sensors (e.g., noise, latency), and rendered images (e.g., reflections, refraction, textures). This disparity between reality and simulation is known as the reality gap [20].

The reality gap has been an open research problem in robotics for years now [16, 31, 32]. With the boost of *Evolutionary Robotics* and the application of reinforcement learning in designing robotic control systems in recent decades, practitioners rely more and more on simulations to evaluate their designs,i.e., test subjects [27, 55]. More specifically, a test subject's *fitness* (e.g., algorithm, trained model) is calculated based on its performance in a simulation for reaching the robot's goals. However, transferring robot skills acquired in a simulated environment to a physical setting, widely referred to as *Sim2Real transfer*, remains an open challenge [16, 31, 32].

To mitigate the simulation-reality gap, Hildebrandt et al. [26] propose a mixed-reality approach for testing UAVs. Their approach, called *world-in-the-loop* simulation, integrates and mixes sensor data from both the simulated and real world, and feeds these mixed sensor inputs to the system under test (UAV). A potential limitation of the *world-in-the-loop* mixed-reality approach proposed by Hildebrandt et al. [26] is the complexity and unpredictability introduced by fusing real and simulated sensor data. This fusion can lead to inconsistencies in timing, noise characteristics, and environmental context, potentially resulting in non-representative or unreliable behavior of the UAV under test. In recent research [32, 33, 36], researchers addressed the problem of realism in simulation-based testing for UAVs by proposing Surrealist, an approach that faithfully replicates real-world test scenarios in simulation environments and generates more challenging test case variants. Complementary, multiple software platforms and frameworks have been introduced to facilitate further research for addressing the aforementioned simulation and operation testing challenges for autonomous systems [9, 33] and have been used and evolved in the context of testing competitions at international conferences and events involving researchers from the software engineering community [14, 15, 34, 36, 37].

Uncertainty Quantification in Autonomous Systems. As discussed in previous chapters (Chapter *Runtime Verification & Uncertainty-Aware DevOps for CPS* provides even more details on this topic), recent studies focused on addressing uncertainty in the context of autonomous systems [39, 56], with strategies assessing (or predicting) uncertainty for CPS [56, 59], or proposing self-healing approaches for them [7, 40, 65]. So far, uncertainty (or confidence) quantification has been addressed mostly in the context of Deep Neural Networks (DNNs) used in perception tasks (e.g., vision components) of autonomous systems. Bayesian Neural Networks (BNN) provide a rigorous framework for modeling and capturing uncertainty [43]. Hence, the general problem of capturing the uncertainty in the system output remains open. Recent research [16, 31, 32] introduced the concept of *Decision Uncertainty*: A black-box uncertainty measurement identified by the inconsistencies in the control signals (i.e., system output) of the autonomous system, potentially leading to unstable, erratic and unpredictable trajectories, and in extreme cases, to safety violations. Complementary, a study from Khatiri et al. conducted the first empirical investigation on the alignment between uncertainty quantification and unsafe UAV states during flights (in deployed environments) [31].

Overview of Next Sections. As follows, the chapter defines test cases within both simulated and real-world environments and highlights the importance of developing new benchmark assets and automated tools specifically tailored to autonomous systems in software engineering and robotics. In addition, the chapter covers: (1) bugs and issues characterizing CPS; (2) strategies for enhancing CPS adaptability using static analysis, monitoring, AI-based methods, and self-healing techniques;

(3) established architectures, toolchains, and frameworks that support cost-effective testing and address ACPS deployment challenges; (4) the validation of these solutions in sectors such as automotive and aviation; and (5) the role of open-source technologies in fostering further advancements, such as frameworks developed through tool competitions.

Finally, the chapter outlines a forward-looking perspective on the key issues the software engineering community must address, discussing practices, expected automation, and emerging paradigms, and suggesting ways to overcome these challenges.

2 Field Testing, Operational, and Deployment Challenges and Issues of CPS

Before we deploy a piece of software, we need to ensure its correctness. The term correctness has many dimensions such as the correct implementation of functional requirements and/or adherence to non-functional requirements. In any case, the correctness of a software needs to be tested. In short, testing is the keyword here. In the context of DevOps, the testing phase precedes the deployment phase to ensure the correct operational behavior of the system on the deployment platform.

During the testing phase, testers execute a set of test cases, i.e., a test suite, consisting of multiple test cases. A test case consists of several parts, such as a test subject, environment, task, and oracle [13]. The test subject is the actual system under test. It is also known as the test object or just SUT. For the execution of the test subject, we need an execution environment that embeds the test subject. Next to the environment, we have to provide the test subject a task (sometimes also known as a mission) that it needs to accomplish. Its result will be compared with the expected outcome, commonly known as the oracle.

So far, we have looked at the general concept of testing. Of course, it also finds its application in the context of CPS, as it is a very generic general testing definition. Nevertheless, for CPS, the environmental aspect needs to have a special focus as testers often use different simulators to simulate the real-world operation environment. And exactly there is the crux of the matter for various challenges in testing CPS in simulation environments.

Software engineers and testers write unit tests for traditional software in the same programming language as the SUT–in most cases, even for system tests. If we think about the environment of the SUT for traditional software, then we see it is the compute platform with an OS and/or runtime environment. However, for system-level tests for CPS such as self-driving cars (SDCs) and unmanned aerial vehicles (UAVs), the operational environment is the real world rather than a computer platform.

3 Bugs, Issues, and Faults of CPS Observed After Deployment

CPS integrate software and hardware, making them susceptible to unique bugs that impact their reliability. Identifying and understanding these bugs is crucial for developing tailored verification and validation (V&V) techniques [16, 22, 35, 68]. Previous studies [68] analyzed over 1,000 issues from 14 open-source CPS projects in domains such as UAVs/drones, automotive, robotics, and Arduino, to create a taxonomy of CPS bugs using a hybrid card-sorting approach. This taxonomy (see Table 1)

Table 1 Taxonomy of CPS bugs (Nr. of bugs for each root cause, Nr. (percentage) of CPS-specific bugs, and other bugs). More details at [68]

Bug Type	Root causes	# of (%) Bugs specific to CPS	# of (%) Other bugs
Hardware bugs	Energy	2 (0.31)	0 (0)
	Faulty sensor data	7 (1.07)	0 (0)
	Hardware failure	4 (0.61)	0 (0)
	HW not supported/not compatible	11 (1.68)	0 (0)
	Memory	4 (0.61)	0 (0)
Total hardware		**28 (4.28)**	**0 (0)**
Network bugs	Connection/communication	5 (0.76)	11 (1.68)
	Packet corrupted/lost	8 (1.22)	1 (0.15)
Total network		**13 (1.98)**	**12 (1.83)**
Interface bugs	External	27 (4.12)	27 (4.12)
	Internal	6 (0.92)	24 (3.66)
Total interface		**33 (5.04)**	**51 (7.78)**
Data bugs	Incorrect data structure	0 (0)	9 (1.37)
	Not persisted	0 (0)	2 (0.31)
Total data		**0 (0)**	**11 (1.68)**
Configuration bugs	Build configuration	2 (0.31)	68 (10.38)
	Wrong parameters	5 (0.76)	13 (1.98)
Total configuration		**7 (1.07)**	**81 (12.36)**
Algorithm	Assignment	19 (2.9)	58 (8.85)
	Concurrency	2 (0.31)	5 (0.76)
	Incorrect condition logic	17 (2.6)	35 (5.34)
	Memory	5 (0.76)	16 (2.44)
	Missing condition check	25 (3.82)	50 (7.63)
	Numerical	18 (2.75)	23 (3.51)
	Programming	26 (3.97)	90 (13.74)
Total algorithm		**112 (17.11)**	**277 (42.27)**
Documentation	–	1 (0.15)	27 (4.12)
Others	–	0 (0)	2 (0.31)
Overall		**194 (33.40)**	**461 (66.56)**

is characterized by 22 root causes grouped into eight categories, covering hardware, interface, configuration, network, data, and application logic [68]. Notably, 33.4% of these bugs are unique to CPS and require specialized attention during V&V as well as tailored solutions for them.

More recent studies focus on UAVs [22, 31, 35], which operate in diverse fields such as agriculture and disaster management but are prone to safety-critical software defects [32]. These defects can pose significant risks to humans, property, and the environment. Ensuring human safety and property protection requires ongoing hazard identification and risk management [35]. Safety concerns often arise during UAV operation, reported by users and developers via issue reports and pull requests. However, UAV platforms receive numerous reports daily, varying in type and quality [35]. The UAV developers must promptly address safety-related issues reported in user and developer feedback, often in the form of issue reports and pull requests [22, 28–30]. Researchers analyzed hazards and accidents linked to 273 safety-related concerns from three GitHub drone projects [22, 35] to better understand safety issues in UAV systems. Using open coding, they categorized the main hazards and accidents described in these issues, as reported in Tables 2 and 3. Specifically, they examined the relationship between hazards and accidents, laying the groundwork for automated tools to aid hazard classification and prioritize resolution based on potential consequences.

Tool support for UAV Issue Management. To streamline this issue management process [28–30, 50, 57] for UAVs, researchers introduced SALIENT [35], a machine learning (ML)-powered tool designed to identify safety-related concerns within issue reports automatically. The tool supports developers in identifying and prioritizing safety-critical issues by detecting safety-related content in issue titles and descriptions, for early detection of hazard and accident categorization.

Table 2 Accident categories and corresponding occurrences in the dataset of 273 safety-related issues and pull requests of UAV systems [22]

Type	Description	Occ.
Crashing/collision issue	The drone crashes on the ground or else collides with a an object while in-flight	35 (12.82%)
Anomalous flight conduct	The drone manifests anomalous behavior while in-flight, e.g., in-flight resets	23 (8.42%)
Landing/rtl issue	The drone has anomalous behavior while landing or returning-to-location	21 (7.69%)
Aircraft lost/ flown away	The drone stops taking actions from the pilot and starts flying autonomously	19 (6.96%)
Stabilization/ orientation/ positioning issue	The drone experiences issues with positional and localization data, e.g., *"you can create congestion on the serial port to the GPS and the position data gets delayed"*	10 (3.66%)
Operator injury	The unexpected behavior of the drone leads to damage to the operator, e.g., motors spin when connecting battery	5 (1.83%)
Takeoff issue	The drone experiences issues during takeoff	2 (0.73%)

Table 3 Hazard categories and corresponding occurrences in the dataset of 273 safety-related issues and pull requests of UAVs. We share only the top, while the remaining ones are detailed in previous studies [22]

Category	Description	Occ.
Event/action allowed in undesired states/configurations	Scenarios where some events, e.g., in-flight reboot, or actions, e.g., disable safety checks, are allowed while they should not	40 (14.65%)
Undesired behavior on failsafe or error condition/configuration	Unexpected behavior of the system in the scenarios where failsafe operations or error conditions occur, e.g., low default speed allowed when radio contact is lost, undesired throttle behavior in case of GPS lock	34 (12.45%)
Undesired failsafe behavior	The behavior of the system to deal with a failsafe operation does not reflect the expected one	32 (11.72%)
Inadequate checks	Parameters, input data from sensors, actions and/or events not checked before activating a specific flight-mode or before enabling a specific action, e.g., battery status not checked before takeoff	25 (9.16%)
Improper parameter setting/initialization/ configuration	System-level parameters, e.g., min-throttle, not or wrongly initialized, configured and set, e.g., improper calibration or incorrect conversions	20 (7.33%)
Misleading or missing data/measurements/ reports	Data coming from external devices and sensors being noisy or missing, e.g., wrong values in transmission channels	18 (6.59%)
Missing or misleading communication with pilot	Conditions and/or events not notified to the pilot, e.g., no alert in presence of unusually high throttle output	16 (5.86%)
Undesired hardware behavior	Unexpected behavior, e.g., failures, of the hardware components affecting the overall behavior of the system, e.g., throttle unclamped when disarmed	12 (4.40%)
Action not allowed in specific states/configurations	Scenarios where some events or actions, e.g., disarm speed controller, are not allowed while they should	11 (4.03%)
Inappropriate mode changes/handling	Incorrect switches between modes, or inappropriate handling of rapid mode switching	9 (3.30%)

As illustrated in Fig. 1, SALIENT offers two primary usage modes through its *CLI* and *GUI*. The GUI is tailored for general users, including those without a development background, whereas the CLI is particularly beneficial for UAV developers seeking to automate the management of safety-related issues. Both interfaces allow users to select, write, and edit issues. Additionally, the CLI commands and corresponding GUI events facilitate the automated identification (or classification) of sentences within issues that concern UAV safety aspects.

To run these functionalities, the CLI and GUI of SALIENT interact with two key components: the `GitHub Issue Parser` and the `ML Component`. (i) Users interact with the `GitHub Issue Parser` via either the CLI or GUI. This component processes issues retrieved from GitHub in multiple formats (discussed in later

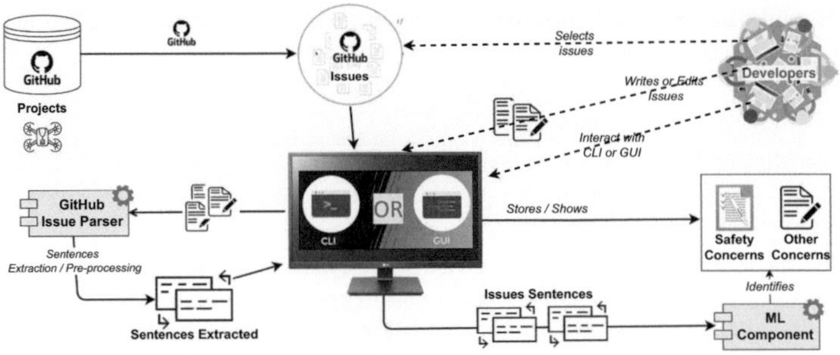

Fig. 1 SALIENT's architecture overview (this is an edited image from [35])

sections) and prepares them for further analysis by logically segmenting the issue text into sentences. (ii) Once the pre-processing is complete, users engage with the `ML Component` through the CLI or GUI of SALIENT to identify sentences with safety-related implications. Specifically, the preprocessed data from the `GitHub Issue Parser` serve as input to SALIENT's `ML Component`, which then classifies individual sentences as safety-related or not.

To assist users in managing issues efficiently, the `ML Component` employs a model trained on a manually curated dataset, as detailed in our prior work [22, 35]. This model enables the classification of safety-related sentences in newly reported UAV issues on GitHub.

Evaluation. Assessing the usefulness of SALIENT on three popular open-source UAV projects (Ardupilot, dRonin, PX4-Autopilot) showed that it effectively identifies and prioritizes critical issues, outperforming baseline strategies such as ChatGPT [22, 35, 48, 49] and Google Bard. SALIENT machine learning techniques achieve 80% precision, recall, and F-measure in identifying safety-related content and highlight key hazard-accident relationships [22, 35].

The next sections (Sects. 4 and 5) Discuss in more detail practical and impactful examples of approaches and tools that have been developed further to automate the testing and deployment phases of CPS [14, 15, 34, 36, 37]. We mainly focus on automotive (SDCs) [9, 16, 18] and aviation (UAVs) [31, 33] examples, while we know that research progress has been made in other domains.

4 Approaches, Open-Source Technologies and Frameworks to Encourage Further DevOps Development for CPS

4.1 Simulation-Based Testing of Unmanned Aerial Vehicles

Ensuring the reliability and safety of Unmanned Aerial Vehicles (UAVs) is paramount as their autonomy and commercial use increase [31, 32]. Testing functional, non-functional, and particularly safety requirements has thus become a critical challenge [22]. While simulation-based testing, especially software-in-the-loop, serves as a foundational practice, the scenarios tested in simulation may not fully capture the complexities encountered during real-world field operations [13, 31, 32, 36].

This section focuses into simulation-based testing for UAVs by first introducing PX4 [44], a widely used open-source flight controller often employed as a research case study. Subsequently, we discuss AERIALIST (unmanned **AERIAL** veh**I**cle te**ST** bench) [33, 34, 36, 37], a test bench designed to streamline the definition, execution, and analysis of UAV tests within simulation environments. Finally, building upon AERIALIST, we will explore SURREALIST (te**S**ting **U**AVs in the neighbo**R**hood of **REAL** fl**I**ght**S**) [32], an approach leveraging search-based techniques to generate more realistic simulation test cases for UAVs.

4.1.1 PX4: UAV Case Study

The PX4 [44] open-source platform provides the flight control software for many UAV systems. It enables control over a simulated vehicle model by interfacing with simulators, such as Gazebo [38]. Through this connection, PX4 receives simulated sensor data and transmits actuator commands, mimicking real-world interaction [32]. Pilots or operators can interact with the simulated UAV via standard interfaces like a ground control station (GCS), radio controller (RC), or programmatically through APIs (e.g., ROS), allowing command input and telemetry reception. PX4 is compatible with various hardware-in-the-loop (HIL) and software-in-the-loop (SIL) simulators [53], with Gazebo [38] being a common choice, particularly for testing functionalities such as obstacle avoidance [33, 34, 36, 37].

PX4 supports different flight modes, which dictate the autopilot's response to user input and its level of autonomy during flight. These modes range from providing assistance for specific maneuvers (e.g.,, takeoff, landing, maintaining position/altitude) to enabling fully autonomous operation based on pre-planned mission paths. The *mission mode*, for instance, allows the UAV to execute a sequence of waypoints and actions defined in a *mission plan* with minimal human oversight, suitable for tasks like mapping or surveys. Core autonomy is managed by PX4-Autopilot, often working alongside specialized modules like PX4-Avoidance [54], which uses camera and distance sensor data for real-time obstacle detection and navigation adjustments during missions.

4.1.2 AERIALIST: UAV Test Bench

AERIALIST [33, 34, 36, 37] is presented as a modular and extensible software test bench specifically for UAVs. Its primary goal is to simplify and automate the entire lifecycle of system-level UAV testing, encompassing test definition, generation, execution, and subsequent analysis. By providing researchers with a readily usable platform centered around a common UAV case study (PX4), AERIALIST facilitates

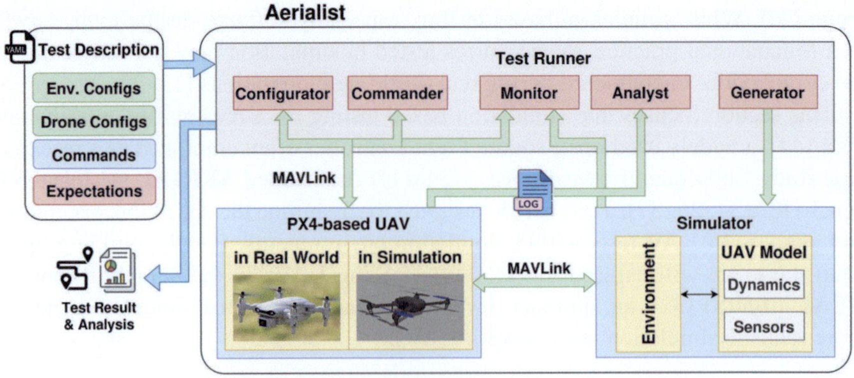

Fig. 2 High-level architecture of AERIALIST [33]

easier entry into UAV software testing research. Its utility is demonstrated by its adoption in academic UAV Testing Competitions [33, 34, 36, 37].

The architecture of AERIALIST, depicted in Fig. 2, is designed for modularity. While the current implementation[1] focuses on the PX4 platform [44], it can potentially be extended to support other UAV and robotic systems. Tests are specified using a *Test Description* file in YAML format [33], detailing configurations for the UAV, the simulation environment (including obstacles), and runtime commands or test steps. AERIALIST's submodules abstract the specific details of the UAV platform and simulator, handling environment setup, connection to the physical or simulated UAV, configuration, command execution, state monitoring during flight, and flight log extraction for analysis. Furthermore, AERIALIST supports execution in containerized environments like Docker and can leverage Kubernetes[2] for large-scale parallel test execution.

4.1.3 SURREALIST: UAV Test Generation Approach

A significant challenge in simulation-based testing arises from the *reality gap* [13, 26, 32]: the inherent differences between the physical attributes and dynamics of *real* UAVs and environments versus their *simulated* counterparts. Factors such as discrepancies in weight, motor performance, sensor accuracy, and unpredictable environmental conditions (e.g., wind) mean that simply replaying commands logged from a physical flight in a simulator will likely not reproduce the same trajectory or behavior [13, 32].

To bridge this gap, SURREALIST (teSting UAVs in the neighboRhood of REAL flIghtS) [32] offers a novel approach specifically for generating more effective simulation-based tests for UAVs. It operates in two main stages: First, starting with

[1] https://github.com/skhatiri/Aerialist.

[2] https://kubernetes.io.

log data from a real-world field test, SURREALIST attempts to *replicate* the observed flight behavior (e.g., the trajectory) within the simulation as closely as possible. This involves searching for the optimal simulation parameters (test properties) that minimize a defined distance metric between the real sensor readings and the simulated ones. Second, using such a replicated simulation as a starting point (or any existing simulation test case), SURREALIST generates *variants* in the immediate neighborhood of the initial test case. The goal here is to create scenarios that are potentially more challenging or safety-critical, achieved by iteratively updating test properties to maximize a *fitness function* representing test difficulty or risk (e.g., minimizing the UAV's distance to obstacles during the flight).

As depicted in Fig. 3, the core of SURREALIST frames both flight replication and challenging test generation as *search problems*. The objective is to find the optimal set of test properties that maximizes a chosen *fitness function*. The search begins with an initial *seed solution* (derived from a real flight log for replication, or an existing simulation test case for generation) and iteratively applies mutations to improve the fitness score. The process continues until a defined *budget* (maximum number of simulation evaluations) is exhausted or no further improvement is found.

The search algorithm employs a global optimization loop that iterates through the available test properties. For each property, it utilizes *mutators*–parameterized operators that modify the property's value (e.g., changing an obstacle's position via $MOVE\_X$). A *local test properties search* procedure, implemented as an adaptive greedy algorithm, is invoked for each mutator. This local search efficiently explores the mutator's parameter space, adjusting the step size adaptively to find better solu-

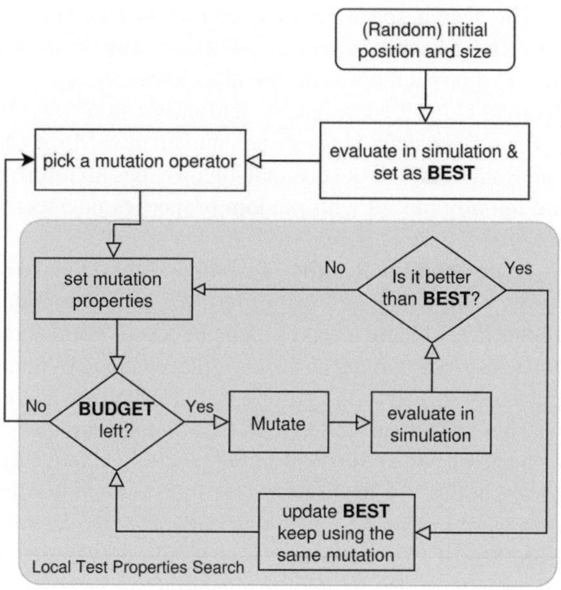

Fig. 3 High-level algorithm of SURREALIST [32]

tions quickly while minimizing the number of computationally expensive simulations required. It terminates based on its local budget or when improvements plateau.

Crucially, evaluating each candidate solution (a set of test properties) involves automatically generating and executing the corresponding simulation using AERIALIST. To mitigate the impact of non-determinism or outliers, each test case is typically executed multiple times (*n* times). The fitness function is then computed based on the average results extracted from the resulting flight logs, guiding the search towards the overall goal (e.g., maximizing replication accuracy or test difficulty).

Flight Replication in Autonomous Mode

This section details a specific application of the SURREALIST flight replication capability, focusing on autonomous flights. The challenge here is to replicate a logged flight where the UAV's trajectory was influenced by *N* obstacles ($\geqslant 1$) whose exact size and position were not recorded. Given the original flight log and mission plan, the goal is to generate a simulated test case by optimizing the properties (size, position, rotation) of these *N* obstacles so that the resulting simulated UAV trajectory closely matches the real-world one.

To guide the search algorithm, a suitable fitness function is needed to quantify the similarity between the trajectory observed in the real flight log and the trajectory produced in a candidate simulation. Since flight trajectories are essentially time series data, Dynamic Time Warping (DTW) [8] is employed. DTW is a well-established algorithm for measuring the similarity between two temporal sequences, even if they vary in speed or length, and has previously been applied to UAV trajectory comparison [4]. The fitness function aims to minimize the DTW distance between the original and simulated flight paths.

The search space for this replication task consists of the properties of the *N* obstacles, assuming a generally flat environment and predefined obstacle shapes (e.g., boxes). For each obstacle, the algorithm can adjust its size (length, width, height), position (x, y, z coordinates), and orientation (rotation angle *r*). Specific mutation operators are defined for these adjustments: Move (Δ_x, Δ_y), Resize (Δ_l, Δ_w, Δ_h), and Rotate (Δ_r). If the original log provides no information about the obstacles, they are initially placed with random properties intersecting the known mission path to serve as a starting point (seed) for the search.

Experimental Results: To evaluate the effectiveness of this approach, experiments were conducted using the PX4 [44] autopilot software controlling a quadcopter. The objective was to replicate a real-world autonomous flight where the UAV had to navigate around an obstacle placed along its planned route. The original logged trajectory served as the ground truth (visualized as the blue line in Fig. 4, left).

The experiment started with seed simulations using a small ($3m \times 3m \times 3m$) box obstacle placed at different initial positions relative to the flight path (one examples shown in Fig. 4, left). SURREALIST then iteratively adjusted the obstacle's properties. As shown in Fig. 4 (right), which displays the best result from 10 runs originating from Seed 1, the algorithm successfully determined obstacle parameters (position, size, rotation) that led to a simulated flight path nearly identical to the original one (achieving a Fréchet distance below 75cm). For instance, in that particular run, the

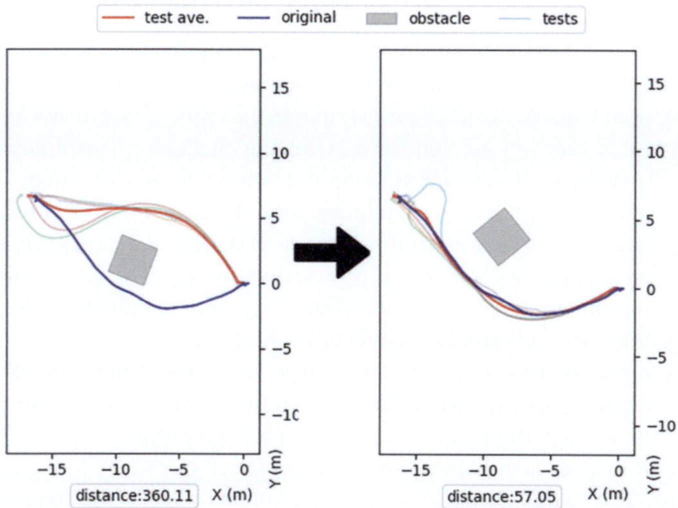

Fig. 4 Flight replication seed (left) show initial simulation attempt with an obstacle placed in the middle compared to the original real flight (blue). Final solution (right) shows the optimized simulation trajectory after SURREALIST adjusted obstacle properties, closely matching the real flight [32]

final obstacle was optimized by moving it 2 m upwards, rotating it 30° clockwise, and increasing its height by 2.8 m compared to the seed. Interestingly, while different runs converged to slightly different final obstacle configurations, they all produced simulated trajectories with very low DTW distances to the original flight. This suggests that achieving behavioral replication (similar trajectory) does not necessarily require reconstructing the *exact* environmental geometry.

> Information contained within flight logs is sufficient for search-based algorithms such as SURREALIST to identify simulation parameters (specifically, obstacle properties) that enable the faithful replication of UAV *autonomous* flight trajectories in a simulated environment.

Test Case Generation in Autonomous Mode

Building upon the flight replication capability, SURREALIST can also be used to proactively generate more challenging test scenarios [32, 34, 36, 37]. This instance of the generic approach aims to discover potentially hazardous flight conditions or expose bugs in the UAV's autonomous controller. Typically, it starts with a baseline simulated test case, such as one produced by the flight replication process described in Sect. 4.1.3.

The specific goal is to modify an existing autonomous flight simulation (defined by mission waypoints and initial obstacle configurations) to increase its difficulty. This is achieved by introducing an *additional* obstacle and optimizing its properties (position, size, rotation) to deliberately create a riskier environment. The objective is to guide the UAV into situations where it flies dangerously close to obstacles (i.e., closer than a predefined safety margin), while still attempting to complete its mission, thereby stress-testing its navigation and collision avoidance logic.

The core search mechanism remains similar to the replication process, but utilizes a different fitness function tailored for maximizing challenge. This fitness function is specifically designed to reward simulation configurations that compel the UAV to navigate through tight spaces or achieve very close proximity to obstacles. By optimizing parameters to maximize this fitness score, the search actively seeks out scenarios representing near-misses or potential collisions. The formulation of the fitness function involves measuring and combining minimal distances between the UAV's trajectory and the surrounding obstacles [32].

Experimental Results: Experiments were performed to demonstrate SURREALIST's ability to generate these challenging conditions. The goal was to take a standard simulated autonomous flight and modify it to provoke unsafe behavior. The setup involved a simulated quad-copter using PX4 in Gazebo, similar to the replication experiments. The initial scenario (seed) was a simple mission with one predefined box obstacle ($8m \times 5m \times 20m$) placed on the direct path (Fig. 5, left). SURREALIST was tasked with adding a second obstacle and optimizing its placement and size based on the test generation fitness function.

The results showed that SURREALIST successfully generated configurations for the second obstacle that induced hazardous situations (Fig. 5, right). These optimized scenarios exhibited several critical behaviors: (i) *Non-determinism*: Repeated simulations of the same final test case produced varying flight paths and outcomes.

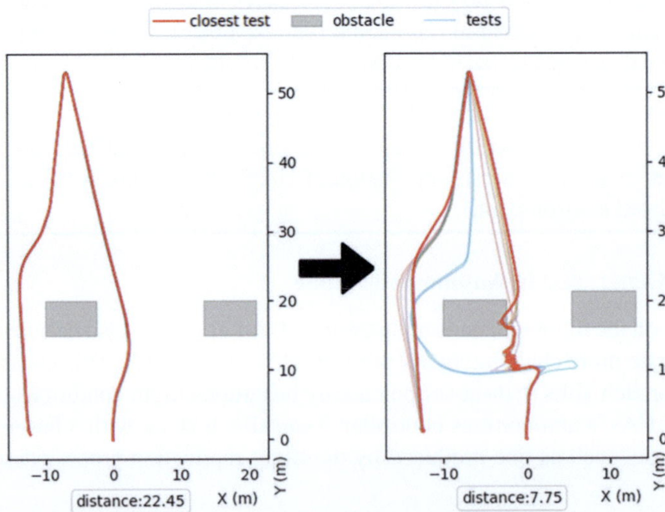

Fig. 5 Test generation seed scenario (left), and the final challenging scenario generated by SURREALIST after adding and optimizing a second obstacle, leading to unsafe and nondeterministic flight (right) [32]

(ii) *Unsafe Proximity*: The UAV was frequently forced too close to the *original* obstacle, violating safety margins. (iii) *Crashes*: In some simulation runs for the generated test case, the UAV actually crashed into the obstacle. In this specific run, the second obstacle was ultimately positioned approximately $8m$ to the left and $1.1m$ higher relative to its initial placement, creating a configuration that was significantly harder for the UAV to navigate safely. Notably, slight variations from this optimized configuration resulted in the UAV behaving safely and deterministically, highlighting that SURREALIST found a specific, hard-to-trigger failure scenario related to safety requirement violations (minimum obstacle distance).

Across 10 independent search runs, SURREALIST consistently discovered test cases leading to crashes. It reduced the minimum achieved obstacle distance from a safe 3.3 m in the seed scenario down to 0 m (crash) in the generated ones. On average, the best test cases found resulted in crashes in about 3 out of 10 repeated simulation executions and unsafe proximity ($<$1.5 m) in another 5 out of 10 executions.

> By systematically modifying simulation-based test cases, specifically through the addition and optimization of environmental features like obstacles, it is possible to generate challenging scenarios that effectively expose unsafe UAV behaviors, including safety distance violations and crashes.

4.2 Runtime Safety Monitoring of Unmanned Aerial Vehicles

While simulation-based testing (as discussed previously, e.g., using approaches such as SURREALIST and AERIALIST [32–34, 36, 37]) are crucial for pre-deployment validation [3, 60, 61], they cannot guarantee flawless operation in unpredictable real-world conditions [22, 66, 67]. Unforeseen factors necessitate runtime monitoring and, often, human oversight [42] to ensure safety during operation.

Recent research addresses this challenge by quantifying *uncertainty* [19, 25, 39, 43, 56, 58, 59, 62], particularly in autonomous systems' perception and decision-making. While initially focused on internal model components like DNNs [6], black-box approaches analyzing external signals like sensor inputs or control outputs [45, 58] offer broader applicability without requiring internal access. A relevant concept in this context is *Decision Uncertainty* [31], a black-box measure derived from inconsistencies observed in high-level control signals. Such uncertainty can manifest as erratic movements (Fig. 6b) and potentially precede or contribute to safety violations (Fig. 6d). However, the precise nature and utility of the relationship between observable, black-box uncertainty and UAV safety requires further investigation.

Figure 6 illustrates different flight behaviors in similar scenarios, highlighting combinations of safety (safe/unsafe proximity to obstacles) and certainty (smooth/hesitant trajectory). These examples motivated Khatiri *et al.* [31] for a deeper exploration of how uncertainty relates to safety for UAVs. They conducted a large-scale data-driven empirical study focusing on the widely used PX4-Avoidance [54] obsta-

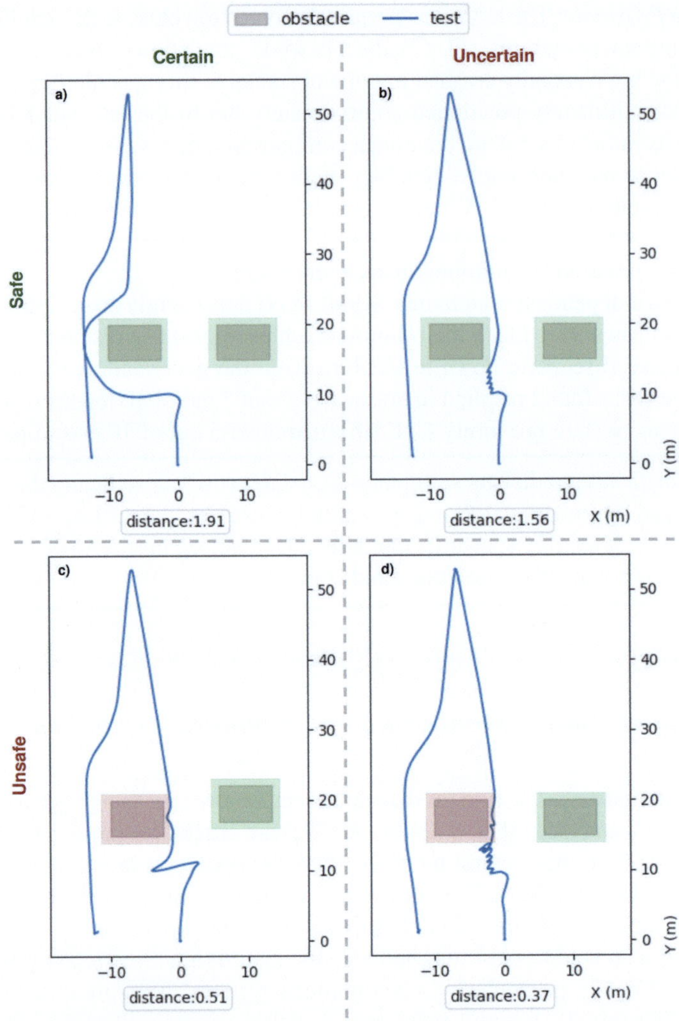

Fig. 6 Examples of flight safety and certainty levels: **a** Safe and Certain, **b** Safe and Uncertain, **c** Unsafe and Certain, **d** Unsafe and Uncertain [31]

cle avoidance system running on PX4-Autopilot [44]. Utilizing evolutionary algorithms inspired by SURREALIST [32] (see Sect. 4.1.3, diverse simulation flight scenarios were generated to capture a wide spectrum of behaviors, including both unsafe and uncertain conditions. Based on this data, they investigated the correlation between safety violations and measurable decision uncertainty. Furthermore, they developed and evaluated SUPERIALISTSupervising Autonomous Aerial Vehicles, a runtime monitoring approach based on anomaly detection using autoencoders, to assess the feasibility of detecting uncertainty and predicting unsafe states using minimal black-box control signals.

The following subsections detail the methodology and findings of this investigation. Section 4.2.1 examines the empirically observed correlation between unsafe states and uncertain decisions. Section 4.2.2 describes the SUPERIALIST approach and evaluates its effectiveness in detecting decision uncertainty in real-time. Finally, Sect. 4.2.3 assesses the extent to which the detected uncertainty can be used to predict impending safety violations, highlighting both the potential and limitations of this black-box approach.

4.2.1 Investigating the Correlation Between Unsafety and Uncertainty

A key question explored in this work is the degree to which uncertainty in a UAV's decision-making correlates with unsafe flight states. Understanding this relationship is crucial for evaluating the potential of using uncertainty measurements for runtime safety prediction [31].

To facilitate this investigation, substantial flight log datasets were required, encompassing a diverse range of scenarios representative of the different conditions outlined in Fig. 6 (*safe*, *unsafe*, *certain*, *uncertain*). They utilized and extended the test generation techniques based on SURREALIST [32], previously discussed, to create datasets that not only push the UAV towards obstacles (potential unsafety) but also encourage non-deterministic, hesitant trajectories (potential uncertainty). This process yielded multiple datasets: one for training (*train_ds*) and two distinct sets for testing (*test1_ds*, *test2_ds*). *test2_ds* specifically incorporates data from the original SURREALIST study [32] to assess the generalizability of the findings across different generation methods.

Flights within these datasets were manually reviewed and labeled to classify their safety and certainty status. Building upon the safety threshold concept from previous work [32], flights were labeled *Unsafe* if the minimum obstacle distance fell below 1 m, or if the UAV exhibited risky maneuvers within 1–3 m of obstacles. Otherwise, flights were labeled *Safe*. Concurrently, flights demonstrating clear, smooth navigation were labeled *Certain*, while those showing erratic or hesitant path segments were labeled *Uncertain*.

Hypothesis: Uncertain decisions by the UAV likely lead to unsafe states.

Statistical analysis of the labeled data reveals a notable but imperfect correlation. The *agreement accuracy* (Table 4), indicating flights that are either (Safe and Certain) or (Unsafe and Uncertain), is high (87–89%). However, the conditional probabilities provide a more nuanced picture.

The probability that a flight state is unsafe given that it was preceded by uncertainty, $p(\text{unsafe} \mid \text{uncertain})$, ranges from 50% to 74% across the test datasets (Table 4). This confirms the hypothesis to a degree but also highlights that a significant portion (26–50%) of uncertain decisions do *not* culminate in unsafe states (see examples in Fig. 7e–f).

Table 4 Statistical metrics for safety-certainty correlation [31]

Metric	*test1_ds* (%)	*test2_ds* (%)
Agreement accuracy (%)	86.8	89.3
p(unsafe | uncertain)	50	74.1
Conf interv (unsafe | uncertain)	[33.6, 66.4]	[66.9, 80.2]
p(uncertain | unsafe)	64	89.1
Conf interv (uncertain | unsafe)	[44.5, 79.8]	[82.8, 93.3]

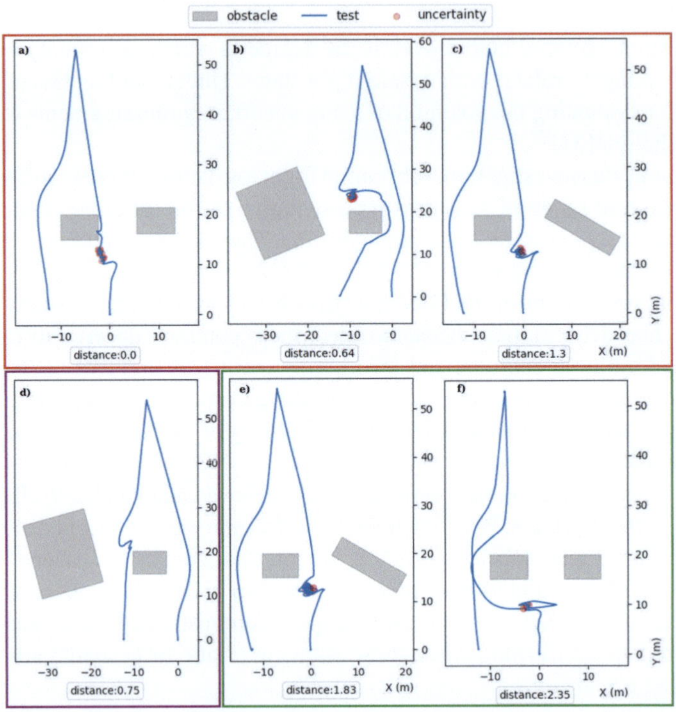

Fig. 7 Uncertainty detection examples [31] ((**a–c**): unsafe flights preceded by uncertainty | (**d**): unsafe flight with high certainty | (**e–f**): safe flights despite periods of uncertainty)

> While up to 74% of uncertain UAV decisions precede unsafe states, a substantial fraction (at least 26%) do not, indicating uncertainty is not a perfect predictor of imminent danger.

Conversely, considering the probability that an unsafe state was preceded by uncertainty, p(uncertain | unsafe), they find values between 64% and 89% (Table 4). This implies that while most unsafe situations show prior signs of uncertainty (Fig. 7a–c), a non-negligible percentage (11–36%) occur without such warnings (Fig. 7d). These latter cases represent scenarios where the UAV fails while acting decisively, posing a challenge for uncertainty-based prediction methods.

Most unsafe states (up to 89%) exhibit prior uncertainty, yet a notable portion (over 11%) occur without clear preceding uncertainty, limiting the recall of uncertainty-based safety monitors.

4.2.2 Real-Time Uncertainty Detection

This section assesses the feasibility and accuracy of detecting UAV decision uncertainty in real-time using anomaly detection techniques [31]. The goal is to identify moments when the UAV's behavior deviates from its typical, certain navigation patterns.

Adopting a *black-box* perspective, the detection focuses on the high-level control outputs logged from the PX4-Avoidance module, specifically the sequence of target waypoints provided to the lower-level controller. Preliminary analysis indicated that the UAV's *heading angle* (yaw, r_s) within these waypoints was the most sensitive indicator of decision uncertainty for the studied system (which uses a forward-facing camera). Therefore, the sequence of heading angles became the primary input for the detection model.

They developed SUPERIALIST, a runtime uncertainty monitor employing a convolutional autoencoder. Trained offline on nominal flight data (specifically, heading angle sequences from the *train_ds* dataset described in Sect. 4.2.1), the autoencoder learns to reconstruct typical heading patterns. At runtime, significant deviations from learned patterns, indicated by a high reconstruction loss exceeding a predefined threshold (θ), are flagged as anomalies, signifying potential decision uncertainty. To reduce false positives during normal maneuvers like turns, the reconstruction loss is averaged over a short time window ($n = 4$).

Figure 8 provides an example where SUPERIALIST identifies periods of high reconstruction loss in the heading angle signal. These detected anomalies correspond to moments where the drone exhibits hesitant or erratic turning behavior as it struggles to find a clear path, often occurring well before it enters a critically unsafe area.

The performance of SUPERIALIST specifically for detecting uncertain behavior is presented in Table 5. The high accuracy (96–97%), precision (90–96%), and recall (84–93%) across both test datasets confirm that this black-box, autoencoder-based approach is highly effective at identifying moments of decision uncertainty based on control signal anomalies.

Anomalies in high-level UAV control signals, detectable by tools like SUPERIALIST, serve as effective real-time indicators of decision uncertainty with high accuracy, precision, and recall.

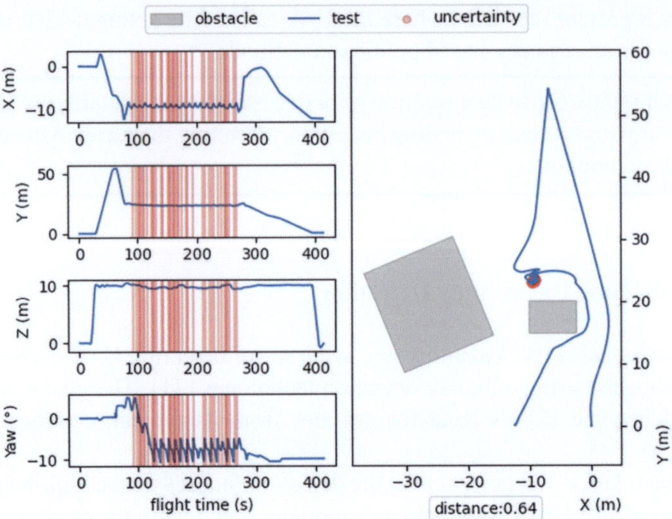

Fig. 8 Example of detected uncertainty (anomalous heading angle reconstruction loss) over flight time [31]

Table 5 Model evaluation metrics for uncertainty detection and unsafety prediction [31]

Task	Dataset	Acc. (%)	Prec. (%)	Recall (%)	F1 (%)
Uncertainty detection	*test1_ds*	95.8	90	84.4	87.1
	test2_ds	96.7	95.7	93.4	94.5
Unsafety prediction	*test1_ds*	84.7	43.3	52	47.3
	test2_ds	88.9	74.1	87	80

4.2.3 Predicting Unsafe States via Uncertainty

Building upon the ability to detect uncertainty, this section evaluates the extent to which these detections can be used to effectively predict upcoming unsafe UAV states. The practical goal is to determine if identifying uncertainty early provides a reliable mechanism for anticipating and potentially preventing safety violations.

Analysis shows that the uncertainty detected by SUPERIALIST often precedes unsafe conditions by a significant margin [31]. On average across the test datasets, the first uncertainty warning occurred 42–50 s before the UAV entered a critical zone (<1 m from an obstacle), at which point the drone was still approximately 3.5–3.7 m away. This provides a substantial time window for potential intervention (automated or manual). Examples where detected uncertainty precedes unsafe states are shown in Fig. 7a–c.

However, using uncertainty detection directly for unsafety prediction faces limitations inherent in the relationship between the two concepts (explored in Sect. 4.2.1).

As shown in Table 5, the precision and recall for predicting unsafe states are considerably lower than for detecting uncertainty itself.

The reduced precision (43–74%) stems from instances where the UAV exhibits uncertainty but ultimately recovers and proceeds safely (Finding 1, Fig. 7e–f). Such cases are correctly flagged as uncertain by SUPERIALIST but count as false positives when the goal is predicting unsafety. The theoretical upper bound for precision is limited by $p(\text{unsafe} \mid \text{uncertain})$ (50–74%, Table 4) [31].

Similarly, the reduced recall (52–87%) is due to unsafe situations that occur without significant preceding uncertainty (Finding 2, Fig. 7d). SUPERIALIST cannot predict these events based on uncertainty anomalies, leading to false negatives for unsafety prediction. The recall is theoretically capped by $p(\text{uncertain} \mid \text{unsafe})$ (64–89%, Table 4).

> While detected control signal anomalies provide early warnings often preceding unsafe states, their direct use for predicting unsafety yields only moderate effectiveness (up to 74% precision, 87% recall), limited by the imperfect correlation between black-box uncertainty and safety violations.

4.3 *Simulation-Based Test Prioritization for Self-Driving Cars*

Simulation-based testing is usually time-consuming and requires a minimum of computational power [11–13]. In certain contexts, such as for end-to-end testing of SDCs in with the BeamNG.tech simulator, test cases can take on average 60 s to execute [17].

With those limiting factors, the objective to prioritize some tests over others becomes obvious. However, to test the system with a specific order of test cases raises some questions: What aspects do we need to consider when defining a test execution order? And, how do we formulate this optimization problem [11, 12]?

Test Case Features. For the former question, we can leverage specific features of test cases. In the context of self-driving cars (SDCs), we can define features describing the road the SDCs should drive along [17, 18]. In Table 6, we have an overview of how such SDC test case features are represented. Based on those features, it is possible to define a fitness function from which an optimal ordering of test cases can be computed.

Optimization Problem. To optimize a test execution order, we need to concretize the objective that needs to be optimized. For our example with SDCs, we want to minimize the execution time of test cases and optimize the diversity of the test cases. Having this in mind, we can define the following function to optimize:

$$max\ f(\tau) = \sum_{i=2}^{n} \frac{diversity(t_i)}{cost(t_i) * i}$$

Table 6 Road characteristics features [10–12, 17]

Feature	Description
Direct distance	Euclidean distance between start and finish
Road distance	Total length of the road
Num. left turns	Number of left turns on the test track
Num. right turns	Number of right turns on the test track
Num. straight	Number of straight segments on the test track
Total angle	Total angle turned in road segments on the test track
Median angle	Median of angle turned in road segment on the test track
Std angle	Standard deviation of angle turned in road segment on the test track
Max angle	The maximum angle turned in road segment on the test track
Min angle	The minimum angle turned in road segment on the test track
Mean angle	The average angle turned in road segment on the test track
Median pivot off	Median of radius of road segment on the test track
Std pivot off	Standard deviation of radius turned in road segment on the test track
Max pivot off	The maximum radius of road segment on the test track
Min pivot off	The minimum radius of road segment on the test track
Mean pivot off	The average radius of road segment turned on the test track

This function includes two aspects such as the test cases' diversity and the execution cost. The test case τ_{max} is the test case that maximizes the function. With these optimal test cases we have defined a test ordering that has the most diverse and cheapest (short runtimes) test cases at the beginning of the testing campaign. However, we have not elaborated yet on how we compute the optimal value. Of course, there are many algorithms available for solving optimization problems. For our case, we want to take a look at *Genetic Algoritms*.

4.3.1 Genetic Algorithm

With genetic algorithms, we have an algorithm in our toolbox for solving optimization problems, leveraging aspects from the evolution's theory. The principle of genetic algorithms is always based on several key steps:

1. **Initialization**: Set up an initial set of solutions, i.e., test orders, from which we start iterating to find the optimal solution, i.e., the order of test executions that is optimal.
2. **Fitness Evaluation**: Evaluate each solution with the fitness function, i.e., the function(s) we want to optimize.
3. **Selection**: We select, according to the fitness evaluation, of the best candidates for the future population, i.e., iteration.
4. **Crossover**: In this step, we create new solutions based on two existing ones by combining them.

5. **Mutation**: The newly created solutions are further mutated we a predefined set of mutation operators. The purpose of this step is to get a more diverse set of solutions and to avoid the algorithm from getting stuck in a local optimum.
6. **Reinsertion**: Inspired by the evolutionary process in nature, genetic algorithms aim to find optimal solutions that fit best and "survive". Depending on the concrete problem formulation, the actual algorithm can vary. For example, in the multi-objective case.

4.3.2 Multi-objective Evolutionary Algorithm

Another way to define the optimization problem is to define two separate optimization functions. The idea is to put each aspect of the optimization problem into separate functions.

$$max\ f_1(\tau) = \sum_{i=2}^{n} \frac{diversity(t_i)}{i}$$

$$min\ f_2(\tau) = \sum_{i=2}^{n} \frac{cost(t_i)}{i}$$

We still have the same aim as in the single-objective case, where we want to have diversity and cheap test cases at the beginning of the testing campaign. However, in the multi-objective case we define two separate functions, which cover one of the two aspects each.

Now with two separate functions, we also need to adapt the algorithm to find the optimal solution(s). Fortunately, the popular NSGA-II algorithm [21] is a genetic algorithm, which is able to solve optimization problems with multiple objectives, i.e., multiple functions to optimize. A major difference between the single and the multi-objective optimization setting is that in the multi-objective case, we get not only a single optimal solution. Instead, we get a set of optimal solutions. Due to the fact that some solutions can favor one objective over the other, we have a set of solutions from which we can pick.

Research [12] has shown that a multi-objective approach can outperform a single-objective one. Depending on the context and setting, splitting up aspects of the test scenarios into multiple functions as objectives is advisable.

4.4 Simulation-Based Test Selection for Self-Driving Cars

Complementary to test prioritization, e.g., with SDC-Prioritizer, as described before in Sect. 4.3, selecting only relevant test cases is relevant as well. But what are the relevant test cases? From a tester's perspective, all distinct tests that make the system fail can be seen as relevant test cases. Hence, we do not need as many test cases as possible but only test cases that are relevant to test a certain feature and with the according specific oracle definition.

Let us take a look at the use case of a lane-keeping system of an SDC. In this context, relevant test cases are those that are challenging for the car to follow the lane. So far, so good, but how do we identify such test cases?

SDC-Scissor [9] is an approach based on machine learning (ML) that consumes the same feature set from Table 6. The ML model then predicts the likelihood of the SDC will drive off the lane or not. With this approach, we have a more selective selection of test cases to test the lane-keeping feature of the SDC.

Of course, there is also a bottleneck with this approach. Since we use ML models, we need data from already executed test cases so that the models can learn from them. Hence, it is important to keep the data of executed test cases for further (re)training of the models.

Although the ML-based test selection approach is the core of SDC-Scissor, the tool can also be used as a simple test runner for simulation-based tests for SDCs. The SDC-Scissor tool is open-source and available on GitHub.[3]

4.5 SDC-Alabaster: Human-in-the-Loop Simulation-Based Test Case Evaluation

In previous sections, we looked at test prioritization and selection strategies. So far, we have not taken a closer look at the test case itself. Using simulation environments for testing raises additional challenges compared to "conventional" software testing [13]. Such challenges are, for example, the perception of safety and realism of simulation environments.

A study [16] involving 50 humans using a virtual reality (VR) headset investigated exactly those aspects. The researchers were interested if the perception of safety and realism from a human's perspective differs from established evaluation metrics such as the out-of-bound (OOB) metric. The study used the SDC-Alabaster framework, which is an extension of SDC-Scissor. With the integration of VR into the framework, the participants could perceive and evaluate several test scenarios.

The study revealed several findings of relevance:

> The passing test cases (i.e., the cases where the OOB metric is not violated) have a higher perception of safety from the participants than those failing (OOB metric is violated).

The results showed that a single meetric such as the out-of-bounds (OOB) metric do reflect the actual human perception of safety to certain degree.

[3] https://github.com/christianbirchler-org/sdc-scissor.

Further findings also clarify that the actual test case setup with additional obstacles next and on the road further impacts the perception significantly by the study participants.

> Overall, participants found the test cases less safe with obstacles.

Next to only oberserving the test scenario, the study participant were also provided a possibility of interaction with the vehicle, i.e., to accelerate or brake the vehicle. Just the fact of having the possibility of intervene the SDCs behavior influences the safety perception.

> Safety perception of test cases is not static: When users can interact with the SDC, participants feel significantly safer compared to when they cannot.

Key takeaways from that study are, for example, that metrics defining if a test passes or fails do not necessarily match with the perception of humans. Hence, defining oracles for such test cases must either be refined or need to have a human-in-the-loop for their assessment. Furthermore, results showed that the possibility of direct interaction of the test subject increases the safety perception significantly. We can say that defining and determining oracles of SDC test cases for simulation environments is a complex and challenging task. Many factors play a role in determining the outcome of a test case. It is subject to future research to investigate those to come up with more automation possibilities.

5 Tools Assessment and Integration in Industrial Use Cases

This section discusses the validation of solutions reported in the aforementioned sections in real-world sectors such as automotive, aviation, etc.

5.1 AERIALIST *and* SURREALIST*: Industrial Evaluation in Aviation*

The AERIALIST [33] and SURREALIST [32] frameworks introduced in Sect. 4.1 are open-source tools initially designed for enhancing the simulation-based testing of Unmanned Aerial Vehicles (UAVs). This section details their adaptation, industrial application, and evaluation within the *COSMOS*[4] *H2020 EU project*, specifically for an aviation use case with industrial partner *GMV*.[5] The GMV use case included a path planning algorithm for airplanes, generating alternative waypoints to navigate between two airports.

[4] https://www.cosmos-devops.org/.

[5] https://www.gmv.com/en.

5.1.1 Adapting AERIALIST for Airplane Simulation

AERIALIST serves as a modular and extensible test bench facilitating the automation of UAV testing processes, from environment setup and firmware execution to runtime monitoring and log analysis. Initially supporting UAVs on the *PX4* platform with the *Gazebo* simulator, AERIALIST's utility in improving testing practices for open-source UAV systems was confirmed through multiple research studies [32–34, 36, 37]. For the *COSMOS* project, AERIALIST was significantly extended to support *GMV*'s aviation use case, which involved manned aircraft simulation using *FlightGear*, an open-source flight simulator. The key adaptation steps included:

- *PX4* and *FlightGear* Integration for Manned Aircraft: The *PX4* flight control software and *FlightGear* simulator were adapted to handle manned airplanes instead of model UAVs. In collaboration with *GMV*, the Cessna 172, a popular civilian airplane model, was chosen as a proof of concept. This involved modifications to the aircraft model controlled by *PX4* and fine-tuning of *PX4* and *FlightGear* parameters to ensure realistic and stable flight control.
- Automation in *FlightGear*: AERIALIST's core functionalities were extended to manage test execution within *FlightGear*, including simulation setup and aircraft monitoring in this new context.
- Extended Test Definition Model: To accommodate *GMV*'s path planning algorithms, utility functions were developed to convert airplane flight paths (composed of waypoints/navaids) into *PX4* flight missions. This enhanced AERIALIST's Test Description model, allowing simpler test definitions using flight waypoints as input.
- Enhanced Flight Analysis Capabilities: As per *GMV*'s requirements, AERIALIST's flight analysis functionalities were augmented to extract and analyze crucial parameters such as distance, time, fuel consumption, and CO2 production.

This extension of AERIALIST for the *GMV* use case proved crucial for enabling large-scale test execution, test generation, and dataset preparation (Fig. 9).

5.1.2 Adapting SURREALIST for Flight Plan Generation

SURREALIST [32] (teSting UAVs in the neighboRhood of REAl flIghtS) is a search-based approach designed to automatically generate realistic simulation test cases from logged real-world flights and to create more challenging variants from these replicated scenarios (as detailed in Sect. 4.1.3). It leverages AERIALIST as its underlying platform for the automated definition, execution, and evaluation of test cases, utilizing parallel execution in a *Kubernetes* cluster to manage non-determinism and ensure reliable test evaluation. The extension of AERIALIST to support *GMV*'s avionics use case unlocked the potential for SURREALIST to be applied to test generation in this new domain. The adaptation involved:

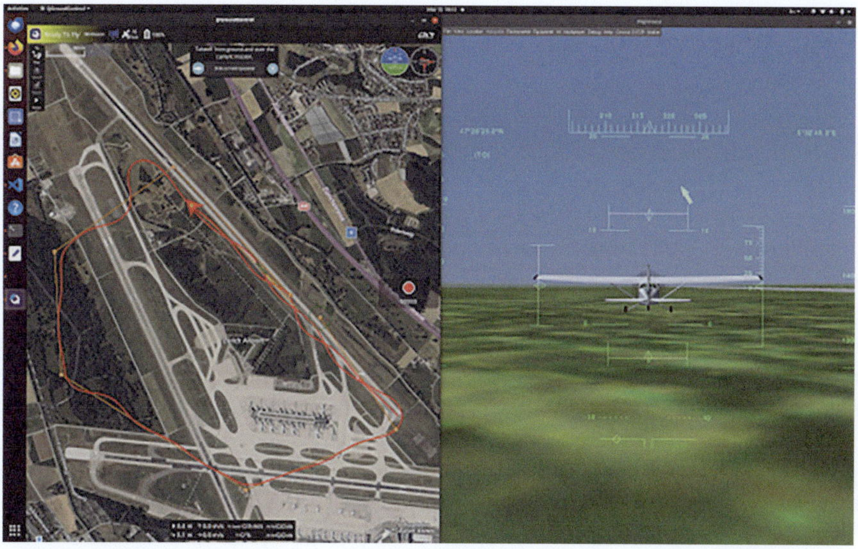

Fig. 9 Sample flight with Cessna 172 airplane in FlightGear conducted with AERIALIST

- Context-Specific Test Case Properties and Mutation Operators: While the original SURREALIST focused on mutating obstacle properties for UAV navigation, the *GMV* use case required different test parameters. In collaboration with *GMV*, test properties were redesigned to focus on flight path waypoints. New mutation operators, *LAT_MOVE* and *LON_MOVE*, were introduced to modify the start or end waypoints of a flight. After each mutation, *GMV*'s path planning tool generated a new flight path, which was then simulated and evaluated using the extended AERIALIST framework.
- Novel Fitness Functions for Aviation: The fitness functions guiding SURREALIST's search were adapted to *GMV*'s objectives. Instead of focusing on UAV proximity to obstacles, new goals included validating the accuracy of fuel consumption and CO2 production estimations provided by *GMV*'s algorithm. The Dynamic Time Warping (DTW) distance of estimated versus simulated fuel consumption over time for alternative flight paths was employed as a fitness function, enabling the validation of flight path rankings generated by *GMV*'s tool.

5.1.3 Evaluation and Industrial Impact

Previous evaluations of AERIALIST in the context of UAV testing demonstrated significant performance benefits. For instance, during a search-based test generation process, an average of 50 different test cases, each executed 10 times in parallel to account for non-determinism, were evaluated. A full experimental run involving 5,000 simulations was completed in approximately 2 days using *Kubernetes* resources (60 VCPUs, 80 GBs of RAM), a task estimated to take at least 20 days on a single machine. This indicates a potential 10x speed-up, with further acceleration possible with more resources.

These performance advantages, alongside the automated test execution, simplified test definition model, and enhanced flight log analysis, directly benefited the *GMV* use case by streamlining their testing and evaluation processes.

Previous evaluations of SURREALIST for autonomous UAVs demonstrated its effectiveness in generating challenging test scenarios that exposed critical system behaviors. For example, by introducing and optimizing an additional obstacle, SURREALIST consistently created test cases where the UAV exhibited non-deterministic behavior, operated unsafely close to obstacles, and in some instances, crashed. This process successfully identified bugs related to safety requirement violations (e.g., maintaining minimum obstacle distance), reducing safe distances from 3.3 m in seed scenarios to 0 m (crash) in generated ones.

In the *GMV* context, this search-based methodology was applied to identify problematic start and destination waypoints that led to significant errors in fuel consumption and CO2 production estimations by *GMV*'s path planning algorithm, potentially causing incorrect path ranking. This application aids in generating diverse test scenarios to validate the routing quality and contributes to the generation of large flight datasets to refine the path planning algorithms.

5.2 SUPERIALIST*: Industrial Evaluation in Utility Management*

The SUPERIALIST framework [31], previously detailed for its application to UAVs (see Sect. 4.2), was also evaluated in an industrial context within the *COSMOS* project, specifically for the *UNPARALLEL*[6] utility management use case. The use case involved applying SUPERIALIST's autoencoder-based anomaly detection to data from Sound Pressure Level (SPL) devices. These devices are part of an acoustic vibration detection system designed to identify and locate water loss events in distribution networks. This section describes the adaptation and performance of SUPERIALIST in this distinct CPS domain.

5.2.1 Adaptation and Experimental Setup

The objective was to adapt SUPERIALIST to monitor time-series data from SPL sensors and detect anomalous behavior caused by electromagnetic interference (EMI). The experimental process involved collecting data from two SPL devices under both normal operating conditions and with artificially induced EMI. Due to the necessary

[6] https://www.unparallel.pt/.

Fig. 10 Injected anomalies in sensor signals

proximity of the devices, EMI affected both, though it was more pronounced on the primary test device (SPL-1). Figure 10 illustrates the dataset used.

The adaptation involved training an autoencoder model on a nominal dataset from SPL-1. The model learned the patterns of normal device operation from preprocessed data, which was segmented into fixed-length windows of approximately 10 s. The anomaly detection threshold was determined empirically and set to the maximum average reconstruction error observed over five consecutive windows on the training data. This setup resulted in zero anomalies being flagged on the training dataset, indicating a stable baseline for detection.

5.2.2 Evaluation and Results

The trained model was evaluated on the remaining datasets: a normal dataset from the second device (SPL-2) and two datasets with injected anomalies (SPL-1-anomaly and SPL-2-anomaly).

- *SPL-2 (Normal Operations)*: When evaluated on the normal operational data from SPL-2 (Fig. 11, left), the system registered 0 false positives out of 150 time windows. This demonstrates the model's specificity in distinguishing normal behavior on a similar but distinct device.
- *SPL-1-anomaly (Induced Anomalies)*: For the dataset with induced EMI (Fig. 11, right), 21 out of 111 time windows were correctly detected as anomalous. All these detections corresponded to the time periods where interference was active.
- *SPL-2-anomaly (Induced Anomalies)*: Similarly, for the second device subjected to EMI, 5 out of 110 time windows were identified as anomalous, all aligning with the anomaly injection periods.

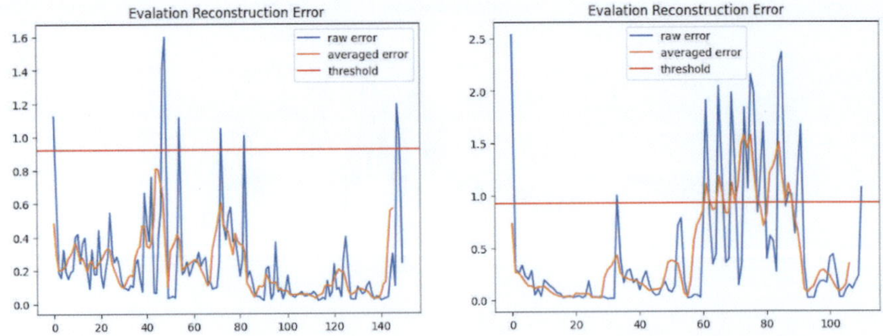

Fig. 11 Comparison of reconstruction errors over SPL-2 nominal data (left) and SPL-1 anomalous data (right)

Based on these evaluations, the SUPERIALIST approach was successfully extended to this utility use case, effectively detecting EMI-induced anomalies in the SPL devices.

> The SUPERIALIST anomaly detection framework, initially developed for UAVs, demonstrated successful adaptation and effectiveness in an industrial utility management scenario. It reliably detected EMI-induced anomalies in sensor readings with no false positives on normal operational data from a separate device, confirming its potential for broader CPS applications.

5.3 Automated Identification of Safety-Critical Concerns in UAVs

Software defects in UAVs can pose serious safety risks, necessitating continuous hazard identification and risk management. Safety-related concerns of UAVs often emerge through issue reports and pull requests, but the high volume of reports in popular projects makes timely identification challenging for developers. To address this, recent studies proposed SALIENT [22, 35], an ML-powered tool that analyzes issue reports at the sentence level to detect safety-related concerns. Evaluations on three major open-source UAV projects showed that SALIENT outperforms baseline approaches like ChatGPT and Google's Bard, providing an effective solution for fast and accurate triage of safety-critical issues. Moreover, an industrial assessment of the tool was conducted with partners of the COSMOS[7] EU project, which further confirmed the validity and practical relevance of the conducted research.

[7] https://www.cosmos-devops.org/.

In the following sections, we provide details on the SALIENT validation conducted in the context of industrial partners of the COSMOS H2020 project.

5.3.1 SALIENT's Open Source and Industrial Evaluation

A summary of the model's training process, tuning, and performance evaluation behind SALIENT is provided in [22, 35]. Specifically, researchers first collected a dataset of issue reports and pull requests from open-source UAV software projects on GitHub, filtering for those with safety-related labels. This resulted in three UAV-related projects. Then, they analyzed 304 closed issues and pull requests labeled as safety-related, manually classifying 1,916 sentences from their titles and descriptions as either safety- or non-safety-related. A strict labeling protocol was followed to minimize subjectivity, leading to 837 (43.7%) sentences identified as safety-related.

To assess AI-based classification, a sample of 17 issues (100 sentences, 40 safety-related) was extracted. Then, GPT-3.5 and PaLM 2 were tested by using a binary classification prompt: Is the following sentence safety-related?' <sentence_here>' Response format: YES/NO. Both models performed poorly, with precision lower than 60%, highlighting the need for a specialized model. Overall, SALIENT best-performing approach, integrating fastText, was assessed by using tenfold cross-validation. It achieved an 81% average F1-score, demonstrating its effectiveness in identifying safety-related issues and supporting developers in issue management.

Industrial assessment from GMV (Aviation company). SALIENT was evaluated for its effectiveness in detecting algorithm limitations and reducing deployment errors, crucial for UAV system safety. The tool demonstrated a detection rate of at least 20% for algorithm limitations and contributed to a 15% reduction in deployment errors. These results highlight SALIENT's superiority over baseline models like ChatGPT and Bard in identifying safety-critical issues.

The internal ML component, utilizing FastText, achieved an average F1-score of 81% via tenfold cross-validation, ensuring high recall and precision in detecting safety-related sentences. These findings highlight SALIENT's role in assisting developers in prioritizing safety-related concerns efficiently.

Prototype Capabilities for UAV/CPS Development evaluated by the GMV company[8] SALIENT is a tool designed to assist developers in analyzing user-reported issues in UAV platforms by automatically detecting safety concerns. Key capabilities include:

- **Automated Safety Issue Detection**: Uses machine learning (ML) to identify safety-related concerns in issue reports.
- **GitHub Integration**: Parses and preprocesses issues from GitHub, cleaning and segmenting text for analysis.

[8] https://www.gmv.com/en.

- **Flexible Usage Modes**: Supports both Command-Line Interface (CLI) for automation and Graphical User Interface (GUI) for general users.
- **ML Component**: Employs FastText for text classification, improving recognition of rare and out-of-vocabulary words.
- **Visualization and Prioritization**: Displays safety concern likelihood in issues, allowing developers to prioritize critical ones.
- **Ease of Setup**: Available as a Python CLI utility with a Dockerfile for simplified deployment.

According to GMV (partner in the COSMOS H2020 EU project), SALIENT enhances UAV/CPS development by improving safety analysis and issue management efficiency.

Evaluation: Usability, Deployment, Complexity, and Performance. Feedback from GMV highlights SALIENT's strengths in usability, deployment, complexity, and performance. In terms of *Usability*:

- GUI and CLI options cater to different user preferences.
- User-friendly interfaces facilitate issue selection, writing, and editing.
- Visualizations aid understanding and prioritization of safety concerns.

In terms of *Deployment Experience*:

- Flexible deployment through CLI and GUI.
- Dockerfile simplifies setup.
- GitHub integration streamlines issue retrieval and preprocessing.

In terms of *Complexity*:

- Uses advanced NLP techniques for text cleaning and classification.
- FastText-based ML model adds complexity but enhances accuracy.
- Customizable hyperparameters provide flexibility but require tuning.

In terms of *Performance*:

- Improves efficiency in safety issue management.
- Outperforms baseline strategies like ChatGPT and Google Bard.
- Enables prioritization of critical issues for faster resolution.

The depth evaluation of SALIENT from GMV focused on the automated detection of algorithm limitations and reduction of deployment errors, both crucial for UAV system safety, particularly in air traffic. The assessment of the *Automated Detection of Algorithm Limitations* conducted by GMV showed the following results:
Measure: Assessed SALIENT's ability to detect algorithm limitations from user-reported issues. **Result**: Achieved a detection rate of at least 20%.

The assessment of the *Reduction of Deployment Errors* conducted by GMV showed the following results:
Measure: Evaluated SALIENT's effectiveness in minimizing deployment errors. **Result**: Reduced errors by at least 15%.

SALIENT significantly enhances UAV safety by aiding developers in identifying and resolving safety concerns. It outperformed baseline strategies (e.g., ChatGPT, Bard) in detecting safety-critical issues. Its internal ML component, utilizing FastText, achieved an average F1-score of 81% (tenfold cross-validation), demonstrating high recall and precision in detecting safety-related sentences. These results highlight SALIENT's effectiveness in prioritizing safety-related issues for rapid resolution. Overall, SALIENT proves valuable for UAV developers and airline operations, offering advanced functionality, flexible deployment, and superior performance in safety issue management.

Recommendations for Improvement from the GMV company:

- **Enhanced Accuracy**: Further refinement of the ML model, including fine-tuning or exploring advanced architectures, could improve performance.
- **Expanded Scope**: Extending classification beyond UAVs to other safety-critical domains would broaden applicability.
- **Customization**: Allowing user-specific training data and hyperparameter tuning could enhance adaptability.
- **Integration**: Compatibility with issue tracking systems such as Jira and GitLab would increase usability.
- **Community Engagement**: Soliciting user feedback and fostering engagement will drive continuous improvement.

Implications and Impact. SALIENT facilitates automated identification and prioritization of safety concerns in UAV development, potentially reducing issue resolution time. Integration into the software development lifecycle can ensure consistent monitoring of safety considerations. Researchers can leverage the tool to analyze UAV safety trends and develop methodologies for mitigating recurring safety-related issues. The provided labeled data can further support advancements in UAV safety research and best practices.

5.4 CPS-Based Tool Competitions

5.4.1 UAV Testing Competition: Fostering Research and Exploitation

The *UAV Testing Competition*[9] actively engages the software testing community, aiming to establish UAV testing as an indispensable field. This initiative provides a structured platform for simulation-based UAV testing, motivating researchers to apply and develop advanced test generation techniques in the novel and challenging area of autonomous vision-based UAV navigation systems. The competition has seen participation from a total of eleven teams across its first two years (six in 2024 [34] and five in 2025 [36, 37]) and is expected to grow in the next editions.

[9] https://github.com/skhatiri/UAV-Testing-Competition/.

The competition offers participants an efficient platform built on top of AERIALIST [33] that simplifies UAV test execution, allowing them to concentrate on developing their test generation strategies. Participants are expected to build their tools on top of this provided infrastructure. The competition challenges participants to generate diverse and effective test cases by modifying simulation environments, for instance, by altering obstacle placements to identify system vulnerabilities. In the first editions, SURREALIST, the state of the art test generation approach for UAVs, has been used as as baseline for the competing tools [34, 36, 37].

By providing a competitive yet collaborative environment, the UAV Testing Competition acts as a catalyst for:

- *Exploitation of Research*: It drives the practical application and refinement of existing research tools and methodologies like AERIALIST and SURREALIST.
- *Benchmarking*: It allows for the comparison of different test generation strategies against established baselines and each other in controlled case studies.
- *Community Building*: It brings together researchers to tackle shared challenges in UAV testing.
- *Future Research Directions*: Insights gained from the competition, such as the importance of handling non-determinism and the need for more diverse test scenarios (e.g., varied obstacle types, environmental factors, directly inform and encourage future research efforts in ensuring the safety and reliability of complex UAV systems.

This initiative not only validates current research but also significantly contributes to the maturation of testing practices for autonomous systems, pushing the boundaries of what can be achieved in simulation-based testing for safety-critical CPS.

5.4.2 SDC Testing Competition

The Self-Driving Car (SDC) Testing Challenge promotes research in simulation-based test selection for autonomous vehicles, aiming to establish cost-effective test selection as a key concern in the autonomous systems testing community. The competition focuses on selecting a subset of test cases that evaluates an SDC most efficiently under resource constraints, addressing the growing demand for scalable and economical validation techniques in safety-critical domains.

The inaugural edition of the competition was held in 2025, attracting seven participating teams from academia and industry [14]. As the complexity of autonomous driving systems increases and exhaustive testing becomes infeasible, the challenge provides a timely platform for exploring prioritization strategies that balance testing cost and effectiveness. Future editions are expected to draw broader participation as interest in intelligent testing solutions continues to rise.

The competition is built on an interface specification. Rather than generating new tests or modifying existing ones, participants were required to implement a simple interface that selects which test case to execute by returning the identifier of the next scenario to run. This abstraction enables a clean separation between test selection logic and simulation infrastructure, allowing participants to focus solely on decision-making strategies for maximizing coverage or fault detection within a limited budget.

6 The Path Forward

This section, inspired by a position paper of Birchler et al. [13], explores future research directions and automation needs in testing Autonomous Cyber-Physical Systems (ACPS), emphasizing the integration of simulation-based testing into development workflows and expanding the notion of test quality. It reviews modern development practices like Agile and Test-Driven Development (TDD), recognizing their value in providing rapid feedback and structured testing. However, the applicability of TDD to simulation-based testing remains uncertain. Regression testing techniques–such as test minimization, selection, and prioritization–are valuable but hard to adapt to simulations due to the lack of clearly defined, computable metrics.

Bridging the reality gap between simulations and real-world performance is a key concern. Domain randomization, hybrid testing with real-world data, and adapting simulator parameters using real measurements are among the techniques proposed to make simulations more representative. Machine learning approaches like domain adaptation and reinforcement learning, alongside hardware advancements, may help make simulated environments more realistic and diverse.

The energy consumption and the environmental aspect may impact our testing practices. With the ICT sector's energy use rising, there's growing interest in making testing pipelines more energy-efficient. Current green software practices largely ignore testing, prompting questions about how to optimize test frequency, suite size, and energy-aware strategies in ACPS development.

In conclusion, while simulation-based testing is essential for evaluating ACPS safety and performance, it introduces new challenges. Addressing issues such as metric development, test automation, environmental impact, and the reality gap is critical for building safer, more efficient, and more sustainable AI-enabled CPS.[10]

Competing Interests The authors have no conflicts of interest to declare that are relevant to the content of this chapter.

Acknowledgements We thank the Horizon 2020 (EU Commission) and the SERI (State Secretariat for Education, Research, and Innovation) support for the project InnoGuard, Marie Sktodowska-Curie Actions Doctoral Networks (HORIZON-MSCA-2023-DN), and the SNSF project entitled "SwarmOps: Human-sensing based MLOps for Collaborative Cyber-physical systems" (Project No. 200021_219732). We also thank the Hasler Foundation for the projects "Bridging the Reality Gap in Testing Unmanned Aerial Vehicles" (Project No.23064) and "Advancing Unmanned Aerial Vehicles Reliability and Societal Trust Through Integrated Testing and Formal Verification" (Project No.2025-02-27-311).

[10] https://www.innoguard.eu/index.html.

References

1. R.B. Abdessalem, S. Nejati, L.C. Briand, T. Stifter, Testing vision-based control systems using learnable evolutionary algorithms, in *International Conference on Software Engineering* (ACM, 2018), pp. 1016–1026
2. A. Afzal, Automated testing of robotic and cyberphysical systems. Ph.D. thesis, Carnegie Mellon University, 2021
3. A. Afzal, D.S. Katz, C. Le Goues, C.S. Timperley, Simulation for robotics test automation: developer perspectives, in *Conference on Software Testing, Verification and Validation* (IEEE, 2021), pp. 263–274
4. A. Afzal, C. Le Goues, C.S. Timperley, Mithra: anomaly detection as an oracle for cyberphysical systems. IEEE Trans. Softw. Eng. (2021)
5. M. Alcon, H. Tabani, J. Abella, F.J. Cazorla, Enabling unit testing of already-integrated AI software systems: the case of apollo for autonomous driving, in *Euromicro Conference on Digital System Design* (IEEE, 2021), pp. 426–433
6. F. Arnez, H. Espinoza, A. Radermacher, F. Terrier, Towards dependable autonomous systems based on bayesian deep learning components, in *2022 18th European Dependable Computing Conference (EDCC)* (IEEE, 2022), pp. 65–72
7. M.N. Asmat, S.U.R. Khan, S. Hussain, Uncertainty handling in cyber-physical systems: state-of-the-art approaches, tools, causes, and future directions. J. Softw. Evol. Process. **35**(7), (2023)
8. D.J. Berndt, J. Clifford, Using dynamic time warping to find patterns in time series, in *KDD Workshop*, vol. 10 (Seattle, WA, USA, 1994), pp. 359–370
9. C. Birchler, N. Ganz, S. Khatiri, A. Gambi, S. Panichella, Cost-effective simulation-based test selection in self-driving cars software with SDC-Scissor, in *IEEE International Conference on Software Analysis, Evolution and Reengineering, SANER 2022, Honolulu, HI, USA, March 15–18, 2022* (IEEE, 2022), pp. 164–168
10. C. Birchler, N. Ganz, S. Khatiri, A. Gambi, S. Panichella, Cost-effective simulation-based test selection in self-driving cars software. Sci. Comput. Program. **226**, 102926 (2023)
11. C. Birchler, S. Khatiri, B. Bosshard, A. Gambi, S. Panichella, Machine learning-based test selection for simulation-based testing of self-driving cars software. Empir. Softw. Eng. **28**(3), 71 (2023)
12. C. Birchler, S. Khatiri, P. Derakhshanfar, S. Panichella, A. Panichella, Single and multi-objective test cases prioritization for self-driving cars in virtual environments. ACM Trans. Softw. Eng. Methodol. **32**(2), 28:1–28:30 (2023)
13. C. Birchler, S. Khatiri, P. Rani, T. Kehrer, S. Panichella, A roadmap for simulation-based testing of autonomous cyber-physical systems: challenges and future direction (2025)
14. C. Birchler, S. Klikovits, M. Fazzini, S. Panichella, ICST tool competition 2025-self-driving car testing track, in *2025 IEEE/ACM International Conference on Software Testing, Verification and Validation (ICST)* (2025)
15. C. Birchler, S. Klikovits, M. Fazzini, S. Panichella, SBFT tool competition 2025-CPS-SDC regression testing track, in *IEEE/ACM International Workshop on Search-Based and Fuzz Testing, SBFT@ICSE 2025* (2025)
16. C. Birchler, T.K. Mohammed, P. Rani, T. Nechita, T. Kehrer, S. Panichella, How does simulation-based testing for self-driving cars match human perception? in *ACM International Conference on the Foundations of Software Engineering* (2024)
17. C. Birchler, C. Rohrbach, T. Kehrer, S. Panichella, Sensodat: simulation-based sensor dataset of self-driving cars, in *21st IEEE/ACM International Conference on Mining Software Repositories, MSR 2024, Lisbon, Portugal, April 15–16, 2024*, ed. by D. Spinellis, A. Bacchelli, E. Constantinou (ACM, 2024), pp. 510–514
18. C. Birchler, C. Rohrbach, H. Kim, A. Gambi, T. Liu, J. Horneber, T. Kehrer, S. Panichella, TEASER: simulation-based CAN bus regression testing for self-driving cars software, in *38th IEEE/ACM International Conference on Automated Software Engineering, ASE 2023, Luxembourg, September 11–15, 2023* (IEEE, 2023), pp. 2058–2061

19. F.Ö. Çatak, T. Yue, S. Ali, Uncertainty-aware prediction validator in deep learning models for cyber-physical system data. ACM Trans. Softw. Eng. Methodol. **31**(4), 79:1–79:31 (2022)
20. J. Collins, R. Brown, J. Leitner, D. Howard, Traversing the reality gap via simulator tuning (2020), arXiv:2003.01369
21. K. Deb, S. Agrawal, A. Pratap, T. Meyarivan, A fast elitist non-dominated sorting genetic algorithm for multi-objective optimisation: NSGA-II, in *Parallel Problem Solving from Nature - PPSN VI, 6th International Conference, Paris, France, September 18–20, 2000, Proceedings*, ed. by M. Schoenauer, K. Deb, G. Rudolph, X. Yao, E. Lutton, J.J. M. Guervós, H. Schwefel. Lecture Notes in Computer Science, vol. 1917 (Springer, 2000), pp. 849–858
22. A. Di Sorbo, F. Zampetti, A. Visaggio, M. Di Penta, S. Panichella, Automated identification and qualitative characterization of safety concerns reported in uav software platforms. ACM Trans. Softw. Eng. Methodol. **32**(3), (2023)
23. J. Garcia, Y. Feng, J. Shen, S. Almanee, Y. Xia, Q.A. Chen, A comprehensive study of autonomous vehicle bugs, in *ICSE '20: 42nd International Conference on Software Engineering, Seoul, South Korea, 27 June–19 July, 2020* (ACM, 2020), pp. 385–396
24. J. García, J.M. Molina. Simulation in real conditions of navigation and obstacle avoidance with px4/gazebo platform. Pers. Ubiquitous Comput. 1–21 (2020)
25. L. Han, S. Ali, T. Yue, A. Arrieta, M. Arratibel, Uncertainty-aware robustness assessment of industrial elevator systems. ACM Trans. Softw. Eng. Methodol. **32**(4), 95:1–95:51 (2023)
26. C. Hildebrandt, S. Elbaum, World-in-the-loop simulation for autonomous systems validation, in *2021 IEEE International Conference on Robotics and Automation (ICRA)* (IEEE, 2021), pp. 10912–10919
27. S. Höfer, K. Bekris, A. Handa, J.C. Gamboa, M. Mozifian, F. Golemo, C. Atkeson, D. Fox, K. Goldberg, J. Leonard et al., Sim2real in robotics and automation: applications and challenges. IEEE Trans. Autom. Sci. Eng. **18**(2), 398–400 (2021)
28. R. Kallis, O. Chaparro, A.D. Sorbo, S. Panichella, Nlbse'22 tool competition, in *2022 IEEE/ACM 1st International Workshop on Natural Language-Based Software Engineering (NLBSE 2022), Co-located with ICSE 2022, Pittsburgh, PA, USA, May 8, 2022*, ed. by A. D. Sorbo, S. Panichella (ACM/IEEE, 2022), pp. 25–28
29. R. Kallis, A.D. Sorbo, G. Canfora, S. Panichella, Ticket tagger: machine learning driven issue classification, in *2019 IEEE International Conference on Software Maintenance and Evolution, ICSME 2019, Cleveland, OH, USA, September 29–October 4, 2019* (IEEE, 2019), pp. 406–409
30. R. Kallis, A.D. Sorbo, G. Canfora, S. Panichella, Predicting issue types on GitHub. Sci. Comput. Program. **205**, 102598 (2021)
31. S. Khatiri, F.M. Amin, S. Panichella, P. Tonella, When uncertainty leads to unsafety. Empirical insights into the role of uncertainty in unmanned aerial vehicle safety. Empir. Softw. Eng. (2025)
32. S. Khatiri, S. Panichella, P. Tonella, Simulation-based test case generation for unmanned aerial vehicles in the neighborhood of real flights, in *International Conference on Software Testing, Verification and Validation* (IEEE, 2023), pp. 281–292
33. S. Khatiri, S. Panichella, P. Tonella, Simulation-based testing of unmanned aerial vehicles with aerialist, in *International Conference on Software Engineering (ICSE)* (2024)
34. S. Khatiri, P. Saurabh, T. Zimmermann, C. Munasinghe, C. Birchler, S. Panichella, SBFT tool competition 2024-cps-uav test case generation track, in *IEEE/ACM International Workshop on Search-Based and Fuzz Testing, SBFT@ICSE 2024* (2024)
35. S. Khatiri, A.D. Sorbo, F. Zampetti, C.A. Visaggio, M.D. Penta, S. Panichella, Identifying safety-critical concerns in unmanned aerial vehicle software platforms with SALIENT. SoftwareX **27**, 101748 (2024)
36. S. Khatiri, T. Zohdinasab, P. Saurabh, D. Humeniuk, S. Panichella, ICST tool competition 2025-CPS-UAV test case generation track, in *IEEE/ACM International Conference on Software Testing, Verification and Validation (ICST)*, p. 2025 (2025)
37. S. Khatiri, T. Zohdinasab, P. Saurabh, D. Humeniuk, S. Panichella, SBFT tool competition 2025-CPS-UAV test case generation track, in *IEEE/ACM International Workshop on Search-Based and Fuzz Testing, SBFT@ICSE 2025* (2025)

38. N.P. Koenig, A. Howard, Design and use paradigms for gazebo, an open-source multi-robot simulator, in *International Conference on Intelligent Robots and Systems* (IEEE, 2004), pp. 2149–2154
39. T. Laurent, S. Klikovits, P. Arcaini, F. Ishikawa, A. Ventresque, Parameter coverage for testing of autonomous driving systems under uncertainty. ACM Trans. Softw. Eng. Methodol. **32**(3), 58:1–58:31 (2023)
40. T. Ma, S. Ali, T. Yue, Testing self-healing cyber-physical systems under uncertainty with reinforcement learning: an empirical study. Empir. Softw. Eng. **26**(3), 52 (2021)
41. T. Mancini, I. Melatti, E. Tronci, Optimizing highly-parallel simulation-based verification of cyber-physical systems. IEEE Trans. Softw. Eng. **49**(9), 4443–4455 (2023)
42. Matternet, Faa grants approval to matternet for single pilot to operate up to 20 drones at test site. Unmanned Publications. Accessed 16 Dec 2023
43. R.T. McAllister, Y. Gal, A. Kendall, M. Van Der Wilk, A. Shah, R. Cipolla, A. Weller, Concrete problems for autonomous vehicle safety: advantages of Bayesian deep learning, in *International Joint Conferences on Artificial Intelligence, Inc.* (2017)
44. L. Meier, D. Honegger, M. Pollefeys, Px4: a node-based multithreaded open source robotics framework for deeply embedded platforms, in *International Conference on Robotics and Automation* (IEEE, 2015), pp. 6235–6240
45. R. Michelmore, M. Wicker, L. Laurenti, L. Cardelli, Y. Gal, M. Kwiatkowska, Uncertainty quantification with statistical guarantees in end-to-end autonomous driving control, in *2020 IEEE International Conference on Robotics and Automation (ICRA)* (IEEE, 2020), pp. 7344–7350
46. A. Ngo, M.P. Bauer, M. Resch, A multi-layered approach for measuring the simulation-to-reality gap of radar perception for autonomous driving, in *24th IEEE International Intelligent Transportation Systems Conference, ITSC 2021, Indianapolis, IN, USA, September 19–22, 2021* (IEEE, 2021), pp. 4008–4014
47. V. Nguyen, S. Huber, A. Gambi, SALVO: automated generation of diversified tests for self-driving cars from existing maps, in *International Conference on Artificial Intelligence Testing* (IEEE, 2021), pp. 128–135
48. S. Panichella, *Enhancing Security Awareness and Education for LLMs* (Springer Nature Switzerland, Cham, 2024), pp. 165–173
49. S. Panichella, *Vulnerabilities Introduced by LLMs Through Code Suggestions* (Springer Nature Switzerland, Cham, 2024), pp. 87–97
50. S. Panichella, A.D. Sorbo, E. Guzman, C.A. Visaggio, G. Canfora, H.C. Gall, How can I improve my app? Classifying user reviews for software maintenance and evolution, in *2015 IEEE International Conference on Software Maintenance and Evolution, ICSME 2015, Bremen, Germany, September 29–October 1, 2015*, ed. by R. Koschke, J. Krinke, M.P. Robillard (IEEE Computer Society, 2015), pp. 281–290
51. M. Park, H. Jang, T. Byun, Y. Choi, Property-based testing for LG home appliances using accelerated software-in-the-loop simulation, in *International Conference on Software Engineering* (ACM, 2020), pp. 120–129
52. A. Piazzoni, J. Cherian, M. Azhar, J.Y. Yap, J.L.W. Shung, R. Vijay, Vista: a framework for virtual scenario-based testing of autonomous vehicles, in *International Conference on Artificial Intelligence Testing* (IEEE, 2021), pp. 143–150
53. PX4, Px4 Simulation (2021), https://docs.px4.io/v1.12/en/simulation/
54. PX4.io. Obstacle Avoidance | px4 User Guide (2022), https://docs.px4.io/master/en/computer_vision/obstacle_avoidance.html. Accessed 07 Feb 2022
55. E. Salvato, G. Fenu, E. Medvet, F.A. Pellegrino, Crossing the reality gap: a survey on sim-to-real transferability of robot controllers in reinforcement learning. IEEE Access (2021)
56. S.Y. Shin, K. Chaouch, S. Nejati, M. Sabetzadeh, L.C. Briand, F. Zimmer, Uncertainty-aware specification and analysis for hardware-in-the-loop testing of cyber-physical systems. J. Syst. Softw. **171**, 110813 (2021)
57. A.D. Sorbo, S. Panichella, C.V. Alexandru, J. Shimagaki, C.A. Visaggio, G. Canfora, H.C. Gall, What would users change in my app? Summarizing app reviews for recommending

software changes, in *Proceedings of the 24th ACM SIGSOFT International Symposium on Foundations of Software Engineering, FSE 2016, Seattle, WA, USA, November 13–18, 2016*, ed. by T. Zimmermann, J. Cleland-Huang, Z. Su (ACM, 2016), pp. 499–510
58. A. Stocco, M. Weiss, M. Calzana, P. Tonella, Misbehaviour prediction for autonomous driving systems, in *Proceedings of the ACM/IEEE 42nd International Conference on Software Engineering*, ed. by G. Rothermel, D. Bae (ACM, 2020), pp. 359–371
59. S. Su, Y. Li, S. He, S. Han, C. Feng, C. Ding, F. Miao, Uncertainty quantification of collaborative detection for self-driving, in *IEEE International Conference on Robotics and Automation, ICRA 2023, London, UK, May 29–June 2, 2023* (IEEE, 2023), pp. 5588–5594
60. C.S. Timperley, A. Afzal, D.S. Katz, J.M. Hernandez, C. Le Goues, Crashing simulated planes is cheap: can simulation detect robotics bugs early? in *2018 IEEE 11th International Conference on Software Testing, Verification and Validation (ICST)* (IEEE, 2018), pp. 331–342
61. D. Wang, S. Li, G. Xiao, Y. Liu, Y. Sui, An exploratory study of autopilot software bugs in unmanned aerial vehicles, in *ACM Joint Meeting on European Software Engineering Conference and Symposium on the Foundations of Software Engineering*, pp. 20–31 (2021)
62. M. Weiss, P. Tonella, Fail-safe execution of deep learning based systems through uncertainty monitoring, in *2021 14th IEEE Conference on Software Testing, Verification and Validation (ICST)* (IEEE, 2021), pp. 24–35
63. F. Wotawa, On the use of available testing methods for verification & validation of ai-based software and systems, in *Workshop on Artificial Intelligence Safety. CEUR Workshop Proceedings*, vol. 2808 (CEUR-WS.org, 2021)
64. L. Wu, Z. Xi, Z. Zheng, X. Li, Application of metamorphic testing on UAV path planning software. J. Syst. Softw. **204**, 111769 (2023)
65. Q. Xu, S. Ali, T. Yue, Digital twin-based anomaly detection in cyber-physical systems, in *Conference on Software Testing, Verification and Validation* (IEEE, 2021), pp. 205–216
66. F. Zampetti, R. Kapur, M. Di Penta, S. Panichella, An empirical characterization of software bugs in open-source cyber–physical systems. J. Syst. Softw. **192**, 111425 (2022)
67. F. Zampetti, D.A. Tamburri, S. Panichella, A. Panichella, G. Canfora, M.D. Penta, Continuous integration and delivery practices for cyber-physical systems: an interview-based study. ACM Trans. Softw. Eng. Methodol. **32**(3), 73:1–73:44 (2023)
68. F. Zampetti, C. Vassallo, S. Panichella, G. Canfora, H. Gall, M. Di Penta, An empirical characterization of bad practices in continuous integration. Empir. Softw. Eng. (2019)

Responsible DevOps for Cyber-Physical Systems

Catia Trubiani, Aldeida Aleti, Birthe Böhm, Zhehua Zhou, and Lei Ma

Abstract Cyber-Physical Systems (CPS) are integral to critical domains such as healthcare, autonomous transportation, and industrial automation, seamlessly bridging the physical and digital worlds. As these systems grow in complexity and impact, there is an urgent need to adopt responsible development and operational practices. This chapter introduces the concept of Responsible DevOps, a framework that extends traditional DevOps methodologies by embedding ethical, social, and sustainability considerations into the lifecycle management of CPS. Unlike conventional DevOps, which primarily focuses on speed, efficiency, and automation, Responsible DevOps emphasizes human-centric values and systemic accountability across all stages of development and deployment. The chapter explores six key dimensions essential for Responsible DevOps in CPS: human interaction, sustainability, bias, fairness, privacy, and explainability. To support practitioners and researchers, the chapter also proposes practical mitigation strategies and guiding practices for each dimension. These include design-time and run-time techniques, organizational policies, and tool-supported interventions that foster more ethical, inclusive, and robust CPS development. By embedding responsibility as a first-class concern in DevOps

C. Trubiani
Gran Sasso Science Institute, L'Aquila, Italy
e-mail: catia.trubiani@gssi.it

A. Aleti (✉)
Monash University, Melbourne, Australia
e-mail: aldeida.aleti@monash.edu

B. Böhm
Siemens AG, Erlangen, Germany
e-mail: birthe.boehm@siemens.com

Z. Zhou · L. Ma
University of Alberta, Edmonton, Canada
e-mail: zhehua1@ualberta.ca

L. Ma
e-mail: ma.lei@acm.org

L. Ma
The University of Tokyo, Tokyo, Japan

S. Panichella et al. (eds.), *Roadmap for DevOps in Cyber-Physical Systems*,
https://doi.org/10.1007/978-981-95-1786-2_7

processes, this framework paves the way for the development of CPS that not only perform reliably but also align with broader societal values and expectations.

1 Introduction and Motivation

Cyber-Physical Systems (CPS) integrate computational and physical processes, interacting closely with their environment through sensing, computation, and actuation [10, 16]. These systems are central to advancements in diverse domains such as healthcare, autonomous transportation, energy management, and industrial automation. However, their inherent complexity and the high stakes associated with their operation demand not only robust software engineering practices but also responsible approaches to their modeling, development and deployment [71, 117].

DevOps, a methodology that combines software development (Dev) and operations (Ops), offers significant potential to improve the lifecycle management of CPS through its focus on collaboration, automation, and continuous delivery [1]. Yet, applying DevOps in the context of CPS introduces unique challenges that go beyond traditional software engineering practices. These challenges arise from the hybrid nature of CPS, where software must seamlessly integrate with physical components to ensure reliability, safety, and real-time responsiveness [60]. Moreover, CPS often operate in unpredictable and dynamic environments, necessitating robust human interaction and adaptability [7, 105].

The concept of Responsible DevOps for CPS extends the traditional DevOps framework by embedding ethical, social, and sustainability principles into its core practices. This chapter examines six critical dimensions: human interaction, sustainability, bias, fairness, privacy, and explainability, which are essential to fostering responsible practices in the development, deployment, and operation of CPS.

Human interaction is vital throughout the DevOps lifecycle, ensuring that human oversight and expertise guide the design, testing, and maintenance of CPS to adapt effectively to real-world complexities [19, 20]. Sustainability [34] emerges as an imperative in the face of the growing energy demands and environmental concerns associated with CPS development and operations, highlighting the need for energy-efficient software and hardware solutions. Similarly, addressing bias and fairness is crucial to preventing the amplification of social inequities and ensuring equitable outcomes in CPS decision-making processes [56].

Privacy [46, 98] is another cornerstone of Responsible DevOps, given the vast amounts of sensitive data that CPS collect and process. Protecting user data and ensuring compliance with privacy regulations are critical to fostering trust and safeguarding against ethical violations. Finally, explainability [26] is central to building user confidence and accountability, particularly in systems incorporating AI components. Transparent and interpretable system behavior allows users to understand and trust CPS decisions, especially in safety-critical scenarios [33, 116].

This chapter discusses each of these dimensions, providing an overview of the existing literature and actionable insights, methodologies, and real-world examples to illustrate the principles of Responsible DevOps. It highlights the interdisciplinary nature of CPS development, where collaboration between software engineers, domain experts, end-users, and policymakers is essential. The responsible DevOps practices discussed in this chapter can help organizations to ensure that CPS operate not only efficiently and effectively but also ethically, equitably, and sustainably.

2 Core Aspects

2.1 Human Interaction

Human interaction is paramount in DevOps for Cyber-Physical Systems (CPS), as these systems often operate in dynamic, complex environments where automated testing and monitoring cannot address every potential scenario. Human oversight, intervention, and judgment play a vital role in ensuring the safety, reliability, and ethical operation of CPS, especially in critical applications such as healthcare, transportation, and industrial automation [48]. CPS equipped with user-centered interfaces could enable operators to make informed decisions, quickly respond to anomalies, and manage system behaviors under unpredictable conditions, offering considerable advantages [108]. Moreover, the continuous involvement of human expertise throughout the DevOps lifecycle allows CPS to adapt effectively to changing environments and various user needs, enhancing their trust, accountability, and resilience [28]. In essence, human interaction is an indispensable aspect of responsible DevOps in CPS, bridging the gap between automated processes and the real-world demands of safety and reliability [75, 122].

Human interaction in CPS can be effectively structured across three critical phases: *development*, *deployment*, and *maintenance*. In the development phase, human roles are integral to designing and rigorously testing systems to ensure they can address a broad spectrum of real-world scenarios, with a focus on edge cases that could impact safety, reliability, and performance [36, 77]. Human experts, including developers, engineers, and domain specialists, contribute their insights to create robust designs that anticipate potential risks and unexpected conditions [121]. The key to effective human interaction in the development phase lies in building a reliable and accurate system model [70]. A representative model serves as the foundation for analysis, design, and testing, allowing developers and engineers to simulate and anticipate real-world challenges. Methods for building system models typically involve a combination of mathematical modeling, simulations, and data-driven approaches. Mathematical models use differential equations and control theory to represent the physical dynamics of the system [31], while simulations enable testing under various scenarios to validate performance and identify potential vulnerabilities [55]. Data-driven models, often incorporating machine learning techniques, are trained on historical or real-time data to enhance the system's predictive capabilities, especially in complex environments [115]. A comprehensive model is able to capture both the physical and computational aspects of a CPS. To increase human interaction in model development, using interactive modeling tools and visualization software could greatly facilitate users to intuitively engage with model parameters, analyze outcomes, and make adjustments, fostering a deeper understanding of the system model [92, 101]. Such a human-centered CPS model empowers developers to rigorously evaluate system behavior across various conditions, ensuring it meets safety and performance standards before deployment. Additionally, a well-constructed model improves transparency, allowing designers to effectively comprehend, diagnose, and refine system processes.

It is worth mentioning that, in recent years, AI techniques have been widely used in modern CPS [112]. These AI-enabled CPS (AI-CPS) are able to process vast amounts of data, learn from their environments, and adapt to complex, dynamic conditions [86]. However, the inclusion of AI components introduces unique challenges in building accurate and reliable system models. Traditional modeling approaches struggle to fully account for the adaptive and often opaque nature of AI decision-making processes, making it difficult to predict system behavior in all scenarios [89]. To address this, Explainable AI (XAI) [110] frameworks could be employed to enhance transparency, providing insights into AI-driven decisions and allowing human operators to understand, evaluate, and guide system actions. Increasing human interaction within AI-CPS development can be achieved by involving domain experts in the training, testing, and interpretation phases, where human feedback helps to refine AI responses [111]. Interactive dashboards and interpretable metrics could also allow operators to engage with AI outputs, strengthening their ability to monitor and adjust system performance as needed. This human-centered development process could make AI-CPS more trustworthy and adaptable to real-world challenges.

During the deployment phase, human interaction centers on the monitoring and adaptation of CPS within real-world settings [69, 73], where operators need clear visualizations, decision-support tools, and the capacity to intervene swiftly if anomalies occur. Human-centered toolchains for system monitoring, version control, and asset management are critical in this phase [108]. Monitoring tools alert operators to unusual patterns, enabling timely intervention, while version control tools ensure software and configuration updates are traceable and reversible if needed. Asset management tools keep track of the physical and digital components of the CPS, giving operators a comprehensive view of system assets and configurations. These toolchains, often designed with intuitive interfaces, real-time alerts, and clear data visualizations, offer valuable insights into system performance and safety compliance, enabling operators to make timely and informed decisions. By streamlining information flow and making critical data easily interpretable, these human-centered toolchains enhance CPS reliability and allow for swift responses to dynamic operational requirements. This structured approach in deployment promotes CPS stability, safety, and adaptability, empowering experts to refine operations in response to evolving conditions and continuous feedback.

Finally, in the maintenance phase of CPS, ongoing human involvement is essential for inspecting and updating systems based on operational feedback, security needs, and evolving regulatory requirements [108]. An interactive software toolchain can significantly aid developers in identifying fault patterns within CPS, enabling them to analyze historical data and real-time performance metrics to quickly pinpoint anomalies and systemic issues. This proactive approach allows for timely interventions and adjustments to enhance system reliability [83]. Moreover, a visualization tool can also play an important role in system enhancement by providing developers with intuitive representations of system behavior and performance trends [50, 79]. These visual tools facilitate the exploration of potential modifications, validation of new models, and assurance that the CPS continues to meet safety standards and operational objectives. Together, these toolchains foster continuous improvement and responsiveness in CPS maintenance.

2.2 Sustainability

The aspect of sustainability got more and more attention over the last years due to environmental concerns but also other reasons such as cost reduction or limited available raw materials. *Sustainable* in general means to be "capable of being maintained or continued at a certain rate or level" [34]. In most sources, three dimensions of sustainability are addressed, which are environmental, social, and economic sustainability [84]. Other dimensions such as institutional, cultural, individual, or technical sustainability were added during the last years [11, 84]. Sustainable DevOps should consider all dimensions of sustainability, however, the influence of DevOps on some of the dimensions is not obvious, e.g., on society. In contrast, technical and environmental sustainability are directly applicable.

Technical sustainability addresses the "longevity of information, systems, and infrastructure and their adequate evolution with changing surrounding conditions" [11]. In fact, technical sustainability has been a requirement in industry for a long time, e.g., in power plants or factories which are usually planned to run for several decades with only few and short interruptions. When it comes to DevOps for CPS, then the technical resources are relevant, e.g., servers, edge devices, scripts, discipline-specific tools, or software code.

Environmental sustainability refers to ensuring the survival of our environment and protect it from possible harm caused by human activities. In terms of CPS, their software as well as their hardware have to be considered to achieve environmental sustainability. Although software does not create emissions by itself, it needs hardware to run on which is responsible for significant emissions. All in all, software-related CO_2 emissions contribute 4–5% of global carbon emissions which roughly is the same as "all aviation, shipping, and rail combined" [42]. And it is expected that electricity consumption will increase moderately during the next years despite efforts to improve hardware efficiency [4].

To assess the impact of software on the environment, the embedded carbon footprint of all hardware products used as well as the caused emissions when running the software have to be taken into account. In addition, all the efforts for creating and maintaining the software, among others, could be added.

Since the first step to improve is usually to measure, over the past years a lot of tools have been developed to measure or estimate the energy consumption or emissions caused by software applications (e.g., see [41]). For hardware products, there are already established Life Cycle Assessments (LCAs) available for assessing their environmental impact [68] and LCA standards were elaborated within the ISO 14040 standard [37].

New guidelines and approaches are currently being developed to transfer LCAs to software, e.g., the Greenhouse Gas standard—ICT Sector [25], an LCA by the European Telecommunications Standards Institute (ETSI) [59], or by the International Telecommunication Union ITU-T [93–96]. However, their implementation takes lots of effort since the whole lifecycle of software is considered in detail including the used hardware. For example, even the impact of traveling for meetings during the development of the software is considered [59]. But what is more, the methodology is not fully defined yet and leaves room for interpretation. And data on caused emissions is sometimes difficult to get, e.g., when the software is running in commercial clouds. That is why organizations like the Green Software Foundation (GSF) are working on a more hands-on approach with their Software Carbon Intensity Specification (SCI) which is currently in the process of standardization as ISO/IEC 21031 [38].

The Green Software Foundation focuses on carbon equivalent emissions of software and defines three general levers to reduce those: energy efficiency, carbon awareness, and hardware efficiency [40].

Hardware efficiency means to use hardware with a minimum embedded carbon footprint. This also includes the provisioning of hardware according to actual needs and selection of hardware according to its embedded carbon footprint. In addition, a maximum device utilization is targeted which results in decreased embedded carbon per unit of work [9]. This relates to the DevOps infrastructure as well as the hardware needed and integrated in the CPS itself either physically or virtually [40].

Carbon awareness targets using green energy whenever possible. Typical measures include the supply with green energy but also location and temporal shifting and shaping of the demand according to the availability of green energy [40]. An example for carbon awareness is to schedule extensive testing during periods or in areas in which green energy is available. For example, testing of CPS software could be shifted to data centers in countries which have a high share of green energy or to time slots when the sun is shining and providing green energy [88].

The third lever energy efficiency aims to minimize the use of energy per unit of work which demands that the software applications themselves get more energy-efficient [40]. Examples cover a wide range such as using an energy-efficient programming language [80], applying green software patterns and guidelines during development [32, 39], CI/CD pipeline optimizations such as change-based testing [87], or searching for alternatives for requirements on CPS that will result in high resource consumption (e.g., strict performance requirements).

Although there is a lot of ongoing research regarding Sustainable DevOps, there are still a lot of challenges to be solved. These challenges range from measuring or estimating the energy consumption of software to identifying potential improvements and implementing these improvements in an optimal way.

Since sustainability is one of numerous qualities of a system, the interplay between these qualities has to be taken into account as well. Finding a balance between these qualities is an optimization problem which requires a lot of insights as input. For example, reducing tests will reduce the carbon footprint immediately but may have impact on the user-perceived quality or even on safety which may not be acceptable. Therefore, the goal may be to remove tests which are not necessary or redundant and do not have any effect on other qualities.

Artificial Intelligence may be a mighty tool in implementing Sustainable DevOps and, vice versa, needs to get more sustainable itself [23].

2.3 Fairness

Humans are inscrutable in a way that algorithms are not. As AI algorithms are created by people, it is inevitable that their biases will end up in code, resulting in biased AI [81]. Unlike humans, however, AI systems can be tested, creating the potential for new forms of transparency and, therefore, opportunities to detect unconscious biases that are otherwise unavailable [44]. The proposed approach will make it possible to discover biases in AI decisions prior to deploying them, and enable companies to develop a strategy on how to address biased AI behavior (e.g., repairing the AI algorithm, manually reviewing and modifying biased decisions, or not using the AI system).

While AI bias is a widely reported issue and has been extensively investigated in the context of Machine Learning algorithms [118], it unfortunately receives very little attention during the development life cycle. Fairness testing [44] is one of the very few works to address this issue by measuring AI discrimination. However, discrimination is different from bias. *Discrimination* is a difference in the software output when changing a field in the input (e.g., from cat to dog). Discrimination has no valuation. *Bias* is our valuation of a discrimination as wrongful, which requires human-in-the-loop approaches for detecting and repairing AI bias.

Bias refers to wrongful discrimination against certain individuals or groups of individuals in favor of others [43]. In numerous forms, bias may infiltrate software systems, and in particular AI-based systems, even if sensitive attributes such as gender, ethnicity or sexual identity are excluded. AI systems learn to make decisions based on training data, which may contain skewed human decisions or represent historical or social inequities. Examples of bias are increasingly prevalent, and in the majority cases, these biases are hidden and unconscious, making them harder to detect. Examples include facial recognition systems that perform poorly on female and African–American faces [67], YouTube's automatic captions for men's speech are more accurate than women's [102], assistant robots in aged care centers have been found to create anxiety in seniors when using pleasant conversations and hiding the truth [3], natural language processing tools to detect hate speech online are biased against African–American people [2], Amazon software decided not to offer same-day delivery to predominantly minority neighborhoods [58], and Staples offered online discounts to customers only in wealthier and more affluent neighborhoods [81].

Existing work on detecting AI bias [44, 81, 106, 119], focus on how to generate test cases that detect bias. These approaches are completely automated and do not consider the human in the loop. Humans have some complex rules about what is a biased decision and when it is okay to consider protected attributes when making decision. For example, it is unlawful for a company to adopt an AI-generated compensation plan with one pay scale for men and a different lower pay scale for women. However, insurance companies treat men and women differently, with one set of rates for male drivers and a different set of rates for female drivers, a disparate treatment that is justified based on statistical differences in accident rates. For an AI programmed to slice enormous amounts of data in every way possible, this distinction may not be as obvious. Hence, bias is highly contextual, making humans an *irreplaceable* part of any potential software bias identification and repair.

Bias is also conditional on time and place. *Cultural bias* has been defined as the tendency to interpret a work or action according to culturally derived meanings [52]. The definition of bias also changes over time as awareness increases and consequently legal measures are put in place. Hence, bias is highly contextual and fluid, which makes humans an *irreplaceable* part of any potential software bias identification.

Various fairness measures have been introduced, such as conditional statistical parity [29], equal opportunity [53], counterfactual fairness [27], and equalized odds [53]. However, these measures are only applicable to classification-based machine learning (ML) systems and are not specifically designed for regression-based ML systems. Furthermore, different fairness measures capture different aspects of bias, making their suitability context- and domain-dependent [76]. For example, Dieterich et al. [35] found that COMPAS, an ML system used by some U.S. courts to predict recidivism, was not biased when assessed with disparate impact, but was later considered unfair when evaluated with other measures, such as the equality of error rates [6].

Similarly, various fairness testing approaches have been introduced in the software engineering literature [119]. These approaches aim to generate discriminatory inputs, which are test cases that reveal biases (i.e., individual discrimination, group discrimination, and causal discrimination) in the ML system under test (SUT). Black-box fairness testing methods, such as random test generation [44], regression testing [12–14, 21], directed and advanced test generation [15, 63, 64, 106], and symbolic generation [5], as well as white-box fairness testing approaches [120], have been proposed. However, these methods are designed primarily for classification-based ML systems and not for regression-based ML systems.

2.4 Explainability

The notion of explainability has been recently reviewed by Chazette et al. [26] that make an effort on understanding what explainability means from a software engineering perspective and how it impacts other quality aspects in a system. The outcome of this study indicates that explainability can be interpreted as an appropriate means of achieving crucial aspects in a system, such as transparency, accountability, and trustworthiness. There exist many quality characteristics that are influenced by the explainability, such as the transparency and the understandability, to mention the most crucial ones. In more concrete terms, explainability is recognized to have a positive impact on users since they can learn how a system works of how to best use a system, and even enhancing their knowledge toward solving problems [26]. Users' needs are recognized to be of key relevance, e.g., privacy awareness and satisfaction, and such needs call for methods and tools that quantify the different users' experiences.

Cyber-Physical Systems (CPS) pose additional challenges for explainability, given that their complexity is exacerbated by the control of different processes in the physical world, possibly with multiple users, changing contexts, and changing environmental conditions [103]. Specifically, software code needs to be distributed across different machines, it may run concurrently, and the interplay between software and hardware components may lead to the management of heterogeneous aspects [104]. All these aspects contribute to make difficult the process of monitoring the behavior of the system [99], and this is the reason why in the following we focus on some recent approaches that try to target explainability in CPS.

Blumreiter et al. [22] propose a framework, namely $MAB - EX$, that executes the following tasks: Monitor (M), Analyze (A), Build (B), and Explain (EX) the behavior of CPS. The overall goal is to support the users on understanding some decisions, e.g., in autonomous driving the vehicles may be stopped given that there is a priority vehicle (i.e., an ambulance or police) authorized to passing an obstacle, and this prevents other vehicles to circulate. The explanation builds upon the system actions, and interestingly not only to the actions taken so far but also to the ones that may happen in a look-ahead vision. This latest characteristic implies knowing in advance which events can happen and the different explanations for the phenomena, leading to predict CPS behavior and promptly act, if needed.

Kanak et al. [61] introduce an approach for advancing explainable and trustworthy AI that outlines a comprehensive six-dimensional concept encompassing transparency, fairness, responsibility, robustness, privacy, and safety. These diverse requirements are analyzed reporting projects that have been funded under the European H2020 programme, and explainability is of high relevance in many projects. This is due to the intrinsic nature of ML models that have been considered reliable [107], but their effectiveness is limited by the current inability of machines to explain their decisions and actions to human users [90].

Yazdanpanah et al. [113] present a study that highlights the centrality of responsibility in cultivating explainability, particularly in developing trustworthy AI systems with socio-technically desirable behavior. In the context of ensuring trustworthy behavior in AI systems, meeting socio-technical requirements entails both technical aspects (e.g., obstacle detection in autonomous vehicles) and the explanation of social considerations (e.g., knowing driving norms in a specific city). It is of key relevance to integrate responsibility in CPS decision-making, for instance systems need to resolve conflicts between individual goals and collective responsibilities, thus explaining the reason behind the taken decisions.

Steindl et al. [100] deal with the challenge of enhancing explainability within CPS. A solution is proposed to keep track of system events while being technology agnostic, in particular (i) a semantic model is foreseen to provide context, (ii) an event broker for capturing the communication among several components, even of different nature, and (iii) a set of components for the detection of system events. These components are applied in different application domains that are smart building and smart grid, and the results support the explainability, i.e., the system decisions are motivated to the users by reporting the set of events leading to such actions.

Weyns et al. [109] present a research agenda for smarter CPS, and explainability is reported as a key challenge for future research. There is a need for CPS to explain autonomous decisions to stakeholders, because this represents a prerequisite to establish trust. CPS require methods and tools that support the capability of keep traceability of the system structure and its behavior, along with the decisions and the rationale behind such choices. Explainability goes in the direction of making available this information, so that the users can comprehend the system behavior, thus improving the human–machine interactivity.

Overall, the explainability is assessed as a crucial aspect to establish human trust. The widely recognized link between explainability, transparency, and human trust is further highlighted in AI systems where people need a clear understanding of data usage and decision-making processes [97], thereby increasing the level of trust in the usage of CPS.

2.5 Privacy in CPS Development

In the fast-evolving landscape of modern CPS, privacy has emerged as a significant concern across various applications due to the growing integration with the Internet of Things (IoT) and big data analytics [46, 98]. Responsible DevOps practices should emphasize privacy protection throughout the entire CPS lifecycle, from design to deployment and beyond. This often encompasses two critical dimensions: data privacy and system privacy [51, 54]. Addressing both dimensions is vital for fostering trustworthiness and ensuring compliance with legal and ethical standards in the development and operation of these interconnected systems.

Data privacy primarily concerns the protection of sensitive information collected, processed, and stored within CPS [51]. As these systems often gather extensive data from users and devices, e.g., personal information and operational metrics, ensuring data privacy is usually both critical and challenging. To enhance data privacy, system designers can implement stringent access controls [74], data anonymization techniques [62, 91], and robust encryption protocols [49, 85] to safeguard data against unauthorized access and breaches. Meanwhile, compliance with established privacy regulations, e.g., the European Union's General Data Protection Regulation (EU GDPR) [45], is also essential, as these regulations typically mandate clear guidelines for data handling practices [8]. Another crucial aspect of data privacy in CPS is the continuous monitoring and assessment of privacy risks [24]. Due to the complexities of these systems, static privacy measures may become inadequate as new vulnerabilities and threats arise. Incorporating automated privacy risk assessments into the DevOps pipeline can facilitate the identification of potential weaknesses in real time [47, 82]. This strategy not only strengthens the resilience of CPS against privacy breaches but also enables system developers to adapt quickly to evolving regulatory requirements and emerging best practices.

On the other hand, system privacy focuses on protecting the integrity and confidentiality of the CPS infrastructure itself [46, 57]. This includes safeguarding the system from malicious attacks that could lead to the exposure of sensitive information. Since CPS involves communication among multiple devices and subsystems, vulnerabilities in one component can potentially affect the entire system. Effective measures should address both software and hardware vulnerabilities, with regular security assessments and risk testing helping to reinforce system safety. Furthermore, system privacy could also be extended to considerations about user consent and control over their interactions with CPS [114]. Users often serve as the first line of defense against privacy infringements, making it essential to equip them with the tools and information necessary to understand their rights and responsibilities concerning data usage [78]. Responsible DevOps practices should support transparent communication about system functionalities and privacy implications, enabling users to make informed decisions regarding their engagement with the CPS.

In summary, both data privacy and system privacy are crucial to ensuring responsible DevOps practices for CPS. By prioritizing these aspects, system developers can create secure and trustworthy systems that respect user privacy while delivering innovative solutions in a complex technological landscape.

3 The Path Forward

The topics discussed in this chapter are qualities that are often neglected for the sake of early results at low effort. Their benefits are often perceived as taking too much effort, and, as a consequence, legislation, the public voice, and the sense of responsibility of individuals or organizations are needed to push these topics forward. This also applies to sustainability. However, there are voices as Martin Lippert from VMware, who states that "most likely software with a much lower carbon intensity will be much more successful in the future than software with a higher one." [72]

There is also an additional benefit of increased sustainability since saving resources goes hand in hand with saving costs in some cases. FinOps is such an approach that “maximizes the business value of cloud, enables timely data-driven decision-making, and creates financial accountability through collaboration between engineering, finance, and business teams” [30]. Such approaches will support the overall goal of sustainability. Apart from costs, also qualities such as performance, maintainability, or modularity enforce or abate sustainability. Therefore, one of the next steps will be to explore the dependencies in this network of enforcing and interfering qualities.

Another pressing challenge is the development and refinement of methods to measure and estimate the sustainability footprint of software development and operations practices, particularly within the DevOps paradigm. Current methodologies for evaluating sustainability impacts are still in their infancy and lack the precision, reliability, and scalability required for widespread adoption. Advancing these methodologies is essential for establishing a foundation upon which organizations can evaluate their sustainability performance and identify areas for improvement. Measurement frameworks [18, 65] must take into account the diverse factors contributing to sustainability, including energy consumption, resource utilization, carbon emissions, and even indirect impacts such as supply chain effects.

Advancing fairness in Cyber-Physical Systems (CPS) requires a multifaceted approach that addresses biases at every stage of development, deployment, and operation. Future efforts should focus on developing fairness-aware testing approaches that can systematically detect and mitigate biases in CPS. Incorporating human-in-the-loop approaches will be crucial, ensuring that fairness considerations align with societal values and ethical principles rather than relying solely on automated algorithms. Additionally, developing new fairness metrics tailored to CPS applications is important, as existing metrics mainly focus on classification-based AI systems. Regulatory frameworks and industry best practices must also evolve to provide clear guidelines on fairness, ensuring that CPS operate equitably in diverse environments. Strengthening interdisciplinary collaboration between software engineers, ethicists, policymakers, and domain experts will further enhance the ability to design CPS that are not only technically robust but also socially responsible.

4 Conclusion

Responsible DevOps for CPS represents a critical shift in the development and operational practices necessary to address the ethical, social, and sustainability challenges posed by these complex systems. Embedding principles such as human interaction, sustainability, bias, fairness, privacy, and explainability into the DevOps framework enhances the trustworthiness, resilience, and equity of CPS.

This chapter explores key dimensions that are essential for adopting a responsible approach to DevOps, and illustrates how such practices can help mitigate risks and enhance trust, thus improving the perception of humans toward such systems. As CPS increasingly shape critical aspects of modern society, the integration of responsible principles into every phase of development and operation becomes paramount.

Moving forward, the emphasis must remain on advancing tools, methods, and frameworks [17, 18, 18, 66] that support these responsible practices. This will ensure that CPS not only meet technical and operational objectives but also align with broader societal values.

Competing Interests The authors have no conflicts of interest to declare that are relevant to the content of this chapter.

Acknowledgements We would like to thank Sebastiano Panichella for his valuable input and insightful suggestions on this chapter. His feedback contributed to improving the clarity and depth of our work.

References

1. Puppet and devops research and assessments (dora). 2016 state of devops report. (2016)
2. The algorithms that detect hate speech online are biased against black people (2019). Accessed 14 Oct 2020
3. Care robots for the elderly are dangerous (2020). Accessed 14 Oct 2020
4. I.E. Agency, Data centres and data transmission networks (2023). Accessed 23 Dec 2024
5. A. Aggarwal, P. Lohia, S. Nagar, K. Dey, D. Saha, Black box fairness testing of machine learning models, in *Proceedings of the 2019 27th ACM Joint Meeting on European Software Engineering Conference and Symposium on the Foundations of Software Engineering* (2019), pp. 625–635
6. J. Angwin, J. Larson, S. Mattu, L. Kirchner, Machine bias. Propublica (2016). Accessed 23 May 2016
7. M.N. Asmat, S. ur Rehman Khan, S. Hussain, Uncertainty handling in cyber-physical systems: state-of-the-art approaches, tools, causes, and future directions. J. Softw. Evol. Process. **35**(7) (2023)
8. S.S. Bakare, A.O. Adeniyi, C.U. Akpuokwe, N.E. Eneh, Data privacy laws and compliance: a comparative review of the eu gdpr and usa regulations. Comput. Sci. & IT Res. J. **5**(3), 528–543 (2024)
9. L.A. Barroso, U. Hölzle, The case for energy-proportional computing. Computer **40**(12), 33–37 (2007)
10. E. Bartocci, J. Deshmukh, A. Donzé, G. Fainekos, O. Maler, D. Ničković, S. Sankaranarayanan, *Specification-Based Monitoring of Cyber-Physical Systems: A Survey on Theory, Tools and Applications* (Springer, 2018), pp. 135–175
11. C. Becker, R. Chitchyan, L. Duboc, S. Easterbrook, B. Penzenstadler, N. Seyff, C.C. Venters, Sustainability design and software: The Karlskrona manifesto, in *2015 IEEE/ACM 37th IEEE International Conference on Software Engineering*, vol. 2 (2015), pp. 467–476
12. C. Birchler, N. Ganz, S. Khatiri, A. Gambi, S. Panichella, Cost-effective simulation-based test selection in self-driving cars software with SDC-Scissor, in *IEEE International Conference on Software Analysis, Evolution and Reengineering, SANER 2022, Honolulu, HI, USA, March 15–18, 2022* (IEEE, 2022), pp. 164–168
13. C. Birchler, N. Ganz, S. Khatiri, A. Gambi, S. Panichella, Cost-effective simulation-based test selection in self-driving cars software. Sci. Comput. Program. **226**, 102926 (2023)
14. C. Birchler, S. Khatiri, B. Bosshard, A. Gambi, S. Panichella, Machine learning-based test selection for simulation-based testing of self-driving cars software. Empir. Softw. Eng. **28**(3), 71 (2023)

15. C. Birchler, S. Khatiri, P. Derakhshanfar, S. Panichella, A. Panichella, Single and multi-objective test cases prioritization for self-driving cars in virtual environments. ACM Trans. Softw. Eng. Methodol. **32**(2), 28:1–28:30 (2023)
16. C. Birchler, S. Khatiri, P. Rani, T. Kehrer, S. Panichella, A roadmap for simulation-based testing of autonomous cyber-physical systems: challenges and future direction (2025)
17. C. Birchler, S. Klikovits, M. Fazzini, S. Panichella, ICST tool competition 2025 - self-driving car testing track, in *IEEE/ACM International Conference on Software Testing*. (ICST, Verification and Validation, 2025), p. 2025
18. C. Birchler, S. Klikovits, M. Fazzini, S. Panichella, SBFT tool competition 2025 - cps-sdc regression testing track, in *IEEE/ACM International Workshop on Search-Based and Fuzz Testing, SBFT@ICSE 2025* (2025)
19. C. Birchler, T.K. Mohammed, P. Rani, T. Nechita, T. Kehrer, S. Panichella, How does simulation-based testing for self-driving cars match human perception? 1(FSE) (2024)
20. C. Birchler, T.K. Mohammed, P. Rani, T. Nechita, T. Kehrer, S. Panichella, How does simulation-based testing for self-driving cars match human perception? in *ACM International Conference on the Foundations of Software Engineering* (2024)
21. C. Birchler, C. Rohrbach, H. Kim, A. Gambi, T. Liu, J. Horneber, T. Kehrer, S. Panichella, TEASER: simulation-based CAN bus regression testing for self-driving cars software, in *38th IEEE/ACM International Conference on Automated Software Engineering, ASE 2023, Luxembourg, September 11–15, 2023* (IEEE, 2023), pp. 2058–2061
22. M. Blumreiter, J. Greenyer, F.J.C. Garcia, V. Klös, M. Schwammberger, C. Sommer, A. Vogelsang, A. Wortmann, Towards self-explainable cyber-physical systems, in *Companion Proceedings of the International Conference on Model Driven Engineering Languages and Systems (MODELS-C)* (2019), pp. 543–548
23. V. Bolón-Canedo, L. Morán-Fernández, B. Cancela, A. Alonso-Betanzos, A review of green artificial intelligence: towards a more sustainable future. Neurocomputing **599**, 128096 (2024)
24. B. Bonakdarpour, J.V. Deshmukh, M. Pajic, Opportunities and challenges in monitoring cyber-physical systems security, in *Leveraging Applications of Formal Methods, Verification and Validation. Industrial Practice: 8th International Symposium, ISoLA 2018, Limassol, Cyprus, November 5–9, 2018, Proceedings, Part IV 8* (Springer, 2018), pp. 9–18
25. G.E.-S.I.G. Carbon Trust, Ict sector guidance built on the ghg protocol product life cycle accounting and reporting standard - chapter 1: Introduction and general principles (2017). Accessed 01 Feb 2025
26. L. Chazette, W. Brunotte, T. Speith, Exploring explainability: a definition, a model, and a knowledge catalogue, in *Proceedings of the International Conference on Requirements Engineering (RE)* (2021), pp. 197–208
27. S. Chiappa, Path-specific counterfactual fairness, in *Proceedings of the AAAI Conference on Artificial Intelligence,* vol. 33 (2019), pp. 7801–7808
28. C. Cimini, F. Pirola, R. Pinto, S. Cavalieri, A human-in-the-loop manufacturing control architecture for the next generation of production systems. J. Manuf. Syst. **54**, 258–271 (2020)
29. S. Corbett-Davies, E. Pierson, A. Feller, S. Goel, A. Huq, Algorithmic decision making and the cost of fairness, in *Proceedings of the 23rd ACM SIGKDD International Conference on Knowledge Discovery and Data Mining* (2017), pp. 797–806
30. F.F.T.A. Council, What is finops? (2023). Accessed 28 Jan 2025
31. P. Derler, E.A. Lee, A.S. Vincentelli, Modeling cyber-physical systems. Proc. IEEE **100**(1), 13–28 (2011)
32. S.W. Design, Web sustainability guidelines (2025). Accessed 28 May 2025
33. A. Di Sorbo, F. Zampetti, A. Visaggio, M. Di Penta, S. Panichella, Automated identification and qualitative characterization of safety concerns reported in uav software platforms. ACM Trans. Softw. Eng. Methodol. **32**(3) (2023)
34. O.E. Dictionary, Sustainable, adj. (2024)
35. W. Dieterich, C. Mendoza, T. Brennan. Compas risk scales: demonstrating accuracy equity and predictive parity. Northpoint Inc **7**(7.4), 1 (2016)

36. C. Emmanouilidis, P. Pistofidis, L. Bertoncelj, V. Katsouros, A. Fournaris, C. Koulamas, C. Ruiz-Carcel, Enabling the human in the loop: Linked data and knowledge in industrial cyber-physical systems. Annu. Rev. Control. **47**, 249–265 (2019)
37. I.O. for Standardization, ISO 14040:2006 Environmental management – Life cycle assessment – Principles and framework (2006). Accessed 23 Dec 2024
38. I. O. for Standardization/IEC (the International Electrotechnical Commission), ISO/IEC 21031:2024 Information Technology - Software Carbon Intensity (SCI) Specification (2024). Accessed 02 Jan 2025
39. G.S. Foundation, Green software patterns (2024). Accessed 02 Jan 2025
40. G.S. Foundation, Green software practitioner (2024). Accessed 23 Dec 2024
41. G.S. Foundation, Awesome green software (2025). Accessed 28 May 2025
42. G.S. Foundation, Software emissions are equivalent to air, rail, and shipping combined (2025). Accessed 06 May 2025
43. B. Friedman, H. Nissenbaum, Bias in computer systems. ACM Trans. Inf. Syst. **14**(3), 330–347 (1996)
44. S. Galhotra, Y. Brun, A. Meliou, Fairness testing: testing software for discrimination, in *Joint Meeting on Foundations of Software Engineering (FSE)* (ACM, 2017), pp. 498–510
45. G. GDPR, General data protection regulation. Regulation (EU) **679** (2016)
46. J. Giraldo, E. Sarkar, A.A. Cardenas, M. Maniatakos, M. Kantarcioglu, Security and privacy in cyber-physical systems: a survey of surveys. IEEE Design & Test **34**(4), 7–17 (2017)
47. G. Gonzalez-Granadillo, S.A. Menesidou, D. Papamartzivanos, R. Romeu, D. Navarro-Llobet, C. Okoh, S. Nifakos, C. Xenakis, E. Panaousis, Automated cyber and privacy risk management toolkit. Sensors **21**(16), 5493 (2021)
48. V. Gunes, S. Peter, T. Givargis, F. Vahid, A survey on concepts, applications, and challenges in cyber-physical systems. KSII Trans. Internet Inf. Syst. (TIIS) **8**(12), 4242–4268 (2014)
49. B.B. Gupta, K.-C. Li, V.C. Leung, K.E. Psannis, S. Yamaguchi et al., Blockchain-assisted secure fine-grained searchable encryption for a cloud-based healthcare cyber-physical system. IEEE/CAA J. Autom. Sinica **8**(12), 1877–1890 (2021)
50. D. Gürdür, J. El-Khoury, T. Seceleanu, L. Lednicki, Making interoperability visible: Data visualization of cyber-physical systems development tool chains. J. Ind. Inf. Integr. **4**, 26–34 (2016)
51. H. Habibzadeh, B.H. Nussbaum, F. Anjomshoa, B. Kantarci, T. Soyata, A survey on cybersecurity, data privacy, and policy issues in cyber-physical system deployments in smart cities. Sustain. Cities Soc. **50**, 101660 (2019)
52. A. Haddad, R. Purtilo, Respect in a diverse society. Health Professional and Patient Interaction, vol. 9 (2019)
53. M. Hardt, E. Price, N. Srebro, Equality of opportunity in supervised learning. Adv. Neural. Inf. Process. Syst. **29**, 3315–3323 (2016)
54. M.U. Hassan, M.H. Rehmani, J. Chen, Differential privacy techniques for cyber physical systems: a survey. IEEE Commun. Surv. & Tutor. **22**(1), 746–789 (2019)
55. P. Hehenberger, B. Vogel-Heuser, D. Bradley, B. Eynard, T. Tomiyama, S. Achiche, Design, modelling, simulation and integration of cyber physical systems: methods and applications. Comput. Ind. **82**, 273–289 (2016)
56. A. Hoenig, K. Roy, Y.T. Acquaah, S. Yi, S.S. Desai, Explainable ai for cyber-physical systems: issues and challenges. IEEE Access **12**, 73113–73140 (2024)
57. A. Humayed, J. Lin, F. Li, B. Luo, Cyber-physical systems security-a survey. IEEE Internet Things J. **4**(6), 1802–1831 (2017)
58. D. Ingold, S. Soper, Amazon doesn't consider the race of its customers. Should it? (2016). Accessed 14 Oct 2020
59. E.T.S. Institute, *ETSI ES 203 199 V1.3.1 (2015-02): Environmental Engineering (EE); Methodology for environmental Life Cycle Assessment (LCA) of Information and Communication Technology (ICT) goods, networks and services* (2015). Accessed 23 Dec 2024

60. D.S. Johnson, H. Koehneman, D. LaFortune, D. Leffingwell, S. Magill, S. Mayner, A. Ofer, R. Stroud, A. Wallgren, R. Yeman, *INDUSTRIAL DEVOPS - Applying DevOps and Continuous Delivery to Significant Cyber-Physical Systems* (National Academies Press, 2017)
61. A. Kanak, S. Ergün, A.S. Atalay, S. Persi, A.E.H. Karcı, A review and strategic approach for the transition towards third-wave trustworthy and explainable AI in Connected, Cooperative and Automated Mobility (CCAM), in *Proceedings of the Asia Pacific Conference on Communications (APCC)*, pp. 108–113 (2022)
62. M. Keshk, B. Turnbull, E. Sitnikova, D. Vatsalan, N. Moustafa, Privacy-preserving schemes for safeguarding heterogeneous data sources in cyber-physical systems. IEEE Access **9**, 55077–55097 (2021)
63. S. Khatiri, S. Panichella, P. Tonella, Simulation-based test case generation for unmanned aerial vehicles in the neighborhood of real flights, in *International Conference on Software Testing, Verification and Validation* (IEEE, 2023), pp. 281–292
64. S. Khatiri, S. Panichella, P. Tonella, Simulation-based testing of unmanned aerial vehicles with aerialist, in *International Conference on Software Engineering (ICSE)* (2024)
65. S. Khatiri, P. Saurabh, T. Zimmermann, C. Munasinghe, C. Birchler, S. Panichella, SBFT tool competition 2024 - cps-uav test case generation track, in *IEEE/ACM International Workshop on Search-Based and Fuzz Testing, SBFT@ICSE 2024* (2024)
66. S. Khatiri, T. Zohdinasab, P. Saurabh, D. Humeniuk, S. Panichella, ICST tool competition 2025 - CPS-UAV test case generation track, in *IEEE/ACM International Conference on Software Testing*. (ICST, Verification and Validation, 2025), p. 2025
67. B.F. Klare, M.J. Burge, J.C. Klontz, R.W.V. Bruegge, A.K. Jain, Face recognition performance: Role of demographic information. IEEE Trans. Inf. Forensics Secur. **7**(6), 1789–1801 (2012)
68. W. Klöpffer, B. Grahl, *Life Cycle Assessment (LCA): A Guide to Best Practice* (Wiley, 2014)
69. S. Kumar, C. Savur, F. Sahin, Survey of human-robot collaboration in industrial settings: awareness, intelligence, and compliance. IEEE Trans. Syst. Man Cybern.: Syst. **51**(1), 280–297 (2020)
70. E.A. Lee, The past, present and future of cyber-physical systems: a focus on models. Sensors **15**(3), 4837–4869 (2015)
71. E.A. Lee, Fundamental limits of cyber-physical systems modeling. Trans. Cyber-Phys. Syst. **1**(1), 3 (2017)
72. B. Linders, How software affects climate change, and what software engineers can do about it (2022). Accessed 28 Jan 2025
73. S.I. Lopes, A.M. Cruz, P.M. Moreira, C. Abreu, J.P. Silva, N. Lopes, J.M. Vieira, A. Curado, On the design of a human-in-the-loop cyber-physical system for online monitoring and active mitigation of indoor radon gas concentration, in *2018 IEEE International Smart Cities Conference (ISC2)* (IEEE, 2018), pp. 1–8
74. J. Lopez, J.E. Rubio, Access control for cyber-physical systems interconnected to the cloud. Comput. Netw. **134**, 46–54 (2018)
75. S. Lou, Z. Hu, Y. Zhang, Y. Feng, M. Zhou, C. Lv, Human-cyber-physical system for industry 5.0: a review from a human-centric perspective. IEEE Trans. Autom. Sci. Eng. 1–18 (2024)
76. N. Mehrabi, F. Morstatter, N. Saxena, K. Lerman, A. Galstyan, A survey on bias and fairness in machine learning (2019). arXiv:1908.09635
77. D.S. Nunes, P. Zhang, J.S. Silva, A survey on human-in-the-loop applications towards an internet of all. IEEE Commun. Surv. & Tutor. **17**(2), 944–965 (2015)
78. S. Oppl, C. Stary, Motivating users to manage privacy concerns in cyber-physical settings-a design science approach considering self-determination theory. Sustainability **14**(2), 900 (2022)
79. R. Penna, M. Amaral, D. Espíndola, S. Botelho, N. Duarte, C.E. Pereira, M. Zuccolotto, E.M. Frazzon, Visualization tool for cyber-physical maintenance systems, in *2014 12th IEEE International Conference on Industrial Informatics (INDIN)* (IEEE, 2014), pp. 566–571

80. R. Pereira, M. Couto, F. Ribeiro, R. Rua, J. Cunha, J.A.P. Fernandes, J.A. Saraiva, Energy efficiency across programming languages: how do energy, time, and memory relate? in *Proceedings of the 10th ACM SIGPLAN International Conference on Software Language Engineering*, SLE 2017, New York, NY, USA, 2017, pp. 256–267. Association for Computing Machinery
81. A. Perera, A. Aleti, C. Tantithamthavorn, J. Jiarpakdee, B. Turhan, L. Kuhn, K. Walker, Search-based fairness testing for regression-based machine learning systems. Empir. Softw. Eng. **27**(3), 1–36 (2022)
82. S.C. Phillips, S. Taylor, M. Boniface, S. Modafferi, M. Surridge, Automated knowledge-based cybersecurity risk assessment of cyber-physical systems. IEEE Access (2024)
83. M. Pinzone, F. Albè, D. Orlandelli, I. Barletta, C. Berlin, B. Johansson, M. Taisch, A framework for operative and social sustainability functionalities in human-centric cyber-physical production systems. Comput. & Indus. Eng. **139**, 105132 (2020)
84. B. Purvis, Y. Mao, D. Robinson, Three pillars of sustainability: in search of conceptual origins. Sustain. Sci. **14**(3), 681–695 (2019). (May)
85. H. Qiu, M. Qiu, M. Liu, G. Memmi, Secure health data sharing for medical cyber-physical systems for the healthcare 4.0. IEEE J. Biomed. Health Inf. **24**(9), 2499–2505 (2020)
86. P. Radanliev, D. De Roure, M. Van Kleek, O. Santos, U. Ani, Artificial intelligence in cyber physical systems. AI & Soc. **36**, 783–796 (2021)
87. R. Ramler, C. Salomon, G. Buchgeher, M. Lusser, Tool support for change-based regression testing: An industry experience report, in *Software Quality*. ed. by D. Winkler, S. Biffl, J. Bergsmann. Complexity and Challenges of Software Engineering in Emerging Technologies. (Springer International Publishing, Cham, 2017), pp.133–152
88. I. Riepin, T. Brown, V.M. Zavala, Spatio-temporal load shifting for truly clean computing. Adv. Appl. Energy **17**, 100202 (2025)
89. J. Sakhnini, H. Karimipour, Ai and security of cyber physical systems: opportunities and challenges, in *Security of Cyber-Physical Systems: Vulnerability and Impact* (2020), pp. 1–4
90. W. Samek, K.-R. Müller, Towards explainable artificial intelligence, in *Explainable AI: Interpreting, Explaining and Visualizing Deep Learning* (2019), pp. 5–22
91. F.C. Sangogboye, R. Jia, T. Hong, C. Spanos, M.B. Kjærgaard, A framework for privacy-preserving data publishing with enhanced utility for cyber-physical systems. ACM Trans. Sensor Netw. (TOSN) **14**(3–4), 1–22 (2018)
92. G.N. Schroeder, C. Steinmetz, R.N. Rodrigues, R.V.B. Henriques, A. Rettberg, C.E. Pereira, A methodology for digital twin modeling and deployment for industry 4.0. Proc. IEEE **109**(4), 556–567 (2020)
93. I.T.U.T.S. Sector, L.1420: Methodology for energy consumption and greenhouse gas emissions impact assessment of information and communication technologies in organizations (2012). Accessed 02 Jan 2025
94. I. T. U. T. S. Sector, L.1430: Methodology for assessment of the environmental impact of information and communication technology greenhouse gas and energy projects (2013). Accessed 02 Jan 2025
95. I. T. U. T. S. Sector. L.1440: Methodology for environmental impact assessment of information and communication technologies at city level (2015). Accessed 02 Jan 2025
96. I. T. U. T. S. Sector. L.1410: Methodology for environmental life cycle assessments of information and communication technology goods, networks and services (2024). Accessed 02 Jan 2025
97. F.N. Sibai, Ai crimes: a classification, in *Proceedings of the International Conference on Cyber Security and Protection of Digital Services (Cyber Security)*, pp. 1–8 (2020)
98. H. Song, G.A. Fink, S. Jeschke, *Security and Privacy in Cyber-physical Systems: Foundations, Principles, and Applications* (Wiley, 2017)
99. M. Stadler, M. Vierhauser, A. Garmendia, M. Wimmer, and J. Cleland-Huang. Flexible model-driven runtime monitoring support for cyber-physical systems. In *Proceedings of the ACM/IEEE 44th International Conference on Software Engineering: Companion Proceedings*, ICSE '22, page 350–351, New York, NY, USA, 2022. Association for Computing Machinery

100. G. Steindl, T. Schwarzinger, K. Schreiberhuber, F.J. Ekaputra, Towards semantic event-handling for building explainable cyber-physical systems. IEEE Open J. Ind. Electr. Soc. (2024)
101. F. Tao, J. Cheng, Q. Qi, M. Zhang, H. Zhang, F. Sui, Digital twin-driven product design, manufacturing and service with big data. Int. J. Adv. Manuf. Technol. **94**, 3563–3576 (2018)
102. R. Tatman, Gender and dialect bias in youtube's automatic captions, in *Proceedings of the First ACL Workshop on Ethics in Natural Language Processing* (2017), pp. 53–59
103. M. Törngren, P.T. Grogan, How to deal with the complexity of future cyber-physical systems? Designs **2**(4) (2018)
104. M. Törngren, U. Sellgren, *Complexity Challenges in Development of Cyber-Physical Systems* (Springer International Publishing, Cham, 2018), pp. 478–503
105. C. Trubiani, P. Jamshidi, J. Cito, W. Shang, Z.M. Jiang, M. Borg, Performance issues? Hey DevOps, mind the uncertainty. IEEE Softw. **36**(2), 110–117 (2019)
106. S. Udeshi, P. Arora, S. Chattopadhyay, Automated directed fairness testing, in *Proceedings of the 33rd ACM/IEEE International Conference on Automated Software Engineering* (2018), pp. 98–108
107. G. Visani, E. Bagli, F. Chesani, A. Poluzzi, D. Capuzzo, Statistical stability indices for lime: obtaining reliable explanations for machine learning models. J. Oper. Res. Soc. **73**(1), 91–101 (2022)
108. B. Wang, P. Zheng, Y. Yin, A. Shih, L. Wang, Toward human-centric smart manufacturing: a human-cyber-physical systems (hcps) perspective. J. Manuf. Syst. **63**, 471–490 (2022)
109. D. Weyns, J. Andersson, M. Caporuscio, F. Flammini, A. Kerren, W. Löwe, A research agenda for smarter cyber-physical systems. J. Integr. Des. Process. Sci. **25**(2), 27–47 (2022)
110. F. Xu, H. Uszkoreit, Y. Du, W. Fan, D. Zhao, J. Zhu, Explainable ai: a brief survey on history, research areas, approaches and challenges, in *Natural language processing and Chinese computing: 8th cCF international conference, NLPCC 2019, Dunhuang, China, October 9–14, 2019, proceedings, part II 8* (Springer, 2019), pp. 563–574
111. W. Xu, M.J. Dainoff, L. Ge, Z. Gao, Transitioning to human interaction with ai systems: New challenges and opportunities for hci professionals to enable human-centered ai. Int. J. Human-Comput. Int. **39**(3), 494–518 (2023)
112. Z. Yang, Z. Ge, On paradigm of industrial big data analytics: From evolution to revolution. IEEE Trans. Industr. Inf. **18**(12), 8373–8388 (2022)
113. V. Yazdanpanah, E.H. Gerding, S. Stein, C. Cirstea, M. Schraefel, T.J. Norman, N.R. Jennings, Different forms of responsibility in multiagent systems: Sociotechnical characteristics and requirements. IEEE Internet Comput. **25**(6), 15–22 (2021)
114. M.K. Yogi, A. Chakravarthy, A novel user centric privacy mechanism in cyber physical system. Comput. & Secur. **149**, 104163 (2025)
115. Y. Yuan, X. Tang, W. Zhou, W. Pan, X. Li, H.-T. Zhang, H. Ding, J. Goncalves, Data driven discovery of cyber physical systems. Nat. Commun. **10**(1), 4894 (2019)
116. F. Zampetti, R. Kapur, M. Di Penta, S. Panichella, An empirical characterization of software bugs in open-source cyber–physical systems. J. Syst. Softw. **192**, 111425 (2022)
117. F. Zampetti, D.A. Tamburri, S. Panichella, A. Panichella, G. Canfora, M.D. Penta, Continuous integration and delivery practices for cyber-physical systems: an interview-based study. ACM Trans. Softw. Eng. Methodol. **32**(3), 73:1–73:44 (2023)
118. R. Zemel, Y. Wu, K. Swersky, T. Pitassi, C. Dwork, Learning fair representations. in *International Conference on Machine Learning* (2013), pp. 325–333
119. J.M. Zhang, M. Harman, L. Ma, Y. Liu, Machine learning testing: survey, landscapes and horizons. IEEE Trans. Software Eng. **48**(1), 1–36 (2022)
120. P. Zhang, J. Wang, J. Sun, G. Dong, X. Wang, X. Wang, J.S. Dong, T. Dai, White-box fairness testing through adversarial sampling, in *Proceedings of the ACM/IEEE 42nd International Conference on Software Engineering* (2020), pp. 949–960
121. S. Zhang, J. Xu, H. Gou, J. Tan, A research review on the key technologies of intelligent design for customized products. Engineering **3**(5), 631–640 (2017)
122. J. Zhou, Y. Zhou, B. Wang, J. Zang, Human-cyber-physical systems (hcpss) in the context of new-generation intelligent manufacturing. Engineering **5**(4), 624–636 (2019)

Standardization for DevOps and Cyber-Physical Systems

Hironori Washizaki and Sebastiano Panichella

Abstract International standards have been documented for DevOps and CPS as reference models and guidelines. These standards capture globally recognized good or best practices as well as reference models for connectivity and interoperability in DevOps and CPS [32, 33] to make DevOps-based organizations and processes (and resulting CPS-based products and services) adhere to established norms consistently, resulting in reduced technical and operational risks and comparable outcomes. This chapter overviews these available standards and discusses how these standards can be adapted to DevOps for CPS so that CPS can be developed, deployed, and evolved efficiently and effectively while having proper communications and collaborations among stakeholders.

1 Chapter Introduction and Motivation

Numerous international standards, such as ISO/IEC standards and IEEE ones, have been documented for DevOps and CPS as reference models and guidelines. These standards capture globally recognized good or best practices as well as reference models for connectivity and interoperability in DevOps and CPS to make DevOps-based organizations and processes (and resulting CPS-based products and services) adhere to established norms consistently, resulting in reduced technical and operational risks and comparable outcomes.

Given the complex and dynamic nature of the integration and bidirectional impact of the cyber and real worlds in CPS, the adoption of DevOps is natural, as it can contribute to quick release and continuous revision of systems based on their operation

H. Washizaki
Waseda University, Shinjuku, Japan
e-mail: washizaki@waseda.jp

S. Panichella (✉)
University of Bern, Bern, Switzerland
e-mail: spanichella@gmail.com

S. Panichella et al. (eds.), *Roadmap for DevOps in Cyber-Physical Systems*,
https://doi.org/10.1007/978-981-95-1786-2_8

and monitoring results [18]. Thus, these standards are expected to be applied solely or together to DevOps for CPS to develop, deploy, and evolve efficiently and effectively.

This chapter overviews the available standards and discusses how they can be adapted to establish DevOps for CPS, enabling the development, deployment, and evolution of CPS efficiently and effectively while ensuring proper communications and collaboration among stakeholders. Complementary, the chapters discuss technologies that can be potentially adopted for addressing some of the standardization actions for CPS.

2 Overview of Standardization Status for DevOps and CPS

Available standards in DevOps for CPS can be roughly classified into three types: DevOps standards, CPS standards, and others. DevOps standards help adopt well-accepted DevOps principles and practices to develop CPS (and non-CPS).

Meanwhile, CPS standards provide reference models for CPS to ensure consistent, interoperable communication among physical sensors, actuators, and cyber systems such as cloud platforms, AI engines, and digital twins. IoT (Internet of Things) standards can apply to the development and maintenance of CPS concerning component connectivity and reusability, as well as data management.

Furthermore, other standards in systems and software engineering, such as general software life cycle standards and quality model standards, should apply to adopt particular principles, practices, and models for DevOps for CPS.

Figure 1 shows the overview of DevOps for CPS with available standards. The subsequent sections overview the standardization status for DevOps and CPS.

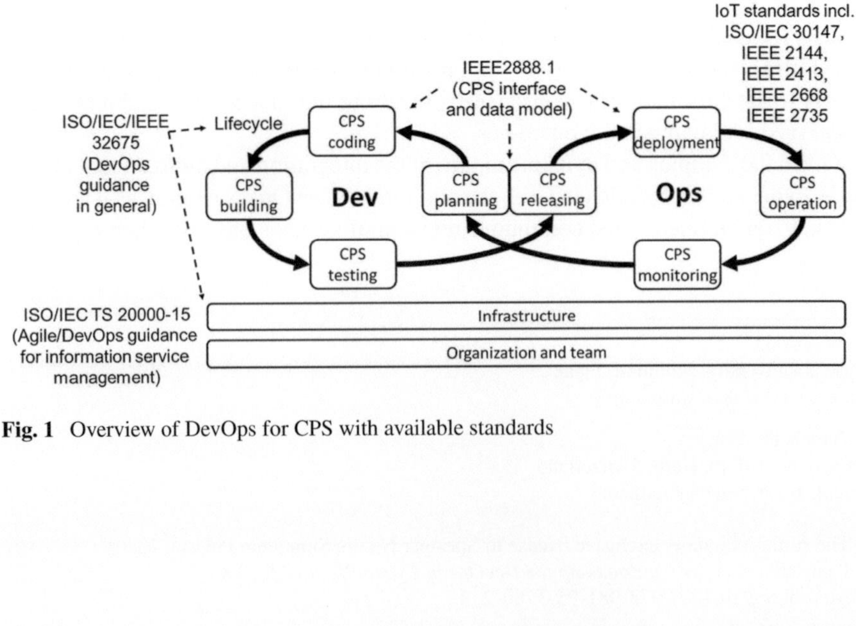

Fig. 1 Overview of DevOps for CPS with available standards

3 Standards for DevOps

DevOps standards are useful for adopting well-accepted DevOps principles and practices to develop, deploy, and evolve software systems and services efficiently and effectively. These principles and practices involve work integration between development and operations teams and proper communication and collaboration among stakeholders.

Table 1 lists some of the major published international standards for DevOps. Among them, as shown in Fig. 1, particularly the ISO/IEC/IEEE 32675:2022 [6] should be available for development and operation of CPS by incorporating DevOps practices into the lifecycle as well as the fundamental infrastructure. ISO/IEC TS 20000-15 [13] might be applicable if the target CPS is connected to be a part of enterprise information systems and services requiring proper management.

Furthermore, several related standards and technical reports are under development in DevOps, such as the ISO/IEC CD 29110-5-5 [12]. In ISO/IEC, a working group dedicated to the standardization in Agile and DevOps has been formed as the SC7/WG29 under JTC1. Under the working group, more standards would be documented in the future.

4 Standards for CPS and IoT

CPS standards provide reference models for CPS to ensure consistent, interoperable communication among physical sensors, actuators, and cyber systems such as cloud platforms, AI engines, and digital twins.

Table 2 lists some of the major published international standards for CPS. IEEE 2888.1 [7] can be helpful in designing sensor interfaces of target CPS in a fast, frequent cycle of development and operation while keeping interoperable among heterogeneous sensor networks. IEEE 2888.2 [8] can be applicable for designing actuator interfaces with standardized data models and message structures.

Furthermore, several related standards and technical reports are under development in CPS, such as the IEEE P3337 [10], IEEE P2888.3 [9], and ISO/IEC AWI TS 5689 [11].

In addition to CPS standards, IoT standards can be applicable to the development and maintenance of CPS with respect to component connectivity and reliability as well as data management. Tables 3 and 4 list some of the major published international standards for IoT.

Table 1 List of DevOps standards

Number	Title	Summary	Key features
ISO/IEC /IEEE 32675:2022	DevOps - Building reliable and secure systems including application build, package and deployment [6]	Guidance on the application of DevOps principles across the software development lifecycle (SDLC), including software engineering and operations, to achieve reliable, secure, and resilient software systems	Suggested key practices include immutable infrastructure and containerization for consistency across environments, version control for infrastructure and configuration, secret management and access control to ensure secure deployments, and rollback mechanisms and canary deployments to manage risk as well as recommends tracking key metrics such as deployment frequency, lead time, mean time to recovery (MTTR), and change failure rate.
ISO/IEC TS 20000-15:2024	Guidance on the application of Agile and DevOps principles in a service management system [13]	Guidance supplementing ISO/IEC 20000 series, which defines requirements for a Service Management System (SMS), to align Agile and DevOps principles with established IT service management (ITSM) practices to improve responsiveness, collaboration, and service quality	Values customer focus, adaptability, collaboration, and continuous learning by introducing Agile practices like Scrum, Kanban, and DevOps principles like CI/CD, IaC, and monitoring into service management workflows, resulting in the promotion of Agile and DevOps-style metrics (e.g., cycle time, deployment frequency, customer satisfaction) to evaluate SMS effectiveness

Table 2 List of CPS standards

Number	Title	Summary	Key features
IEEE 2888.1-2023	IEEE Standard for Specification of Sensor Interface for Cyber and Physical Worlds [7]	A unified sensor interface model for CPS to ensure consistent, interoperable communication between physical sensors and cyber systems such as cloud platforms, AI engines, and digital twins	Standardizing sensor data structure as well as quality indicators (e.g., accuracy, confidence), protocol-agnostic design, supporting mapping to standard communication protocols such as MQTT, HTTP, and CoAP, lightweight format suitable for resource-constrained devices, in order to integrate with IEEE 2888.2 (Actuator Interface) to enable full CPS loop (sense-analyze-actuate) and enables plug-and-play interoperability among heterogeneous sensor networks
IEEE 2888.2-2023	IEEE Standard for Actuator Interface for Cyber and Physical Worlds [8]	A common interface model and protocols for actuators used in CPS to support seamless interoperability, integration, and control of actuators from the cyber world, such as cloud applications or AI systems	Standardizing data models and message structures for actuator interfaces, communication protocols for issuing commands from cyber systems to physical actuators, and framework to enable interoperability among various types of actuators (e.g., motors, valves, servos) regardless of vendor or technology

Table 3 ISO/IEC standard for IoT

Number	Title	Summary	Key features
ISO/IEC 30147:2021	Internet of Things (IoT) - Integration of IoT trustworthiness activities in ISO/IEC/IEEE 15288 system engineering processes [3]	Guidance on the integration of IoT trustworthiness activities throughout the entire system life cycle to align with ISO/IEC/IEEE 15288, which defines system life cycle processes, ensuring a standardized and comprehensive engineering approach	Emphasizing five key trustworthiness characteristics in IoT, including security for protection against threats and attacks, privacy for safeguarding personal or sensitive information, safety for prevention of harm to people or the environment, reliability for consistent and correct operation over time, and resilience for recovering from disruptions or attacks, to be mapped to relevant stages of the system engineering process

5 Supporting Standardization of CPS Through Testing Tools

The emergence of tools such as AERIALIST [26, 27], SURREALIST [26], SUPERIALIST [25], SDc-Scissor [14, 15, 15–17, 22] and competition infrastructures [19, 20, 23, 28, 30, 31] provides crucial technical enablers to support standardization efforts in CPS, especially for Unmanned Aerial Vehicles (UAVs) and self-driving cars (SDC). These tools align with the objectives of standards like IEEE 2888.1/2888.2 for sensor and actuator interoperability by offering reproducible and configurable test environments that capture interactions between physical UAVs and cyber systems.

Supporting Standardization of UAVs through Testing Tools. AERIALIST supports modular test specification, execution, and analysis pipelines over PX4-based UAVs, thus providing a platform to validate standardized communication models and actuator control protocols. Furthermore, SURREALIST contributes to the development of realistic and challenging simulation scenarios via search-based techniques, which can help in benchmarking safety-critical behaviors in accordance with standards like ISO/IEC 30147:2021, which emphasize trustworthiness characteristics such as safety [24, 29, 32], reliability, and resilience. SUPERIALIST enables runtime analysis of decision uncertainty through control signal monitoring, aiding in the detection and classification of unsafe states, thus supporting the development of safety

Table 4 List of IEEE standards for IoT

Number	Title	Summary	Key features
IEEE 2144.1-2020	IEEE Standard for Framework of Blockchain-based Internet of Things (IoT) Data Management [2]	Standardized framework that integrates blockchain technology with IoT data management to enhance data security, trust, and traceability in IoT environments	Standardizing multiple layers to integrate blockchain and IoT components, including the perception layer for IoT devices and sensors that generate data, the network layer for communication between devices and the blockchain infrastructure, the data management layer for blockchain mechanisms for data integrity, traceability, and access control, and the application layer for services and user-facing applications that utilize the trusted IoT data
IEEE 2413-2019	IEEE Standard for an Architectural Framework for the Internet of Things (IoT) [1]	Common architectural framework to support cross-domain interaction, system interoperability, and functional integration across different IoT domains, resulting in a reduction of fragmentation and promotion of reusability of architectural components	Standardizing three main architectural views, including the functional view for IoT functions such as sensing, actuation, data processing, and user interfaces, the information view for the structure and flow of data, data models, and semantics, and the communication view for communication protocols, networking, and interoperability, together with crosscutting concerns incorporated throughout the architecture, such as security, privacy, and safety

(continued)

Table 4 (continued)

Number	Title	Summary	Key features
IEEE 2668-2022	IEEE Standard for Maturity Index of the Internet of Things - Evaluation, Grading, and Ranking [4]	A standardized framework for assessing the maturity of IoT systems using a quantifiable index called the IoT Maturity Index (IDex) by establishing a method to evaluate, grade, and rank IoT systems based on their maturity, helping stakeholders make informed decisions	Standardizing the maturity index based on core dimensions, including interoperability as the system's ability to interact with other systems and devices, trustworthiness including security, privacy, safety, and reliability; performance efficiency including latency, throughput, and resource usage; usability as the ease of use and user satisfaction, scalability as the system's ability to grow and handle increasing loads, maintainability as the ease of updating, debugging, and adapting the system, and the cost efficiency as the evaluation of economic feasibility and ROI
IEEE 2735-2022	IEEE Standard for Interoperability of Complex Virtual Instruments for Internet of Things [5]	Standard framework to ensure interoperability and semantic consistency among complex virtual instruments (CVIs) used in IoT environments by establishing standardized data representations and metadata models for virtual instruments in IoT	Standardizing CVI referring to a software-based representation of a real or conceptual measuring instrument for aggregating multiple data sources, performing advanced analytics or simulations, and presenting output as if from a physical instrument, exemplified by virtual sensors, data fusion engines, and AI-based diagnostic tools

validation benchmarks for autonomous UAVs. Together, these tools offer an integrated framework for evaluating UAV systems under standardized metrics, fostering cross-platform reproducibility, traceability of unsafe behaviors, and evidence-based compliance with evolving CPS and IoT standards.

Supporting Standardization of Self-Driving Cars through Testing Tools. Simulation-based testing tools such as SDC-Prioritizer [17] and SDC-Scissor [15, 16, 22] play a crucial role in supporting the standardization of SDCs and IoT systems by providing structured, reproducible, and feature-based methodologies for test case prioritization and selection. These tools contribute to the formulation of standardized test frameworks and performance evaluation criteria that align with CPS standards like IEEE 2888.1/2 and IoT frameworks such as IEEE 2668 and IEEE 2144.1. By enabling multi-objective optimization of test executions and utilizing machine learning for identifying critical test cases (e.g., in the context of lane-keeping systems), these tools support the development of metrics and oracles necessary for defining standardized validation procedures. Additionally, SDC-Alabaster's integration of virtual reality provides human-in-the-loop feedback [21], supporting trustworthiness dimensions such as safety and perception–key concerns emphasized in standards like ISO/IEC 30147 and IEEE 2413. As testing requirements become more sophisticated, such tools can inform and accelerate the standardization of simulation-based testing environments, test case relevance criteria, and oracle definitions within CPS and IoT domains.

6 Conclusion and Future Prospective

This chapter overviews ISO/IEC and IEEE standards, which have been documented for DevOps and CPS as reference models and guidelines. These standards are expected to be adopted for DevOps for CPS so that CPS can be developed, deployed, and evolved in an efficient and effective way while having proper communications and collaborations among stakeholders.

DevOps standards such as ISO/IEC/IEEE 32675 are expected to be useful for adopting well-accepted DevOps principles and practices to develop, deploy, and evolve CPS in an efficient and effective way. CPS standards such as IEEE 2888.1 and 2888.2 are expected to provide reference models for ensuring consistent, interoperable communication among physical sensors, actuators, and cyber systems constituting the entire CPS. In addition, IoT standards can be applicable to the development and maintenance of CPS with respect to component connectivity and reliability, as well as data management.

In the future, the synergy and challenges of using both standards for DevOps and CPS are expected to be examined further, resulting in empirical studies and subsequent standards development. Particularly, it is expected to examine how much DevOps principles and practices in DevOps standards are effectively applicable to CPS development and operations, specifically, which address the dynamic nature and complexity in the blend of the cyber and physical world. Meanwhile, it is necessary to examine how CPS standards contribute to connectivity and interoperability in CPS while shortening development time and life cycle.

Competing Interests The authors have no conflicts of interest to declare that are relevant to the content of this chapter.

Acknowledgements We thank the Horizon 2020 (EU Commission) and the SERI (State Secretariat for Education, Research, and Innovation) support for the project InnoGuard (https://www.innoguard.eu/index.html), Marie Sktodowska-Curie Actions Doctoral Networks (HORIZON-MSCA-2023-DN), and the SNSF project entitled "SwarmOps: Human-sensing based MLOps for Collaborative Cyber-physical systems" (Project No. 200021_219732). We also thank the Hasler Foundation for the projects "Bridging the Reality Gap in Testing Unmanned Aerial Vehicles" (Project No.23064) and "Advancing Unmanned Aerial Vehicles Reliability and Societal Trust Through Integrated Testing and Formal Verification" (Project No.2025-02-27-311).

References

1. IEEE 2413-2019 IEEE Standard for an Architectural Framework for the Internet of Things (IoT) (2019)
2. IEEE 2144.1-2020 IEEE Standard for Framework of Blockchain-based Internet of Things (IoT) Data Management (2020)
3. ISO/IEC 30147:2021 Internet of Things (IoT) - Integration of IoT trustworthiness activities in ISO/IEC/IEEE 15288 system engineering processes (2021)
4. IEEE 2668-2022 IEEE Standard for Maturity Index of the Internet of Things–Evaluation, Grading, and Ranking (2022)
5. IEEE 2735-2022 IEEE Standard for Interoperability of Complex Virtual Instruments for Internet of Things (2022)
6. ISO/IEC/IEEE 32675:2022 DevOps - Building reliable and secure systems including application build, package and deployment (2022)
7. IEEE 2888.1-2023 IEEE Standard for Specification of Sensor Interface for Cyber and Physical Worlds (2023)
8. IEEE 2888.2-2023 IEEE Standard for Actuator Interface for Cyber and Physical Worlds (2023)
9. IEEE P2888.3 IEEE Draft Standard on Orchestration of Digital Synchronization between Cyber and Physical World (2024)
10. IEEE P3337 Standard for Requirements for Designing Accessible Intelligent Cyber-Physical Systems (AICS) for Well-Being (2024)
11. ISO/IEC AWI TS 5689 Cybersecurity - Security frameworks and use cases for cyber physical systems (2024)
12. ISO/IEC CD 29110-5-5: Systems and software engineering - Life cycle profiles for Very Small Entities (VSEs) - Part 5-5: Agile/DevOps guidelines (2024)
13. ISO/IEC TS 20000-15:2024 Guidance on the application of Agile and DevOps principles (2024)
14. C. Birchler, N. Ganz, S. Khatiri, A. Gambi, S. Panichella. Cost-effective simulation-based test selection in self-driving cars software with SDC-Scissor, in *IEEE International Conference on Software Analysis, Evolution and Reengineering, SANER 2022, Honolulu, HI, USA, March 15-18, 2022* (IEEE, 2022), pp. 164–168
15. C. Birchler, N. Ganz, S. Khatiri, A. Gambi, S. Panichella, Cost-effective simulation-based test selection in self-driving cars software. Sci. Comput. Program. **226**, 102926 (2023)

16. C. Birchler, S. Khatiri, B. Bosshard, A. Gambi, S. Panichella, Machine learning-based test selection for simulation-based testing of self-driving cars software. Empir. Softw. Eng. **28**(3), 71 (2023)
17. C. Birchler, S. Khatiri, P. Derakhshanfar, S. Panichella, A. Panichella, Single and multi-objective test cases prioritization for self-driving cars in virtual environments. ACM Trans. Softw. Eng. Methodol. **32**(2), 28:1–28:30 (2023)
18. C. Birchler, S. Khatiri, P. Rani, T. Kehrer, S. Panichella, A roadmap for simulation-based testing of autonomous cyber-physical systems: challenges and future direction (2025)
19. C. Birchler, S. Klikovits, M. Fazzini, S. Panichella, ICST tool competition 2025 - self-driving car testing track, in *IEEE/ACM International Conference on Software Testing*. (ICST, Verification and Validation, 2025), p. 2025
20. C. Birchler, S. Klikovits, M. Fazzini, S. Panichella, SBFT tool competition 2025 - cps-sdc regression testing track, in *IEEE/ACM International Workshop on Search-Based and Fuzz Testing, SBFT@ICSE 2025* (2025)
21. C. Birchler, T.K. Mohammed, P. Rani, T. Nechita, T. Kehrer, S. Panichella, How does simulation-based testing for self-driving cars match human perception? in *ACM International Conference on the Foundations of Software Engineering* (2024)
22. C. Birchler, C. Rohrbach, T. Kehrer, S. Panichella. SensoDat: Simulation-based sensor dataset of self-driving cars, in *21st IEEE/ACM International Conference on Mining Software Repositories, MSR 2024, Lisbon, Portugal, April 15–16, 2024*, ed. by D. Spinellis, A. Bacchelli, E. Constantinou (ACM, 2024), pp. 510–514
23. C. Birchler, C. Rohrbach, H. Kim, A. Gambi, T. Liu, J. Horneber, T. Kehrer, S. Panichella, TEASER: simulation-based CAN bus regression testing for self-driving cars software, in *38th IEEE/ACM International Conference on Automated Software Engineering, ASE 2023, Luxembourg, September 11–15, 2023* (IEEE, 2023), pp. 2058–2061
24. A. Di Sorbo, F. Zampetti, A. Visaggio, M. Di Penta, S. Panichella, Automated identification and qualitative characterization of safety concerns reported in uav software platforms. ACM Trans. Softw. Eng. Methodol. **32**(3) (2023)
25. S. Khatiri, F.M. Amin, S. Panichella, P. Tonella, When uncertainty leads to unsafety. empirical insights into the role of uncertainty in unmanned aerial vehicle safety. Empir. Soft. Eng. (2025)
26. S. Khatiri, S. Panichella, P. Tonella. Simulation-based test case generation for unmanned aerial vehicles in the neighborhood of real flights, in *International Conference on Software Testing, Verification and Validation* (IEEE, 2023), pp. 281–292
27. S. Khatiri, S. Panichella, P. Tonella, Simulation-based testing of unmanned aerial vehicles with aerialist, in *International Conference on Software Engineering (ICSE)* (2024)
28. S. Khatiri, P. Saurabh, T. Zimmermann, C. Munasinghe, C. Birchler, S. Panichella, SBFT tool competition 2024 - cps-uav test case generation track, in *IEEE/ACM International Workshop on Search-Based and Fuzz Testing, SBFT@ICSE 2024* (2024)
29. S. Khatiri, A.D. Sorbo, F. Zampetti, C.A. Visaggio, M.D. Penta, S. Panichella, Identifying safety-critical concerns in unmanned aerial vehicle software platforms with SALIENT. SoftwareX **27**, 101748 (2024)
30. S. Khatiri, T. Zohdinasab, P. Saurabh, D. Humeniuk, S. Panichella, ICST tool competition 2025 - CPS-UAV test case generation track, in *IEEE/ACM International Conference on Software Testing*. (ICST, Verification and Validation, 2025), p.2025
31. S. Khatiri, T. Zohdinasab, P. Saurabh, D. Humeniuk, S. Panichella, SBFT tool competition 2025 - CPS-UAV test case generation track, in *IEEE/ACM International Workshop on Search-Based and Fuzz Testing, SBFT@ICSE 2025* (2025)
32. F. Zampetti, R. Kapur, M. Di Penta, S. Panichella, An empirical characterization of software bugs in open-source cyber–physical systems. J. Syst. Softw. **192**, 111425 (2022)
33. F. Zampetti, D.A. Tamburri, S. Panichella, A. Panichella, G. Canfora, M.D. Penta. Continuous integration and delivery practices for cyber-physical systems: an interview-based study. ACM Trans. Softw. Eng. Methodol. **32**(3), 73:1–73:44 (2023)

Future Directions of DevOps for Cyber-Physical Systems

Sebastiano Panichella, Paolo Arcaini, Myra B. Cohen, and Aitor Arrieta

Abstract This chapter summarizes the insights and contributions presented throughout the book on DevOps for Cyber-Physical Systems (CPS), offering a cohesive summary of key developments across the DevOps lifecycle–from traceability and testing to deployment and ethics. It highlights emerging research themes such as runtime-aware validation, uncertainty modeling, sustainable DevOps practices, and fairness in CPS operations. Drawing on contributions from EU projects and recent academic advances, the chapter reflects on the evolving needs of CPS engineering and identifies actionable future directions, including simulation realism, green DevOps, and standardization. By advocating a holistic, responsible, and data-driven approach to DevOps, this chapter aims to guide researchers and practitioners toward dependable and ethically sound CPS development.

1 Summary of Previous Chapters

This book has explored the multifaceted dimensions of integrating DevOps into the development and operation of Cyber-Physical Systems (CPS). The introductory chapter provided essential context and motivation, grounding readers in the terminology, challenges, and structure of the book. The chapter on challenges and needs

S. Panichella (✉)
University of Bern, Bern, Switzerland
e-mail: spanichella@gmail.com

P. Arcaini
National Institute of Informatics, Tokyo, Japan

M. B. Cohen
Iowa State University, Ames, IA, USA

A. Arrieta
Mondragon University, Mondragon, Spain

S. Panichella et al. (eds.), *Roadmap for DevOps in Cyber-Physical Systems*,
https://doi.org/10.1007/978-981-95-1786-2_9

for DevOps in CPS, based on insights from EU projects such as COSMOS and Adeptness,[1] laid out the foundational gaps and open challenges in current practice.

Subsequent chapters examined specific phases of the DevOps lifecycle in the CPS domain. The chapter on cross-domain traceability introduced reactive links as a novel method for managing consistency across tools and domains, while noting the need for refinement to handle cyclic links and precision discrepancies. Testing for CPS was covered with a focus on runtime reliability and the use of production data for generating targeted test inputs and feedback-driven validation [7], supported by emerging tools such as DeepAtash [16, 17].

Uncertainty-aware DevOps practices were presented as essential for bridging design-time and runtime knowledge, emphasizing runtime monitoring and iterative refinement of system models [2, 10]. Deployment challenges and their tight coupling with testing and monitoring were explored [10], particularly in the context of simulation-based evaluation of autonomous CPS and the persistent reality gap [4].

The responsible DevOps chapter urged inclusion of ethical, fairness, and sustainability considerations in the DevOps lifecycle, advocating for cross-disciplinary collaborations and new measurement methodologies [5, 6, 12, 13]. Standardization efforts, reviewed in the final technical chapter, underscored the relevance of IEEE and ISO standards for guiding interoperable, efficient CPS development and maintenance [1].

2 The Path Forward from the Book on DevOps for CPS

The future of DevOps for CPS lies in maturing foundational research, operationalizing innovations, and institutionalizing cross-cutting concerns across the DevOps lifecycle. Key trends and future directions include:

- **From Static to Continuous Validation:** As advocated by recent studies [3, 4, 8, 11, 15], the shift from development-time validation to continuous field-driven testing is pivotal. Runtime feedback mechanisms such as anomaly detection and confidence-based oracles [10, 13, 14] must inform both testing and retraining pipelines to ensure dependable CPS operation.
- **Uncertainty-Aware Engineering:** The integration of uncertainty modeling from design to operation offers a promising research avenue. Future work should focus on making runtime data interpretable and actionable to support automated feedback loops in DevOps cycles [4, 10].
- **Sustainable DevOps:** Increasing attention must be paid to the carbon footprint of DevOps pipelines, particularly in simulation-based testing [4]. Research should explore green DevOps strategies, energy-aware test suite optimization, and FinOps-inspired methods for sustainable resource management [9].

[1] https://www.cosmos-devops.org/ and https://www.adeptness.eu.

- **Simulation Realism and Testing Automation:** Bridging the reality gap remains an urgent need [4, 10]. Machine learning-based simulation adaptation, domain randomization, and hardware-in-the-loop approaches are expected to converge toward higher fidelity and utility of virtual testing [4].
- **Fairness and Ethics in CPS DevOps:** Technical robustness must be complemented with fairness-aware testing, new ethical metrics tailored for CPS, and mechanisms for stakeholder involvement in decision-making [5, 6, 12, 13]. This demands deeper collaboration between developers, ethicists, and regulators.
- **Toward Standardized Practice:** Existing standards like ISO/IEC/IEEE 32675 and IEEE 2888.1/.2 provide a starting point. However, empirical studies are needed to evaluate how effectively these standards support the dynamic, interconnected areas of DevOps in CPS, particularly in safety-critical domains [1].

Overall, this book advocates for a holistic view of DevOps tailored to CPS: one that emphasizes operational reliability, ethical responsibility, sustainable development, and the seamless integration of monitoring, testing, and deployment. Realizing this vision will require coordinated efforts across academia, industry, and standardization bodies.

Competing Interests The authors have no conflicts of interest to declare that are relevant to the content of this chapter.

Acknowledgements We thank the Horizon 2020 (EU Commission) and the SERI (State Secretariat for Education, Research, and Innovation) support for the project InnoGuard (https://www.innoguard.eu/index.html), Marie Sktodowska-Curie Actions Doctoral Networks (HORIZON-MSCA-2023-DN), and the SNSF project entitled "SwarmOps: Human-sensing based MLOps for Collaborative Cyber-physical systems" (Project No. 200021_219732). We also thank the Hasler Foundation for the projects "Bridging the Reality Gap in Testing Unmanned Aerial Vehicles" (Project No.23064) and "Advancing Unmanned Aerial Vehicles Reliability and Societal Trust Through Integrated Testing and Formal Verification" (Project No.2025-02-27-311). P. Arcaini is supported by the ASPIRE grant No. JPMJAP2301, JST; and also by Engineerable AI Techniques for Practical Applications of High-Quality Machine Learning-based Systems Project (Grant Number JPMJMI20B8), JST-Mirai.

References

1. ISO/IEC/IEEE 32675:2022 DevOps - Building reliable and secure systems including application build, package and deployment (2022)
2. R. Amaro, R. Pereira, M.M. da Silva, Capabilities and practices in devops: a multivocal literature review. IEEE Trans. Software Eng. **49**(2), 883–901 (2023)
3. C. Birchler, S. Khatiri, P. Derakhshanfar, S. Panichella, A. Panichella, Single and multi-objective test cases prioritization for self-driving cars in virtual environments. ACM Trans. Softw. Eng. Methodol. **32**(2), 28:1–28:30 (2023)
4. C. Birchler, S. Khatiri, P. Rani, T. Kehrer, and S. Panichella, A roadmap for simulation-based testing of autonomous cyber-physical systems: challenges and future direction (2025)
5. C. Birchler, S. Klikovits, M. Fazzini, S. Panichella, ICST tool competition 2025 - self-driving car testing track, in *IEEE/ACM International Conference on Software Testing*. (ICST, Verification and Validation, 2025), p. 2025

6. C. Birchler, S. Klikovits, M. Fazzini, S. Panichella, SBFT tool competition 2025 - cps-sdc regression testing track, in *IEEE/ACM International Workshop on Search-Based and Fuzz Testing, SBFT@ICSE 2025* (2025)
7. C. Birchler, T.K. Mohammed, P. Rani, T. Nechita, T. Kehrer, S. Panichella, How does simulation-based testing for self-driving cars match human perception? in *ACM International Conference on the Foundations of Software Engineering* (2024)
8. C. Birchler, C. Rohrbach, H. Kim, A. Gambi, T. Liu, J. Horneber, T. Kehrer, S. Panichella, TEASER: simulation-based CAN bus regression testing for self-driving cars software, in *38th IEEE/ACM International Conference on Automated Software Engineering, ASE 2023, Luxembourg, September 11–15, 2023* (IEEE, 2023), pp. 2058–2061
9. F.F.T.A. Council, What is finops? (2023). Accessed 28 Jan 2025
10. S. Khatiri, F.M. Amin, S. Panichella, P. Tonella, When uncertainty leads to unsafety. empirical insights into the role of uncertainty in unmanned aerial vehicle safety. Empir. Softw. Eng. (2025)
11. S. Khatiri, S. Panichella, P. Tonella, Simulation-based test case generation for unmanned aerial vehicles in the neighborhood of real flights, in *International Conference on Software Testing, Verification and Validation*, pp. 281–292 (IEEE, 2023)
12. S. Khatiri, P. Saurabh, T. Zimmermann, C. Munasinghe, C. Birchler, S. Panichella, SBFT tool competition 2024 - cps-uav test case generation track, in *IEEE/ACM International Workshop on Search-Based and Fuzz Testing, SBFT@ICSE 2024* (2024)
13. S. Khatiri, T. Zohdinasab, P. Saurabh, D. Humeniuk, S. Panichella, ICST tool competition 2025 - CPS-UAV test case generation track, in *IEEE/ACM International Conference on Software Testing*. (ICST, Verification and Validation, 2025), p. 2025
14. A. Stocco, P. Tonella, Confidence-driven weighted retraining for predicting safety-critical failures in autonomous driving systems. J. Softw.: Evol. Proc. **34**(10), e2386 (2022)
15. P. Tonella, The road toward dependable ai based systems, in *2023 IEEE/ACM 45th International Conference on Software Engineering (ICSE)*, pp. 2–2 (IEEE, 2023)
16. T. Zohdinasab, V. Riccio, P. Tonella, DeepAtash: focused test generation for deep learning systems, in *Proceedings of the 32nd ACM SIGSOFT International Symposium on Software Testing and Analysis, ISSTA 2023, Seattle, WA, USA, July 17-21, 2023* ed. by R. Just, G. Fraser. (ACM, 2023), pp. 954–966
17. T. Zohdinasab, V. Riccio, P. Tonella, Focused test generation for autonomous driving systems. ACM Trans. Softw. Eng. Methodol. **33**(6), 1–32 (2024)

Conclusion

Sebastiano Panichella, Paolo Arcaini, Myra B. Cohen, and Aitor Arrieta

This book has presented a comprehensive, multi-dimensional exploration of DevOps practices for Cyber-Physical Systems (CPS), focusing on the integration of software engineering principles with the operational and physical realities of CPS. Throughout, we have emphasized that applying DevOps to CPS is not a simple matter of transplanting practices from traditional software contexts—it requires significant adaptation, innovation, and cross-domain collaboration. The chapters collectively highlight that success in DevOps for CPS is contingent on reconciling the diverse needs of safety, sustainability, traceability, uncertainty, standardization, and operational reliability.

Several recurring themes have emerged from the chapters and their prospective directions:

- **Runtime Awareness and Continuous Feedback**: There is a consensus that DevOps for CPS must move from static, design-time validation to continuous, runtime-informed processes. Testing, verification, and deployment practices must embrace runtime feedback through mechanisms such as monitoring, anomaly detection, and online retraining to ensure the ongoing dependability of systems that operate in uncertain, dynamic environments.
- **Uncertainty and Adaptation as First-Class Concerns**: Unlike purely digital systems, CPS inherently interact with the physical world, making uncertainty

S. Panichella (✉)
University of Bern, Bern, Switzerland
e-mail: sebastiano.panichella@unibe.ch

P. Arcaini
National Institute of Informatics, Tokyo, Japan

M. B. Cohen
Iowa State University, Ames, USA

A. Arrieta
Mondragon University, Mondragón, Spain

S. Panichella et al. (eds.), *Roadmap for DevOps in Cyber-Physical Systems*,
https://doi.org/10.1007/978-981-95-1786-2_10

management critical. DevOps pipelines must not only be able to handle uncertain conditions at runtime but also incorporate mechanisms for learning from operational feedback and iteratively improving models, assumptions, and system configurations.
- **Traceability and Cross-Domain Consistency**: Maintaining coherent links across tools, abstraction levels, and engineering domains remains a key technical challenge. Approaches like reactive links are a promising step, but further work is needed to support cyclic dependencies, semantic mismatches, and precision constraints, especially in AI-enhanced CPS.
- **Sustainability and Ethics in Practice**: DevOps pipelines must evolve to reflect societal responsibilities. As systems scale and grow in complexity, so do their energy demands and environmental impacts. Responsible DevOps embraces green practices, fairness-aware engineering, and financial accountability frameworks like FinOps. Moreover, it demands new methodologies to assess and improve the sustainability and ethical implications of CPS across their lifecycle.
- **Simulation and Testing Evolution**: Simulation-based testing plays a central role in CPS development, especially for safety-critical domains like autonomous systems. Yet, the "reality gap" between simulation and deployment hinders effectiveness. Bridging this gap with domain adaptation, hybrid real-sim strategies, and hardware-in-the-loop testing is an open frontier for research and tool development [1].
- **Standardization as a Catalyst**: Standards play a crucial role in ensuring consistency, interoperability, and quality across CPS lifecycles. However, they must keep pace with fast-evolving DevOps practices and the complexity of cyber-physical integration. Continued empirical studies and feedback from practice are vital to evolve existing standards and ensure their effective applicability.

Final Remarks

DevOps for CPS is not merely a convergence of two fields—it is the synthesis of software agility with the rigorous demands of the physical world. This synthesis demands not only technical excellence but also a cultural shift toward interdisciplinary collaboration, lifelong learning, and a proactive embrace of uncertainty, ethics, and sustainability. The path forward is clear: build systems that are not only efficient and reliable, but also adaptable, equitable, and environmentally conscious.

We hope this book will serve as both a foundation and a springboard—for researchers, practitioners, and policy-makers alike—to continue advancing the state of the art in DevOps for CPS. Let this be a call to action: to architect development processes that are as dynamic and resilient as the systems they aim to build.

Competing Interests The authors have no conflicts of interest to declare that are relevant to the content of this chapter.

Acknowledgements We thank the Horizon 2020 (EU Commission) and the SERI (State Secretariat for Education, Research, and Innovation) support for the project InnoGuard (https://www.innoguard.eu/index.html), Marie Sktodowska-Curie Actions Doctoral Networks (HORIZON-MSCA-2023-DN), and the SNSF project entitled "SwarmOps: Human-sensing based MLOps for Collaborative Cyber-physical systems" (Project No. 200021_219732). We also thank the Hasler Foundation for the projects "Bridging the Reality Gap in Testing Unmanned Aerial Vehicles" (Project No. 23064) and "Advancing Unmanned Aerial Vehicles Reliability and Societal Trust Through Integrated Testing and Formal Verification" (Project No. 2025-02-27-311). P. Arcaini is supported by the ASPIRE grant No. JPMJAP2301, JST; and also by Engineerable AI Techniques for Practical Applications of High-Quality Machine Learning-based Systems Project (Grant Number JPMJMI20B8), JST-Mirai.

Reference

1. C. Birchler, S. Khatiri, P. Rani, T. Kehrer, S. Panichella, A roadmap for simulation-based testing of autonomous cyber-physical systems: challenges and future direction (2025)

MIX
Papier aus verantwortungsvollen Quellen
Paper from responsible sources
FSC® C105338

If you have any concerns about our products,
you can contact us on
ProductSafety@springernature.com

In case Publisher is established outside the EU,
the EU authorized representative is:
Springer Nature Customer Service Center GmbH
Europaplatz 3, 69115 Heidelberg, Germany

Printed by Libri Plureos GmbH
in Hamburg, Germany